HOME EMERGENCY GUIDE

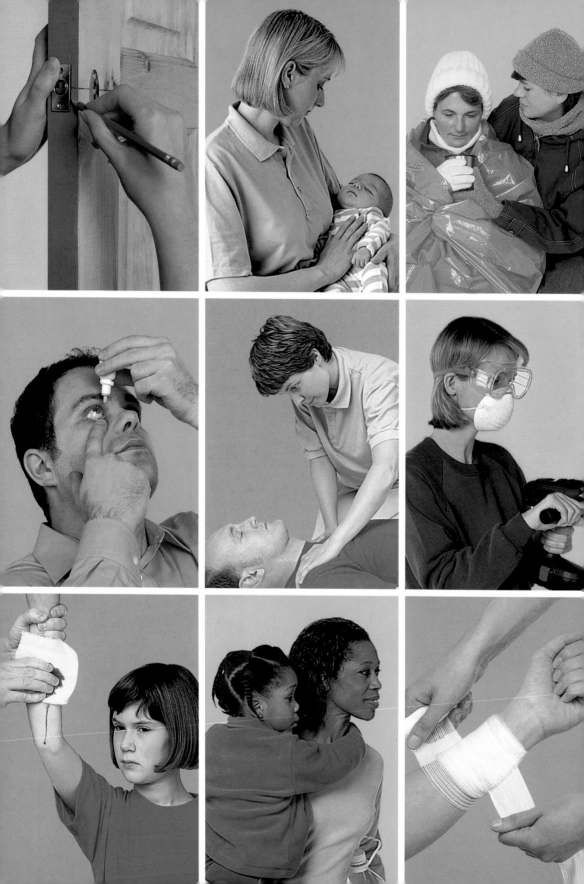

HOME EMERGENCY GUIDE

DK Publishing

LONDON, NEW YORK,
MUNICH, MELBOURNE, AND DELHI

CONTRIBUTORS

Dr. Vivien Armstrong • Dr. Sue Davidson • Professor Ian Davis
David Holloway • John McGowan • Tony Wilkins
David R.Goldmannn MD FACP • Allen R.Walker MD • John Cunningham

Produced for Dorling Kindersley by
COOLING BROWN
9–11 High Street, Hampton,
Middlesex TW12 2SA

Project Editor • Alison Bolus
Senior Designer • Tish Mills
Creative Director • Arthur Brown
Managing Editor • Amanda Lebentz

DORLING KINDERSLEY
Senior Managing Editor • Jemima Dunne
Managing Art Editor • Louise Dick
Senior Art Editor • Marianne Markham
DTP Designer • Julian Dams

DK PUBLISHING
Senior Editor • Jill Hamilton
Senior Art Editor • Susan St. Louis
Editorial Assistant • Kate Hamill

First published in the United States in 2003 by
DK Publishing, Inc.
375 Hudson Street, New York, New York 10014

00 01 02 03 04 05 10 9 8 7 6 5 4 3 2

A catalog record for this book is available from the Library of Congress.

ISBN 0-7894-9346-2

Color reproduction by GRB Editrice, Verona, Italy
Printed and bound in Singapore by Star Standard Industries (Pte.) Ltd.

See our complete product line at
www.dk.com

CONTENTS

① FIRST AID

② FAMILY ILLNESS

③
HOUSEHOLD EMERGENCIES

④
NATURAL DISASTERS

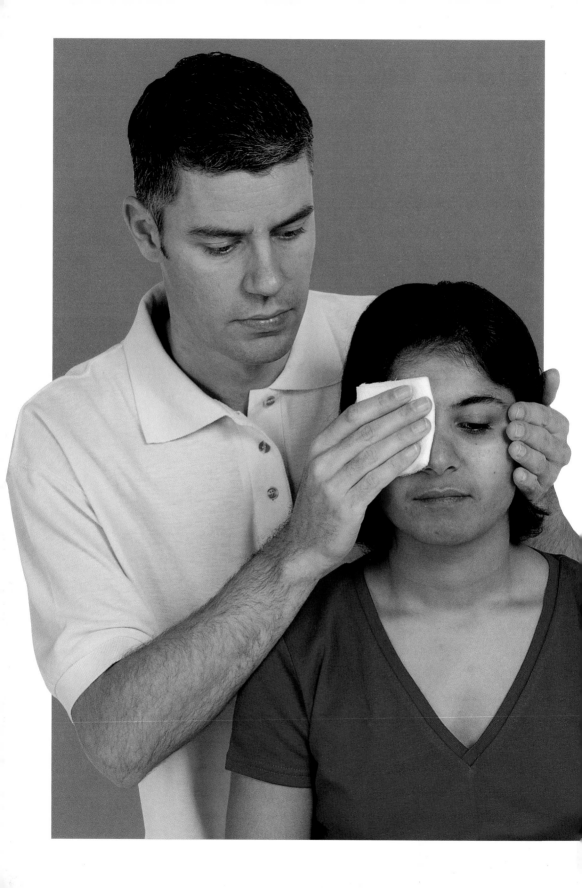

1
FIRST AID

Knowing what to do in a medical emergency, such as when someone suffers a heart attack, a deep chest wound, or a snake bite, could save the victim's life. This section tells you how to recognize important symptoms and give appropriate first-aid treatment in a wide range of situations, with full details on resuscitating an unconscious person.

Action in an emergency

When faced with an emergency, try to remain calm and controlled so that you can act effectively. Before assessing the victim's condition and carrying out the appropriate first aid, make sure that you are not putting yourself in danger. You will not be able to help anyone else if you become a victim yourself. If possible, have someone else dial 911 while you deal with the situation.

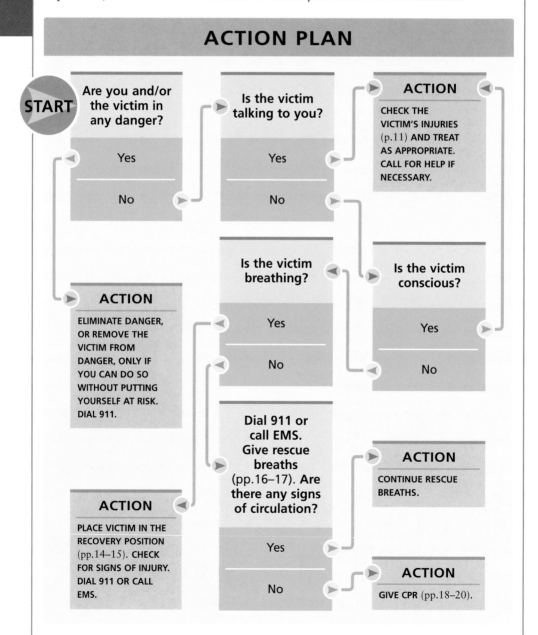

ACTION PLAN

START

Are you and/or the victim in any danger?
- Yes
- No

ACTION
ELIMINATE DANGER, OR REMOVE THE VICTIM FROM DANGER, ONLY IF YOU CAN DO SO WITHOUT PUTTING YOURSELF AT RISK. DIAL 911.

Is the victim talking to you?
- Yes
- No

ACTION
CHECK THE VICTIM'S INJURIES (p.11) AND TREAT AS APPROPRIATE. CALL FOR HELP IF NECESSARY.

Is the victim conscious?
- Yes
- No

Is the victim breathing?
- Yes
- No

ACTION
PLACE VICTIM IN THE RECOVERY POSITION (pp.14–15). CHECK FOR SIGNS OF INJURY. DIAL 911 OR CALL EMS.

Dial 911 or call EMS. Give rescue breaths (pp.16–17). Are there any signs of circulation?
- Yes
- No

ACTION
CONTINUE RESCUE BREATHS.

ACTION
GIVE CPR (pp.18–20).

ASSESSING A VICTIM'S INJURIES

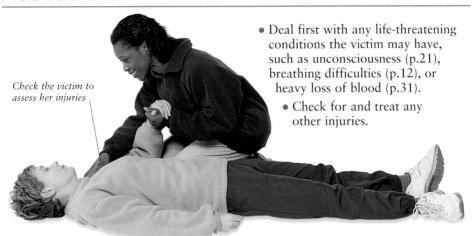

Check the victim to assess her injuries

- Deal first with any life-threatening conditions the victim may have, such as unconsciousness (p.21), breathing difficulties (p.12), or heavy loss of blood (p.31).
  - Check for and treat any other injuries.

CALLING AN AMBULANCE

1 Dial 911

- Check the victim's breathing before calling for help.
- If possible, send someone else to make the call and ask him or her to confirm that help is on the way.
- *If you are alone with a child who is unconscious or an adult who has drowned, choked, or been injured*, give rescue breaths (pp.16–17) and/or CPR (pp.18–20) for 1 minute before making the call.
- *If you are alone with an adult who is not breathing and you suspect a heart attack*, dial 911 immediately.
- If you have to leave a victim who is breathing, place him in the recovery position (pp.14–15).

2 Give information

- Tell the ambulance dispatcher where you are, your telephone number, what has happened, the age, sex, condition, and injuries of the victim(s), and whether any hazards are still present, such as a fire or gasoline on the road.

3 Give first aid

- Give the appropriate first-aid to the victim.
- Stay with the victim until medical help arrives.
- Monitor the victim's breathing (p.68 for an adult, p.71 for a child), pulse (p.68 for an adult, p.70 for a child), and consciousness (p.12) until the ambulance arrives.

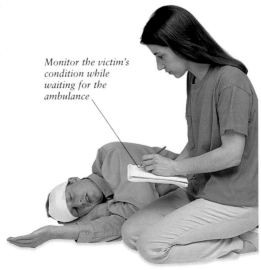

Monitor the victim's condition while waiting for the ambulance

Resuscitation techniques

The techniques on the following pages, used in sequence, can help maintain a victim's oxygen supply until help arrives. Upon finding an unconscious person, you need to open and, if necessary, clear the victim's airway so that air can enter the lungs. If the victim is not breathing, give rescue breaths to maintain the oxygen supply, thereby sustaining the victim's vital organs. If the victim also has no circulation, give cardiopulmonary resuscitation (CPR) – rescue breaths with chest compressions – to ensure that air enters the body and is circulated by the blood. An unconscious victim who is breathing should be placed in the recovery position, a secure position that keeps the airway open and the head, neck, and back aligned.

CHECKING FOR CONSCIOUSNESS (all ages)

1 Seek reaction

- Ask a simple question, or give a simple command, such as "Open your eyes."
- Shake an adult's shoulders gently.

! Important

- Never shake a baby or child. Instead, gently tap the shoulder or flick the sole of the foot.

2 Assess response

- If the victim responds to speech, assess whether he is alert and aware of the situation or confused and sleepy.
- If he responds to touch, assess whether he reacts readily to your touch or is sluggish in response.
- If there is no reaction at all, open the victim's airway (p.13).

3 Monitor victim

- During first-aid treatment, you will need to repeat steps 1–2 every 10 minutes to check the victim's level of consciousness.
- Note any changes in the victim's responses to speech or gentle shaking (adult victims only), and whether these indicate an improvement or a deterioration in his condition, then pass this information on to the paramedics when the ambulance arrives.
- If a conscious victim becomes unconscious, open the airway (p.13), check breathing (p.14), and dial 911 or call EMS.

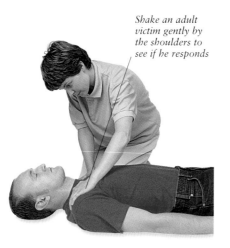

Shake an adult victim gently by the shoulders to see if he responds

OPENING THE AIRWAY (adults and children)

BEFORE YOU START

Make sure that you have:
- Checked for consciousness but had no response (p.12).

1 Tilt head back

- Gently place one hand on the victim's forehead.
- Tilt the head back by pressing down on the forehead.

! Important

- If you suspect that there are head or neck injuries, handle the head carefully. Tilt the head back slightly.
- Do not sweep your fingers blindly around the mouth.

2 Remove any obstruction

- Look inside the victim's mouth. Carefully pick out any obvious obstruction with your fingers.

3 Lift chin

- Place two fingers of the other hand under the chin and lift it gently.
- Tilt the head to open the airway. Check breathing (p.14).

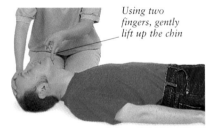

Using two fingers, gently lift up the chin

OPENING THE AIRWAY (babies under 1)

BEFORE YOU START

Make sure that you have:
- Checked for consciousness but had no response (p.12).

1 Tilt head back

- Place one hand on the baby's forehead, then tilt the head by pressing on the forehead.

2 Remove any obstruction

- Pick out any obvious obstruction in the mouth with your fingertips.

3 Lift chin

- Place one finger of the other hand under the chin and lift it gently.
- Tilt the head slightly. If you tilt it too far, you may block the airway again. Check breathing (p.14).

Do not over-extend the baby's neck

! Important

- Always be very gentle with a baby's head when tilting it back.

CHECKING FOR BREATHING (all ages)

2 Treat victim

- If breathing has stopped, begin rescue breaths (pp.16–17).
- If the victim is breathing but unconscious, place him in the recovery position (see below and opposite), then check for injuries.

1 Look for movement

- Kneel beside the victim and put your cheek close to his mouth. Listen and feel for any signs of breathing, while looking along his chest for signs of movement.
- Do this for up to 10 seconds.

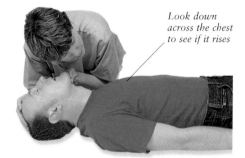

Look down across the chest to see if it rises

RECOVERY POSITION (adults and children)

2 Prepare to turn victim

- Bring the arm farther from you across the victim's chest, and place the back of his hand under his near cheek.
- Pull his far leg into a bent position; keep his foot on the floor.
- Pull his knee toward you.

1 Position arms and legs

- Kneel next to the victim.
- If the victim is wearing eyeglasses, remove them. Also remove any bulky objects from his pockets.
- Position the arm closer to you so that it lies at a right angle to his body, with his elbow bent at a right angle and the palm facing upward.

Keep palm facing up

Use leg as lever to turn body

3 Turn victim

- Continue to pull the upper leg so that the victim rolls onto his side. If necessary, support his body with your knees so that he does not roll too far forward.
- Leave the victim's hand supporting his head, and tilt the head so that the airway stays open.

Keep leg bent

4 Support victim

- Adjust the victim's hand so that it supports his head. Bend the hip and knee of his upper leg at right angles so that this leg supports his body.
- Check that an ambulance is on the way.
- Check and record the victim's breathing (p.68 for an adult, p.71 for a child), pulse (p.68 for an adult, p.70 for a child), and consciousness (p.12) until help arrives.

! Important

- If you suspect a spinal injury, do not move the victim unless his breathing is impeded or he is in danger. Maintain his open airway.

RECOVERY POSITION (babies under 1)

BEFORE YOU START

Make sure that you have carried out the following steps:

- Checked for consciousness but had no response (p.12).
- Opened the baby's airway (p.13).
- Checked for breathing and found definite signs (see p.14).

! Important

- If you suspect a spinal injury, do not move a baby unless the breathing is impeded or he is in danger.

2 Monitor baby

- Monitor the baby's breathing (p.71), pulse (p.70), and level of consciousness (p.12) until help arrives.

1 Pick up baby

- Hold the baby securely in your arms so that his head is lower than his body.
- Tilt the baby's head back to keep the airway open and to allow any vomit to drain from his mouth.
- Ensure that you keep the baby's head, neck, and back aligned and supported at all times.

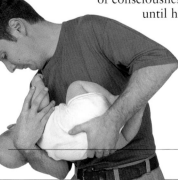

Keep the baby's head tilted downward to let fluid drain

GIVING RESCUE BREATHS (adults and children)

BEFORE YOU START

Make sure that you have carried out the following steps:
- Checked for consciousness but had no response (p.12).
- Opened the victim's airway (p.13).
- Checked for breathing but found no signs (p.14).

1 Breathe into victim's mouth

- Check that the victim's airway is still open.
- Pinch the victim's nose closed with your thumb and index finger.
- Take a deep breath, then place your open mouth tightly around his so that you form a good seal.
- Blow air into his mouth for about 2 seconds.

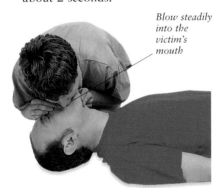

Blow steadily into the victim's mouth

2 Watch chest

- Lift your mouth away from the victim's mouth, keeping your hands in place to maintain his head position.
- Glance at the victim's chest; you should see his chest fall as the air leaves his lungs. This is called an effective breath. Repeat the breath.

3 Repeat breathing

- If there is no chest movement, readjust his head and try again.
- Repeat rescue breaths up to five times or until you achieve two effective breaths. Then check for signs of circulation (see step 4). OR
- If his chest fails to move even after rescue breathing, check for signs of circulation. If you know that the victim has choked and his chest still does not move, do not check for circulation but go straight to CPR (pp.18–20).

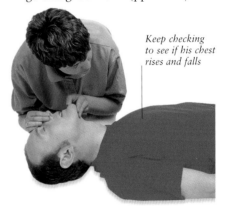

Keep checking to see if his chest rises and falls

4 Check for signs of circulation

- Look for any signs that indicate circulation – breathing, coughing, and movement of limbs – for up to 10 seconds.
- If there are signs of circulation, continue rescue breathing, giving 10 breaths per minute for adults and 20 for children. Recheck for signs of circulation every minute.
- If the victim starts breathing again, place him in the recovery position (pp.14–15).
- If there are no signs of circulation, begin CPR (pp.18–20).

❗ Important

- If you have a face shield (p.60), use this when giving rescue breaths to prevent cross-infection.
- If the victim has swallowed a corrosive poison, use a face shield to protect yourself from the effects of the chemical.
- Before giving the first breath, make sure that the victim's head is tilted back and the airway is open.

Place the shield on the victim's face, with the filter over her mouth

GIVING RESCUE BREATHS (babies under 1)

BEFORE YOU START

Make sure that you have carried out the following steps:
- Checked for consciousness but had no response (p.12).
- Opened the baby's airway (p.13).
- Checked for breathing but found no signs (p.14).

1 Breathe into baby's mouth

- Make sure that the baby's airway is still open.
- Take a breath. Seal your lips around both the mouth and nose.
- Attempt to give about one breath per second.

2 Watch chest

- Glance at the baby's chest; it should rise and fall. Repeat rescue breaths.
- If the chest does not move, readjust the airway and try again.
- Try up to five times or until you achieve two effective breaths. Check for signs of circulation. OR
- If the chest still does not move, check for signs of circulation.
- If you know the baby has choked and the chest still does not move, do not check for circulation but go straight to CPR (p.20).

3 Check circulation

- Look for any signs that indicate circulation – breathing, coughing, and movement of limbs – for up to 10 seconds.
- If there are signs of circulation, continue rescue breathing (at a rate of one breath per 3 seconds). If there are no signs of circulation, begin CPR (p.20).

❗ Important

- When giving rescue breaths to a baby, be careful not to blow too hard.

GIVING CPR (adults and children over 7)

② Position hands

- Lift away the fingers of your first hand and lay this hand on top of your other hand.
- Interlock your fingers, so that the fingers of your bottom hand are not touching the chest.
- Kneel upright with your shoulders directly above the victim and your elbows locked straight.

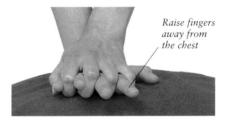

Raise fingers away from the chest

① Find compression point

- Lay the victim on a firm surface.
- Kneel beside the victim, level with his chest. Slide your fingers (using the hand farther from his head) along the lowest rib to the point where it meets the breastbone.
- Position your middle and index fingers at this point.
- Place the heel of your other hand on the breastbone, just above your index finger. This is the area of the chest where you must apply the compressions.

③ Compress chest

- Press downward, depressing the breastbone by $1\frac{1}{2}$–2 inches (4–5 cm) on an average adult, then release the pressure but do not remove your hands from the chest.
- Compress the chest in this way 15 times at a rate of about 100 compressions per minute (roughly three every 2 seconds), maintaining an even rhythm.

Place fingers where the victim's lower rib and breastbone meet

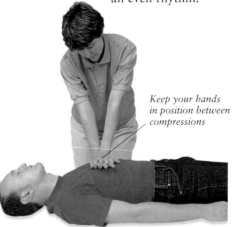

Keep your hands in position between compressions

4 Give rescue breaths

- Give the victim two rescue breaths (p.16).

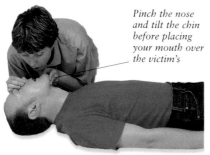

Pinch the nose and tilt the chin before placing your mouth over the victim's

5 Repeat CPR cycles

- Continue giving cycles of 15 chest compressions and two rescue breaths until help arrives.
- If the circulation returns or the victim starts breathing at any time, stop CPR and place him in the recovery position (pp.14–15).
- Stay with the victim and monitor his breathing (p.68), pulse (p.68), and level of consciousness (p.12) until help arrives.

GIVING CPR (children 1–7)

BEFORE YOU START

Make sure that you have carried out the following steps:

- Checked for consciousness but had no response (p.12).
- Opened the victim's airway (p.13).
- Checked for breathing but found no signs (p.14).
- Given two effective rescue breaths and checked for signs of circulation but found none (p.16) **OR**
- Attempted two rescue breaths and checked for signs of circulation but found none (p.16).

2 Give compressions

- Kneel upright with your shoulders directly above the child's chest and your elbow locked straight.
- Press downward, so that you are depressing the breastbone by one-third of the depth of the chest, then release the pressure without removing your hands.
- Compress the chest five times at a rate of about 100 compressions per minute, keeping an even rhythm.
- Give one rescue breath.

1 Find compression point

- Lay the child on a firm surface.
- Find the base of the breastbone (see opposite), then position one hand on the lower half of the child's breastbone.

Position one hand ready for compressions

3 Repeat CPR cycles

- Continue giving cycles of five chest compressions to one rescue breath.
- If the child's circulation and/or breathing return, place him or her in the recovery position (pp.14–15).
- Stay with the child and monitor his or her breathing (p.71), pulse (p.70), and level of consciousness (p.12) until help arrives.

GIVING CPR (babies under 1)

BEFORE YOU START

Make sure that you have carried out the following steps:

- Checked for consciousness but had no response (p.12).
- Opened the baby's airway (p.13).
- Checked for breathing but found no signs (p.14).
- Given two effective rescue breaths and checked for signs of circulation but found none (p.17). **OR**
- Attempted two rescue breaths and checked for signs of circulation but found none (p.17).

1 Find compression point

- Lay the baby on a firm surface.
- Position the tips of two fingers of one hand on the baby's breastbone, a finger's width below the nipples. This is the point where you must apply the compressions.

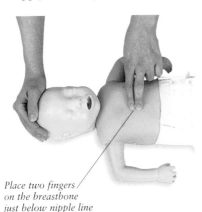

Place two fingers on the breastbone just below nipple line

! Important

- When giving rescue breaths to a baby, be careful not to blow too hard.

2 Compress chest

- Press downward, so that you depress the breastbone by one-third of the depth of the chest, then release the pressure without moving your hands.
- Compress the chest five times at a rate of about 100 compressions per minute, keeping an even rhythm.
- Give one effective rescue breath.

Seal your mouth over the baby's nose and mouth

3 Repeat CPR cycles

- Continue giving cycles of five chest compressions and one rescue breath.
- If the baby's circulation and/or breathing return, stop CPR and hold him or her in the recovery position (p.15).
- Stay with the baby and monitor his or her breathing (p.71), pulse (p.70), and level of consciousness (p.12) until help arrives.

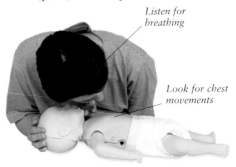

Listen for breathing

Look for chest movements

Unconsciousness

An interruption in the normal activity of the brain results in unconsciousness. This potentially life-threatening condition requires immediate medical help. The aims of first-aid treatment are to check the victim's level of consciousness, open the airway and check breathing, then, if the victim is breathing, to put him or her in a stable position until help arrives.

SIGNS & SYMPTOMS

- No response to loud noise or gentle shaking
- Closed eyes
- No movement or sound

TREATING UNCONSCIOUSNESS (all ages)

1 Check consciousness

- Check the victim for signs of consciousness (p.12).
- Open the victim's airway (p.13) and check her breathi. g (p.14).
- If the victim is not brea hing, begin rescue breaths (p.16 for adults and children, p.17 for babies).
- If the victim is breathing, place her in the recovery position (pp.14–15 for adults and children, p.15 for babies) and treat any injuries (see step 3).

Keep leg bent

2 Summon help

- Dial 911 or call EMS.
- Look for clues to the cause of the condition, such as needle marks, medical warning bracelets, or identification cards.
- Ask bystanders for any information they may have that you can give to the emergency services.

3 Treat injuries

- Examine the victim gently for any serious injuries.
- Control any bleeding (p.31). Check for and support suspected broken arms or legs (pp.44–45).

4 Monitor victim

- Stay with the victim until medical help arrives.
- Monitor her breathing regularly (p.68 for an adult, p.71 for a child or baby) and pulse (p.68 for an adult, p.70 for a child or baby) every 10 minutes.
- Check for any changes in the victim's level of consciousness by asking simple questions or shaking her gently every 5–10 minutes.

! Important

- Do not move the victim unnecessarily in case there is spinal injury.
- If you need to leave the victim to get help, place her in the recovery position (pp.14–15 for adults and children, p.15 for babies).
- Do not shake a baby or child.
- Be prepared to begin resuscitation (pp.12–20).
- Do not give an unconscious victim anything to eat or drink.

Choking (adults and children)

An obstruction of the airway, usually caused by food or a foreign object, can result in choking. The aim of first-aid treatment for choking is to dislodge the object as quickly as possible. This involves encouraging the victim to cough, then, if necessary, using thrusts. If the obstruction is not removed, the victim will stop breathing and lose consciousness.

TREATING CHOKING
(adults and children over 7)

1 Encourage coughing

- Ask the victim to cough. This may dislodge whatever is blocking the victim's windpipe.
- Check a child's mouth to see if anything has been dislodged.

Encourage victim to cough

! Important

- If the victim becomes unconscious, open the airway, check breathing, and be prepared to begin resuscitation (pp.12–20).
- If the victim is pregnant or obese, or you cannot reach around the victim's abdomen, give chest thrusts instead of abdominal thrusts. Position your fist in the middle of the victim's chest, grab your fist with the other hand, and pull sharply inward up to five times.

2 Give abdominal thrusts

- If the victim is becoming weak, or stops breathing or coughing, carry out abdominal thrusts. Stand behind the victim and put both arms around the upper part of the abdomen. Make sure he is bending forward.
- Clench your fist and place it (thumb inward) between the navel and the bottom of the breastbone. Grasp your fist with your other hand. Pull sharply inward and upward up to five times.

3 Check mouth

- Check his mouth. If the obstruction is still not cleared, repeat steps 2 and 3 up to three times, checking his mouth after each step.
- If the obstruction still has not cleared, Dial 911 or call EMS. Continue until help arrives or the victim becomes unconscious.

TREATING CHOKING (children 1–7)

①Encourage coughing

- If the child is still able to breathe, encourage him to cough. This may help dislodge the obstruction, and should always be tried before other method, such as abdominal thrusts, are used.

Encourage child to cough

②Check mouth

- Check the child's mouth carefully to see if anything has been dislodged. Encourage him to spit it out, then make sure that the obstruction has been cleared.

❗ Important

- Do not sweep your finger around the child's mouth since you might push an object farther down the throat.
- If the child becomes unconscious, open the airway, check breathing, and be prepared to begin resuscitation (pp.12–20).

③Give abdominal thrusts

- If the child shows signs of becoming weak, or stops breathing or coughing, carry out abdominal thrusts.
- Put your arms around the child's upper abdomen. Make sure that he is bending well forward.
- Place your fist between the navel and the bottom of the breastbone, and grasp it with your other hand. Pull sharply inward and upward up to five times. Stop if the obstruction clears.

Give five abdominal thrusts

④Check mouth

- Check the victim's mouth again to see if anything has been dislodged, and remove the object carefully.
- If the obstruction is still not cleared, repeat steps 3 and 4 up to three times.
- If the obstruction still has not cleared, dial 911 or call EMS.
- Continue giving abdominal thrusts until help arrives or the child becomes unconscious.

Choking (babies under 1)

Babies under 1 can easily choke on small objects. A choking baby may squeak, turn red then blue in the face, or appear to cry without making a noise. The aim of first-aid treatment is to dislodge the object as quickly as possible, using chest thrusts. If the obstruction is not removed, the baby will stop breathing and lose consciousness.

> **SIGNS & SYMPTOMS**
>
> - High-pitched squeak-like sounds, or no noise at all
> - Difficulty in breathing
> - Red face and neck, turning gray-blue

TREATING CHOKING

1 Give back slaps

- Position the baby face down along your arm, with your hand supporting her head.
- Slap her back sharply up to five times.
- Turn her over and look in her mouth to see if anything has been dislodged.
- If it has, pick it out carefully.

Give five back slaps

2 Give chest thrusts

- If the baby is still choking, lay her face upwards and place two fingers on her breastbone, just below nipple level.
- Push sharply into her chest with your fingers up to five times.
- Check her mouth again and remove anything that you can see.

Give five sharp chest thrusts

3 Repeat treatment

- If the obstruction still has not been dislodged, repeat the sequence of back slaps and chest thrusts three more times.
- If the obstruction has not been cleared after all efforts have been made, call an ambulance.
- Take the baby with you when you go to call the ambulance.
- Repeat the treatment sequence while you are waiting for the ambulance to arrive.

! Important

- Do not blindly sweep your finger around the mouth.
- If the baby becomes unconscious, open the airway, check breathing, and prepare to begin resuscitation (pp.12–20).
- Do not attempt to use abdominal thrusts on a baby.

Heart attack

A heart attack is usually caused by a blockage of the blood supply to the heart. The aims of first-aid treatment for a heart attack are to make the victim comfortable and to arrange for prompt transport to the hospital. The chances of surviving a heart attack have improved significantly in recent years, but it is still vital that the victim be treated by medical professionals as soon as possible.

SIGNS & SYMPTOMS

- Sharp chest pain often extending down left arm
- Nausea and vomiting
- Feeling faint and breathless
- Gray skin and blueish lips
- Pulse that quickens and then weakens

TREATING A HEART ATTACK

1 Make victim comfortable

- Raise the victim's shoulders so that he is half-sitting and support him with cushions or pillows.
- Bend his knees and support them with more pillows.
- Reassure him and keep him as calm as possible.

2 Summon help

- Dial 911 or call EMS. Tell the dispatcher that you are with someone who is probably having a heart attack.
- Call the victim's doctor, if you are requested to do so.

3 Help with medication

- If the victim has medication for angina, help her take it.

4 Monitor condition

- Keep the victim calm and rested.
- Check and record the victim's breathing (p.68), pulse (p.68), and level of consciousness (p.12) until medical help arrives.

Support victim's back with cushions or pillows

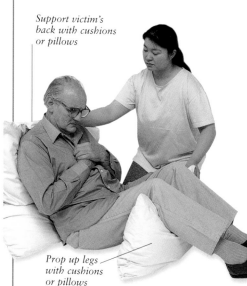

Prop up legs with cushions or pillows

! Important

- Do not allow the victim to eat or drink.
- If the victim falls unconscious, open his airway, check breathing, and be prepared to begin resuscitation (pp.12–20).

Asthma attack

During an asthma attack, muscle contractions cause the airways of the lungs to narrow, leading to swelling and inflammation of the airways' linings. This results in difficulty breathing, which can be life-threatening. The aims of first-aid treatment for an asthma attack are to help the victim to breathe and to seek medical help if symptoms do not improve.

SIGNS & SYMPTOMS

- Breathing becomes difficult
- Frequent dry, wheezy cough
- Difficulty talking
- Gray-blue tinge to skin

TREATING AN ASTHMA ATTACK

1 Calm victim

- Sit the victim down in a comfortable position. Leaning forwards is usually best.
- Reassure and calm her.
- Tell her to breathe slowly and deeply.

2 Provide medication

- Give the victim her reliever inhaler, and ask her to take a dose.
- If the victim is a child, he or she may need to have a spacer attached to the inhaler (p.167).
- The effect of the inhaler should be obvious within minutes if it is a mild asthma attack.

3 Repeat the dose

- If the inhaler has eased the symptoms, ask the victim to repeat the dose.
- Encourage her to continue breathing slowly and deeply.
- Tell her to inform her doctor if the attack was unusually severe.

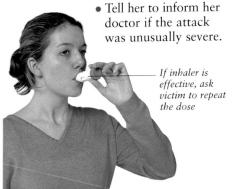

If inhaler is effective, ask victim to repeat the dose

! Important

- Do not use a preventive inhaler during an attack.
- If the victim becomes unconscious, open her airway, check breathing, and be prepared to begin resuscitation (pp.12–20).

Call an ambulance if

- This is the first attack and the victim does not have an inhaler.
- The asthma does not improve after two doses of reliever inhaler.
- The victim is exhausted and is finding breathing increasingly difficult.

Shock

Any severe injury or illness, such as severe bleeding or burns, that dramatically reduces the flow of blood around the body can cause shock. If shock is not treated rapidly, vital organs may fail. The aims of first-aid treatment are to treat any obvious cause of shock, to improve the blood supply to the vital organs, and then to get the victim to the hospital.

SIGNS & SYMPTOMS

- Fast, then weakening, pulse
- Gray-blue tinge to lips and skin
- Sweating and cold, clammy skin
- Dizziness and weakness

TREATING SHOCK

1 Treat cause of shock

- If the cause of shock is obvious, for example severe bleeding (see p.31), treat it accordingly.

2 Make victim comfortable

- If the victim is breathing normally, lay him on the floor or another firm surface, on top of a blanket if the surface is cold.
- If his legs are not injured, raise and support them so that they are above the level of his heart.
- Keep the victim still.
- Loosen any restrictive clothing around his neck, chest, and waist.
- If he is cold, cover him with a blanket or clothing.

3 Summon help

- Dial 911 or call EMS.

4 Monitor victim

- Monitor the victim's breathing (p.68 for an adult, p.71 for a child or baby), pulse (p.68 for an adult, p.70 for a child or baby), and level of consciousness (p.12) every 10 minutes until help arrives.

! Important

- Stay with the victim at all times, except if you need to dial 911 or call EMS.
- Keep the victim still.
- Do not let the victim eat, drink, or smoke.
- If the victim becomes unconscious, open his airway, check breathing, and be prepared to begin resuscitation (pp.12–20).

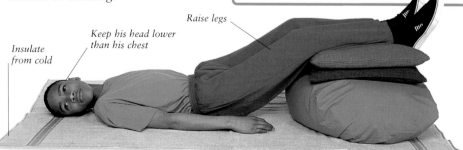

Raise legs

Keep his head lower than his chest

Insulate from cold

Anaphylactic shock

People who have an extreme sensitivity to a specific substance can suffer a rare and severe type of allergic reaction known as anaphylactic shock. The reaction spreads through the body, causing a sudden drop in blood pressure and narrowing of the airways, and can be fatal. The aims of first-aid treatment are to help the victim inject epinephrine (Epipen) and to summon help.

SIGNS & SYMPTOMS

- Itchy red skin rash
- Swollen face, lips, and tongue
- Anxiety
- Difficulty breathing, wheezing

TREATING ANAPHYLACTIC SHOCK

1 Summon help

- Dial 911 or call EMS, or ask someone else to do so.
- Tell the dispatcher if you know what has caused the reaction.

2 Make victim comfortable

- If the victim is conscious, help him into a sitting position to ease difficulty breathing.

Sitting up should aid victim's breathing

3 Look for Epipen

- If the victim has an Epipen, get it for him so that he can administer it.

- Epinephrine is usually administered into the outer thigh, through any clothing.

Place Epipen against thigh and depress needle

4 Monitor victim

- Monitor victim's breathing (p.68 for an adult, p.71 for a child or baby), pulse (p.68 for an adult, p.70 for a child or baby), and level of consciousness (p.12) every 10 minutes until help arrives.

! Important

- Stay with the victim at all times, except if you have to leave him to dial 911 or call EMS.
- If the victim becomes unconscious, open his airway, check his breathing, and be prepared to begin resuscitation (pp.12–20).

Head injury

Although a head injury sometimes leaves no visible wound, there may be obvious bruising or bleeding at the site. The victim may have a headache. The aims of first-aid treatment are to control bleeding, dress the wound, and seek medical help. Even apparently minor head injuries should always be seen by a doctor.

SIGNS & SYMPTOMS

- Bleeding or bruising at the site of the wound
- Depression in the skull
- Dizziness or nausea
- Headache and memory loss

TREATING A HEAD INJURY

1 Treat visible wounds

- If there is a scalp wound, replace any skin flaps.
- Press a clean pad firmly over the wound to control the blood flow.
- Maintain the pressure for at least 10 minutes until the blood flow has been controlled.
- Secure a bandage around the victim's head to hold the pad in position.

Lie victim down in case of shock

3 Monitor victim

- Monitor the victim's breathing (p.68 for an adult, p.71 for a child or baby), pulse (p.68 for an adult, p.70 for a child or baby), and level of consciousness (p.12) every 10 minutes until help arrives.

Use a pillow to support her head and shoulders

2 Assess victim

- Check that the victim is fully conscious by asking simple, direct questions in a clear voice.
- If she answers your questions, lay her down in a comfortable position, then arrange for transport to the hospital.
- If the victim does not respond, ask someone to dial 911 or call EMS.
- If you need to leave an unconscious victim, place her in the recovery position first (pp.14–15) unless you suspect a spinal injury.

! Important

- Use disposable gloves and/or wash your hands well when dealing with body fluids.
- If the victim becomes unconscious, open her airway, check her breathing, and be prepared to begin resuscitation (pp.12–20).

Dial 911 or call EMS if

- The victim is unconscious, appears confused, or her condition is deteriorating.
- There is a depression or soft patch in her skull, or blood or watery fluid is leaking from her ears or nose; these indicate a skull fracture.

Stroke

An interruption of the blood supply to the brain, caused by a blood clot or a ruptured artery in the brain, is known as a stroke. The effect of a stroke depends on which part, and how much, of the brain is affected. Although a major stroke can be fatal, a minor stroke is not life-threatening, and a full recovery is possible. Whether the victim is conscious or unconscious, it is important that he or she is taken to hospital as soon as possible in order to minimize any brain damage caused by the stroke.

SIGNS & SYMPTOMS

- Acute headache
- Confusion, which could be mistaken for drunkenness
- Weakness or paralysis, possibly on just one side of the body, manifested in slurred speech, drooping mouth, and a loss of limb, bladder, or bowel control
- Possible unconsciousness

TREATING A STROKE

1 Lay victim down

- Make the victim comfortable by laying her down and supporting her head and shoulders slightly with cushions or rolled-up blankets.
- Tilt her face to one side to allow any fluid to drain out of her mouth, and wipe her face with a washcloth. Alternatively, place something absorbent on her shoulder to soak up the fluid.
- Loosen restrictive clothing around her neck and chest.

2 Summon help

- Ask someone to dial 911 or call EMS immediately.

3 Monitor victim

- Check and record the victim's breathing (p.68), pulse (p.68), and level of consciousness (p.12) every 10 minutes until help arrives.

! Important

- Do not allow the victim to have anything to eat or drink.
- If the victim is or falls unconscious, open her airway, check breathing, and be prepared to begin resuscitation (pp.12–20).

Use washcloth to absorb any fluid

Severe bleeding

A heavy loss of blood is often distressing and can be life-threatening. The aims of first-aid treatment are to stop the bleeding, dress the wound as quickly as possible, and respond to any condition, such as shock or unconsciousness, that may result from heavy loss of blood or from the wound itself.

TREATING SEVERE BLEEDING

1 Control blood flow

- If necessary, remove or cut away any clothing to expose the wound.
- Cover the injury with a sterile wound dressing, a clean pad if you have one, or with your hand.
- Press the wound firmly for 10 minutes, or longer if necessary, until the bleeding stops. Use disposable gloves if available.
- If possible, raise injured part above the victim's heart level. If part may be fractured, handle it with care.

Keep part raised above heart level

Keep firm, even pressure on the wound until bleeding stops

2 Lay victim down

- If the bleeding does not stop, lay the victim on a firm surface, keeping the injured part raised.
- Loosen any restrictive clothing.

3 Secure dressing

- Bandage the wound dressing firmly but not too tightly (p.61, checking circulation).
- If blood seeps through the dressing, cover it with another one. If bleeding continues, remove both dressings and apply a fresh one.

4 Summon help

- Ask someone to dial 911, or do so yourself.

5 Monitor victim

- Watch for signs of shock (p.27).
- Monitor the victim's breathing (p.68 for an adult, p.71 for a child or baby), pulse (p.68 for an adult, p.70 for a child or baby), and level of consciousness (p.12) every 10 minutes until help arrives.

! Important

- Use disposable gloves and/or wash your hands well when dealing with body fluids.
- Do not apply a tourniquet.
- If there is an object in a wound, place padding on either side of the object so that the dressing will rest on the pads, not the object.
- If the victim becomes unconscious, open her airway, check her breathing, and be prepared to begin resuscitation (pp.12–20).

Penetrating chest wounds

A deep wound to the chest can cause direct or indirect damage to the lungs, which may lead to a collapsed lung, and damage to the heart. The aims of first-aid treatment for a penetrating chest wound are to stop the bleeding, to help prevent the victim from going into shock, and to get the victim to the hospital for treatment as quickly as possible.

SIGNS & SYMPTOMS

- Difficult, painful breathing
- Acute distress
- Presence of frothy blood at mouth
- Possible signs of shock

TREATING PENETRATING CHEST WOUNDS

1 Control blood flow

- Expose the wound and press the palm of your hand against it, or get the victim to do it himself.
- Support the victim in a semi-upright or half-sitting position.

2 Dress wound

- Cover the wound with a sterile dressing or clean pad.
- Cover the dressing with a piece of aluminum foil, plastic wrap, or a plastic bag to prevent air from entering the chest cavity.
- Secure the dressing with a bandage or strips of adhesive or micro-porous tape. Apply the tape to three sides of the dressing only.

3 Make victim comfortable

- Encourage the victim to lean toward the side of the wound.
- Try to make him as comfortable as possible, using additional cushions or pillows to support him as necessary.
- Loosen any restrictive clothing around his waist.

4 Summon help

- Dial 911 or call EMS. Tell the dispatcher where the injury is and describe the extent of the bleeding.
- Watch carefully for any signs of shock developing (p.27).

! Important

- Use disposable gloves and/or wash your hands well when dealing with body fluids.
- If the victim is or falls unconscious, open his airway, check his breathing, and be prepared to begin resuscitation (pp.12–20).
- If you need to put him in the recovery position (pp.14–15), lay him on his injured side.

Cover pad with plastic wrap and secure with tape

Cuts and scrapes

Small wounds, such as cuts and scrapes, rarely bleed for long and require little in the way of first-aid treatment. What is important, however, is to clean the wound and apply a sterile wound dressing as quickly as possible in order to minimize the risk of infection. Check, too, that the victim's tetanus immunization is up to date, and arrange a booster dose if necessary.

SIGNS & SYMPTOMS

- Oozing blood
- Localized pain
- Scraped area containing dirt and dust particles

TREATING CUTS AND SCRAPES

1 Clean wound

- Sit the victim down and reassure her. Even a minor fall can leave a victim feeling shaky.
- Rinse dirt from the cut or scrape under cold running water.
- Gently clean the entire wound area with sterile gauze swabs. Use a new swab for each stroke and work from the wound outward.
- Lift any loose material, such as glass, gravel, or metal with the corner of a gauze swab.
- Carefully pat the area dry with a clean gauze swab.

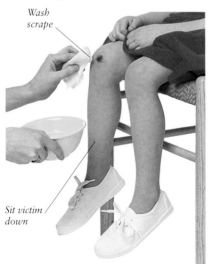

Wash scrape

Sit victim down

2 Dress wound

- For smaller cuts and scrapes, cover the injured area with an adhesive bandage.
- For larger injuries, place a sterile wound dressing over the injury and bandage it in place (p.61).
- Rest the injured limb, preferably in a raised position.

Protect scrape with an adhesive bandage

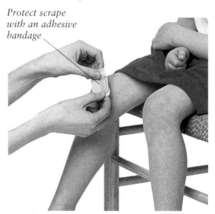

! Important

- Use disposable gloves and/or wash your hands well when dealing with body fluids.
- Do not touch the cut or scrape with your fingers to avoid infecting the wound.
- Avoid using cotton or any other dry fluffy material to clean a cut or scrape – such material is likely to stick to the wound.

Splinters

It is very common to find small splinters of wood embedded in the skin of hands, knees, and feet, especially those of children. It is usually possible to remove splinters by hand or using tweezers, having made sure that the wound has first been cleaned and the tweezers sterilized. If splinters remain embedded or lie over a joint, seek medical help.

TREATING SPLINTERS

1 Sterilize tweezers

- Using soap and warm water, clean the affected area thoroughly.
- Sterilize a pair of tweezers by heating them in a flame.

Sterilize tweezers in a flame

2 Pull out splinter

- Grip the splinter with the tweezers, then pull it out in a straight line in the opposite direction to which it entered.
- Try not to break the splinter.

Grasp splinter and pull it straight out

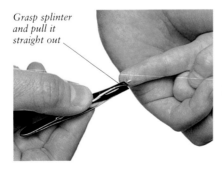

3 Clean wound

- Squeeze the area around the wound to make it bleed. This helps to flush out any remaining dirt.
- Clean the affected area and cover it with an adhesive bandage.
- Check that the victim's tetanus immunization is up to date.

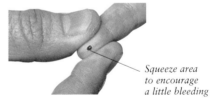

Squeeze area to encourage a little bleeding

4 Dress embedded splinter

- If the splinter breaks, or will not come out, place pads on either side, and a bandage over it, taking care not to press down on the splinter.
- Seek medical help.

! Important

- Do not attempt to use a needle to lever out the splinter.
- Use disposable gloves and/or wash your hands well when dealing with body fluids.

Eye wound

Any wound to the eye is potentially serious. Blows to the eye can cause bruising or cuts, and sharp fragments of materials, such as glass, can become embedded in the eye's surface. Even a superficial scrape can result in scarring and vision deterioration. The aims of first-aid treatment for an eye wound are to prevent any further damage, to dress the wound, and to get the victim to the hospital.

SIGNS & SYMPTOMS

- Sharp pain in injured eye
- Visible wound or bloodshot eye
- Partial or total loss of vision
- Blood or clear fluid leaking from injured eye

TREATING AN EYE WOUND

1 Keep victim still

- Lay the victim on a firm surface, placing a blanket underneath him if it is cold.
- Kneel down and support his head on your knees, holding it as still as possible.
  - Tell him to keep both his eyes shut and still.

Tell victim to keep both eyes still

Support his head

2 Dress wound

- Hold a sterile wound dressing or clean pad over the injured eye, or ask the victim to do it, and ask him to keep his uninjured eye still.
- Keep his head steady.

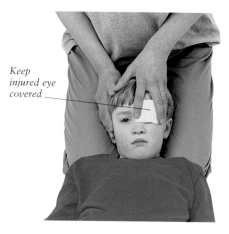

Keep injured eye covered

3 Summon help

- Ask someone to dial 911 or call EMS. If you call yourself, first place some cushions under the victim's head for support.
- Alternatively, if you can keep the victim still and laying down, take him to the hospital yourself.

! Important

- Do not touch the affected eye or allow the victim to touch it.

Foreign object in the eye

Eyelashes, bits of dust, and dislodged contact lenses are common eye irritants. They usually float on the white of the eye, and can be easily removed. Anything that rests on the coloured part of the eye or is stuck on or embedded in the eye's surface, however, will demand hospital attention. Your aims are to prevent injury to the eye and seek hospital care, if necessary.

SIGNS & SYMPTOMS

- Eye pain or discomfort
- Blurred vision
- Red or watering eye

TREATING A FOREIGN OBJECT IN THE EYE

1 Examine eye

- Sit the victim down so that she is facing the light.
- Using two fingers, gently separate the upper and lower eyelids so that you can examine the eye.

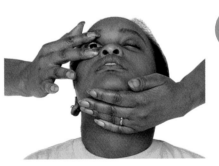

2 Flush out object

- If you can see something floating on the white of the eye or trapped under the lower lid, try to flush it out with clean water.
- Tilt the head so that the injured eye is lower than the other one.
- Pour water carefully into the corner of the injured eye, allowing the liquid to drain away.
- Alternatively, tell the victim to immerse her face in a sinkful of water and try blinking.

3 Lift off object

- If flushing does not work, use the corner of a clean, dampened handkerchief or tissue to lift the foreign object off the eye.
- Do not use any pressure.

4 Inspect upper eyelid

- Look under the upper eyelid to see if a foreign object has lodged there. To remove it, ask the victim to grasp the upper lashes and pull the eyelid over the lower one.
- If this fails to help, bathe the eye in water and ask the victim to blink.

5 Seek medical help

- If all your efforts to remove the foreign object are unsuccessful, take the victim to the hospital.

! Important

- If anything is stuck to the eye, penetrating the eyeball, or resting on the colored part of the eye, treat as for an eye wound (p.35).
- Do not touch the affected eye or allow the victim to touch it.

Chemicals in the eye

When splashes of chemicals get into the eyes, they can cause serious damage, resulting in scarring and even blindness. The primary aim of first-aid treatment is to effectively irrigate the eye, or flush it with water, in order to disperse hazardous substances. The next step is to dress the eye, and then seek hospital care for the victim.

SIGNS & SYMPTOMS
• Eye redness and swelling
• Watering of the eye
• Sharp pain in the eye
• Signs of chemicals nearby

TREATING CHEMICALS IN THE EYE

1 Rinse eye

- If the victim cannot open his eye, use your finger and thumb to gently separate the two eyelids.
- Hold the affected eye under gently running cold water for at least 10 minutes.
- Be careful that water being rinsed from the injured eye does not drain into the other eye or splash either you or the victim.
- If it is easier, use a jug or glass to pour water onto the eye.

2 Seek medical help

- Ask the victim to hold a sterile pad, or one made from clean, nonfluffy material, such as a handkerchief, over the injured eye.
- If possible, identify the chemical.
- Take or send him to the hospital.

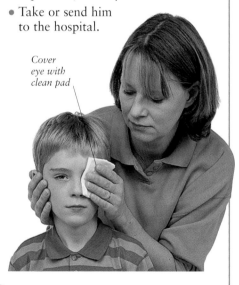

Cover eye with clean pad

Wear protective gloves

Wash eye with cold water for 10 minutes

! Important

- Do not touch the affected eye or allow the victim to touch it.
- If chemical spray is the irritant, face the victim into the wind. Do not attempt to flush it out using water.
- Wear gloves to protect yourself.

Bleeding from the mouth

Damage to a tooth and cuts to the mouth lining, lips, or tongue are common causes of bleeding from the mouth. The aim of first-aid treatment is to control severe bleeding; large amounts of blood, if swallowed, can cause vomiting, while inhalation of blood can cause choking.

TREATING BLEEDING FROM THE MOUTH

1 Control bleeding

- Ask the victim to sit with his head tilted forward. This helps the blood to drain away. Give him a bowl to spit into.
- Press a gauze pad on the wound for up to 10 minutes to stop the bleeding.

Press a pad on the wound

2 Monitor wound

- If the wound continues to bleed, take a fresh gauze pad and reapply pressure for 10 more minutes.
- Encourage the victim to spit out blood rather than swallow it.

TREATING A KNOCKED-OUT TOOTH

1 Replant tooth

- If an adult tooth is knocked out, replant it in its socket as soon as possible and tell the victim to see a dentist right away.
- If you cannot replant the tooth, keep it in milk or water until the victim reaches a dentist or doctor.
- If a baby tooth is knocked out, do not attempt to replant it.

Reposition missing adult tooth in its socket

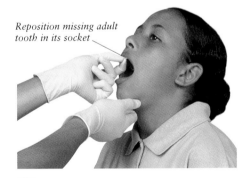

! Important

- Do not wash the mouth out, as this may disturb a clot.
- If the wound is large, or if it is still bleeding after 30 minutes of pressure, consult a dentist or doctor.

2 Control bleeding

- If the knocked-out tooth cannot be found, place a thick gauze pad across the socket, making sure that the pad stands higher than the teeth on either side of the gap.
- Tell the victim to bite on the pad.

Nosebleed

A nosebleed is most often caused by the rupturing of blood vessels inside the nostrils. This can happen following a blow to the nose, sneezing or blowing the nose. Nosebleeds occur more frequently during bouts of cold or flu when the blood vessels are more fragile. The aims of first-aid treatment for a nosebleed are to control the bleeding and to comfort the victim. A child, in particular, may find the sight and smell of the blood upsetting.

TREATING A NOSEBLEED

1 Control bleeding

- Seat the victim with her head leaning forward over a bowl.
- Ask her to pinch her nose just below the bridge and to breathe through her mouth. If the victim is a child, pinch it for her.
- Tell her to avoid coughing, spitting, sniffing, swallowing, or speaking, since any of these actions could disturb a blood clot.

Pinch her nostrils together for 10 minutes

Tell her to spit into a bowl

3 Clean victim

- When the bleeding has stopped, clean the blood away with lukewarm water, ensuring that the victim is still leaning forward.
- Tell the victim to rest for a while.
- Advise her not to blow her nose as it could disturb the blood clots.

Clean gently with cotton

2 Assess situation

- After 10 minutes, release the pressure on the victim's nose.
- If the bleeding continues when the pressure is released, pinch her nose for 10 more minutes.
- If, after 30 minutes, the nose is still bleeding, take her to the hospital. Keep her leaning forward.

! Important

- Do not allow the victim to lie down or tilt her head back; the blood could trickle down her throat and cause vomiting.
- If the blood is thin and watery, this indicates a fractured skull. Seek medical help immediately.

Emergency childbirth

Childbirth is rarely an emergency, since the very nature of labor means that it usually lasts for hours, therefore there is generally plenty of time to summon medical help. In the event that you do have to care for a woman who is about to give birth, however, your aims should be to call for medical help, to support the woman and keep her calm, and to care for the baby when he or she is born.

TREATING EMERGENCY CHILDBIRTH

1 Summon help

- Dial 911 or call EMS, telling the dispatcher the name of the hospital where the woman is due to give birth, her expected delivery date, and any other relevant information.

2 Make woman comfortable

- Try to make the woman reasonably comfortable as she copes with the contractions. She may want to sit propped up, with her knees drawn up, or she may prefer to kneel, with her upper body leaning on some pillows or folded blankets. It is best to take the lead from her as to what is comfortable.

- Encourage her to breathe slowly during and after the contractions. Regular breathing should calm her and help with the pain; it also gives her something to concentrate on.

3 Prepare equipment

- Assemble as many of the following items as possible: disposable gloves; face mask or piece of cotton material; sanitary napkins; plastic bags; warm water; plastic sheeting or newspapers; clean towels; pillows; blankets.

- Wash your hands and nails thoroughly, even if you will be wearing disposable gloves.

- Put on a face mask or improvise one out of clean cotton material.

- Cover whatever surface the mother is laying on with plastic sheeting or newspapers. Add a layer of towels on top for comfort and absorbency.

Leaning forwards from a kneeling position can help to reduce back ache

Support her with pillows

4 Monitor birth

- If the woman feels the urge to push, encourage her to bear down with each contraction.
- Tell her when the widest part of the baby's head is visible. At this point she needs to stop pushing and change her breathing technique to panting.
- Check for a layer of membrane over the baby's face. If there is one, tear it away.
- Check that the umbilical cord is not wrapped around the baby's neck. If it is, then very gently pull it over the baby's head to prevent strangulation.
- Once the baby's head and shoulders are visible, the next contraction should expel the rest of the baby's body.

5 Check baby

- Lift up the baby very carefully and lay her on her mother's stomach.
- Newborn babies will appear blue initially. Look for signs of circulation (p.17). If the baby remains blue and shows no signs of life, begin resuscitation (pp.12–20).

6 Wrap baby

- Wrap the baby in a clean blanket or towel, still with the umbilical cord attached, and give her to the mother to hold.
- If the mother cannot hold the baby, place the baby on her side on a firm but soft surface.

7 Deliver afterbirth

- Mild contractions will continue after the baby is born until the placenta is delivered.
- Put the placenta into a plastic bag so that a doctor or midwife can check that it is complete.
- Clean the mother with warm water and towels and give her sanitary napkins to absorb any further bleeding.
- Some bleeding is normal, but if the bleeding seems excessive, massage the mother's stomach just below the navel to help control the flow.
- Advise the mother to breastfeed, if possible, because it encourages the uterus to contract.

! Important

- Do not give the mother anything to eat.
- Do not pull the baby's head and shoulders out.
- Do not cut the umbilical cord.
- Do not dispose of the afterbirth.
- Do not smack the baby.

Major seizures

A convulsion, or major seizure, is the result of an electrical disturbance in the brain and consists of muscular spasms and loss of body control. Seizures that are recurrent usually indicate the brain disorder epilepsy. The aims of first-aid treatment for major seizures are to protect the victim from injuring herself and to summon medical help if necessary.

SIGNS & SYMPTOMS

- Rigid body with arched back and clenched jaw
- Eyes rolled upwards
- Convulsive shaking
- Seizure followed by sleep

TREATING MAJOR SEIZURES

1 Protect victim

- If you see the victim falling at the beginning of the seizure, try to prevent injury as she falls.
- Do not move her while she is having the seizure.
  - Loosen the clothing around her neck and try to protect her head with something soft, such as a piece of folded clothing.

Protect the victim's head

Do not try to restrain the victim during the seizure

3 Summon help

- If you know the victim has epilepsy, and she only has one seizure at this time, stay with her until she has recovered.
- If you are not certain that the victim is susceptible to epileptic seizures, dial 911 or call EMS.
- If the victim remains unconscious for more than 10 minutes or convulses for more than 5 minutes, or if she has repeated seizures, dial 911 or call EMS.
- Monitor the victim's breathing (p.68 for an adult, p.71 for a child or baby), pulse (p.68 for an adult, p.70 for a child or baby), and level of consciousness (p.12) until help arrives.

2 Monitor victim

- After the seizure, the victim may fall into a deep sleep. Check her breathing (p.14), open her airway, and be prepared to resuscitate her.
- If the victim is breathing, place her in the recovery position (pp.14–15).

! Important

- Move sharp objects away from the victim.
- Do not use force to restrain the victim.
- Do not put anything in the victim's mouth.

Febrile seizures

Seizures that occur in young children as a result of a very high temperature are known as febrile seizures. Children under the age of 5 are most likely to suffer from a seizure, which is alarming to watch but is rarely dangerous to the child. The aims of first-aid treatment are to lower the child's temperature, protect her from injury, and summon medical help.

SIGNS & SYMPTOMS

- Arched back, clenched fists, stiff legs and arms
- Eyes rolled upwards
- Head and body jerking
- High fever

TREATING FEBRILE SEIZURES

1 Protect child

- Place pillows, rolled-up blankets, towels, or clothing around the child to help protect her from injury.
- Do not move the victim while she is having a seizure.

2 Cool child

- Remove clothing or bedcovers to cool the child down.
- Working from the head down, sponge the child's body all over with tepid water.
- Do not dry the child; instead, allow the moisture to evaporate from her skin.
- Do not let her get too cold.

3 Get help

- Dial 911 or call EMS.

4 Monitor victim

- Monitor the child's temperature at regular intervals (p.70).
- Give the recommended dose of acetaminophen liquid when the seizures have stopped.
- Stop cooling her down as soon as her temperature reaches a normal 98.6°F (37°C).

! Important

- Do not use force in an attempt to restrain the child.
- Do not put anything in the child's mouth.

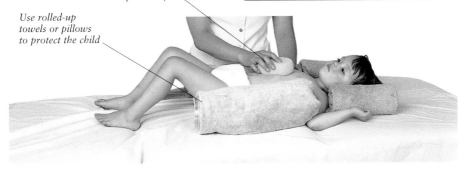

Sponge the child with tepid water until her temperature falls

Use rolled-up towels or pillows to protect the child

Broken arm

The fracture of an arm bone is not as serious as that of a leg bone (p.45) because the victim is usually able to walk and get to the hospital relatively easily. The aims of first-aid treatment for a broken arm are to control any bleeding, to support the injured arm with a sling, and to transport the victim to the hospital, keeping the arm as still as possible.

SIGNS & SYMPTOMS

- Limb held at awkward angle
- Limb cannot be moved
- Severe pain
- Swelling and bruising
- Possible wound above fracture site

TREATING A BROKEN ARM

1 Support arm

- Sit the victim down.
- If there is a wound, treat any bleeding (p.31).
- Ask the victim to support the injured arm across his chest so that it feels comfortable. Tell him to hold the injured hand a little higher than the elbow.

Keep the arm raised slightly

2 Put arm in sling

- Put some padding between the arm and the chest for comfort, then support the injured arm with a sling (p.63).
- To keep the arm still, tie another folded triangular bandage around the chest and over the sling.

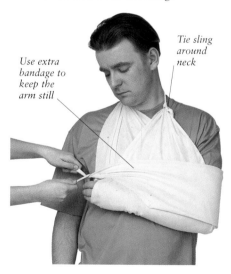

Tie sling around neck

Use extra bandage to keep the arm still

! Important

- Do not give the victim anything to eat, drink, or smoke.
- If the elbow is injured, do not attempt to bend the arm. Lay the victim down, surround the limb with padding, and dial 911 or call EMS.
- An injured arm may not be fractured, but if you are in doubt, treat it as a fracture until it can be x-rayed.

3 Seek medical help

- Take or send the victim to the hospital to have the injury assessed.
- Make sure that the arm is kept still during the trip to the hospital.

Broken leg

The fracture of a leg bone is a serious injury that requires immediate hospital treatment. It is important that the victim does not put any weight on the injured limb. Thigh bone fractures may involve severe internal bleeding, which can cause shock. The aims of first-aid treatment are to control any bleeding, to support the limb, and to dial 911 or call EMS.

SIGNS & SYMPTOMS

- Limb held at awkward angle
- Limb cannot be moved
- Severe pain
- Swelling and bruising
- Possible wound or internal bleeding if thigh is injured

TREATING A BROKEN LEG

1 Support leg

- Help the victim to lie down.
- If there is a wound, treat any bleeding (p.31).
- Put plenty of soft padding, such as rolled-up blankets or towels, on each side of the fractured leg.
- Dial 911 or call EMS.

Hold the injured leg steady

Use a rolled-up towel to support the leg

2 Immobilize leg

- If you can stay with the victim, and there is no need to move her, leave the padding in place and, if necessary, support the leg with your hands.
- If you need to move the victim out of danger, immobilize the injured leg by bandaging it to the other one. Tie folded triangular bandages around the joints above and below the fracture site.

! Important

- Do not give the victim anything to eat, drink, or smoke.
- Do not move the victim unless she is in danger.
- An injured leg may not be fractured, but if you are in doubt, treat it as a fracture until it can be x-rayed.

3 Monitor victim

- Watch for signs of shock (p.27).
- Check her breathing (p.68 for an adult, p.71 for a baby or child) and pulse (p.68 for an adult, p.70 for a baby or child) while waiting for help to arrive.

Spinal injuries

Damage to the spinal cord can cause permanent loss of movement below the injured area, therefore all spinal injuries are potentially serious. The aims of first-aid treatment of a suspected spinal injury are to dial 911 or call EMS, and to keep the victim immobile until medical help arrives, because even the slightest movement could damage the spinal cord.

SIGNS & SYMPTOMS

- Pain in neck or back
- Burning sensation or tingling in a limb
- Loss of feeling in a limb
- Inability to move legs

TREATING SPINAL INJURIES

1 Summon help

- Dial 911 or call EMS.

2 Immobilize victim

- Leave the victim in the position in which you found her.
- Reassure her and support her head to prevent any movement.
- Ask someone to place rolled-up clothes or towels on either side of the victim's head and body to help keep her still.
- Stay with her until help arrives.

3 Monitor victim

- Monitor her breathing (p.68 for an adult, p.71 for a child or baby), pulse (p.68 for an adult, p.70 for a child or baby), and level of consciousness (p.12) every 10 minutes while waiting for help.

! Important

- Do not move the victim unless she is in danger or needs to be resuscitated.
- If she loses consciousness, open her airway by tilting her head only slightly, and monitor her breathing.
- If breathing becomes difficult for her, have several other people help to move the victim into the recovery position. Put your hands over her ears to keep her head aligned and, working as a team, roll her over very gently, making sure that you keep the neck and back aligned at all times.

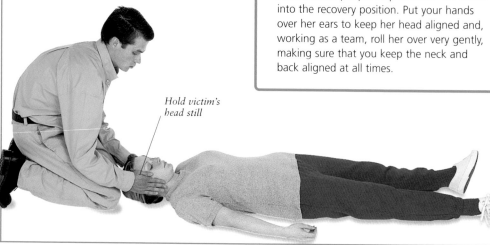

Hold victim's head still

Sprains and strains

Sprains occur when ligaments and other tissues that surround and support a joint are torn or stretched. A strain refers to muscles or tendons that are damaged or overstretched. Both injuries may lead to pain, swelling, deformity, and discoloration. Treatment follows the "RICE" procedure: rest, ice (or cold pack), compression, and elevation.

SIGNS & SYMPTOMS

- Pain and swelling in the affected area
- Deformity and discoloration

TREATING SPRAINS AND STRAINS

1 Support injury

- Steady and support the injured part.
- For extra support, place the injured limb on your knee or in your lap.

2 Cool injury

- Prepare a cold compress: either soak a washcloth or towel in cold water and wring it out lightly, wrap a towel around a packet of frozen peas, or fill a plastic bag with small ice cubes. Apply the compress to the affected area to reduce swelling, bruising, and pain.
- Do not apply ice directly to the skin, because this can burn it.

3 Apply compression

- Place a thick layer of padding, such as cotton wool, around the injury.
- Secure the padding in place with a roller bandage (p.62) to apply a gentle, even pressure to the injured area. Make sure that the bandage is not too tight (p.61).

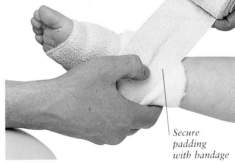

Secure padding with bandage

Use cold compress to reduce swelling

4 Elevate injury

- Raise and support the limb to help reduce bruising and swelling.
- Advise the victim to rest the limb and to see a doctor.

! Important

- When you apply compression, make sure that you do not obstruct the blood supply to the tissues surrounding the injured area (p.61).

Severe burns

A burn that affects all the layers of the skin or covers a large area of the body is a severe burn. The aim of first-aid treatment is to cool down the affected area rapidly to minimize damage and loss of body fluids, and therefore reduce the risk of developing shock. Any burn larger than the palm of the victim's hand, whatever the depth, needs hospital treatment.

SIGNS & SYMPTOMS

- Skin that is red, brown and charred, or white
- Blisters
- Unconsciousness
- Clear fluid dripping from skin
- Signs of shock (p.27)

TREATING SEVERE BURNS

1 Put out fire

- If the victim's clothing is on fire, force her to the ground and use a wool or cotton blanket, rug, or coat to smother the flames (p.182).
- If possible, have someone dial 911 or call EMS for medical help and, if necessary, the fire department.

2 Cool burn

- Immerse the burn in cool water, douse it with water, or cover it with cold, wet towels for at least 10 minutes.
- If there is no water, use cold milk or a canned drink to cool the burn.

3 Expose injury

- Gently remove any clothing, shoes, belts, or jewelry near the burn, but leave anything that is stuck to it.
- Cover the burn with a sterile wound dressing or clean nonfluffy material.

4 Make victim comfortable

- Lay the victim down, keeping the burn away from the ground and, if possible, above heart level.
- Dial 911 or call EMS if help is not already on the way.

5 Monitor victim

- Monitor the victim's breathing (p.68 for an adult, p.71 for a child or baby), pulse (p.68 for an adult, p.70 for a child or baby), and level of consciousness (p.12) every 10 minutes while waiting for help.
- Watch for signs of shock (p.27).

! Important

- Do not apply any ointments to the burn.
- Do not touch the burn or burst any blisters.
- Do not put ice or iced water on the burn.

Minor burns and scalds

A burn that damages only the outer layer of the skin or affects a relatively small area is a minor burn or scald. Although such burns can be red and painful and may swell and blister, most heal well within a few days if treated promptly. Your aims are to cool the burn and to cover it with a sterile wound dressing to minimize the risk of infection.

SIGNS & SYMPTOMS

- Red and painful skin
- Blisters dripping clear fluid

TREATING MINOR BURNS AND SCALDS

1 Cool burn

- Pour cool water over the injured area for at least 10 minutes.
- If there is no water, use cold milk or a canned drink to cool the burn.

Cool the burn with water

2 Expose injury

- Gently remove any clothing, shoes, belts, or jewelry near the burn before the area starts to swell and blister.
- Do not remove anything that is stuck to the burn because this could worsen the injury.

3 Dress burn

- Cover the burn with a sterile wound dressing or clean nonfluffy material.
- Wrap a bandage loosely over the dressing to secure it (p.61).

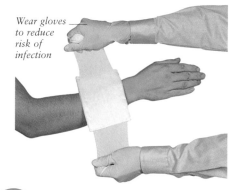

Wear gloves to reduce risk of infection

4 Monitor wound

- Check the wound daily for any signs of infection, such as pain, swelling, redness, or pus.
- If you suspect that it has become infected, advise the victim to see a doctor at once.

! Important

- Do not apply anything other than cool liquid to the burn.
- Do not touch the burn or burst any blisters.
- Do not put ice or iced water on the burn.

Sunburn

Ultraviolet rays in sunlight can damage cells in the outer layer of human skin, causing soreness, redness, and blistering. Skin can burn after just 30 minutes of exposure to the sun and sunburn is most likely to occur in the middle of the day, though symptoms may not develop immediately. The aims of treatment are to move the victim out of the sun, to cool the affected area, and to apply soothing lotions or creams.

SIGNS & SYMPTOMS

- Very red, hot skin
- Soreness
- Swelling
- Blistering
- Possible signs of heatstroke (p.52)

TREATING SUNBURN

1 Move victim inside

- If the victim is outside, move him into the shade or indoors.

2 Cool burn

- Get the victim into a cold bath, or apply damp towels or cold water to the burn for at least 10 minutes.

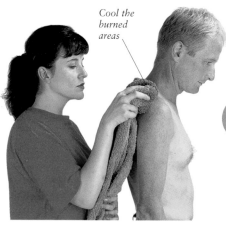

Cool the burned areas

3 Give fluid

- See that the victim sips plenty of cold water while you cool his skin.

Ensure that he takes small sips of fluid

4 Apply lotion

- Gently smooth calamine lotion or after-sun cream onto the burned areas. Reapply as necessary.

Put cream on burn

! Important

- If the skin is badly blistered, advise the victim to see a doctor.
- If the victim has severe sunburn and heatstroke (p.52), call 911.

Heat exhaustion

Caused by excessive sweating, heat exhaustion occurs when vital salt and water are lost through the skin. People who are unused to hot and humid conditions, and those suffering from any illness that causes diarrhea and vomiting, are often the most susceptible. The aims of first-aid treatment are to cool the victim and to replace lost salts and water. Heat exhaustion can develop into heatstroke.

SIGNS & SYMPTOMS

- Feeling dizzy or confused
- Headache and nausea
- Sweating, with pallid, clammy skin
- Arm, leg, or abdominal cramps
- Fast but weak pulse

TREATING HEAT EXHAUSTION

1 Make victim comfortable

- Move the victim to a cool place.
- Lay him down and support his legs in a raised position to improve the blood flow to vital organs.

2 Replace lost fluids

- Give him cool, salty drinks. Ideally, offer isotonic drinks or a weak salt and sugar solution (1 teaspoon of salt and 4 teaspoons of sugar to 1 liter of water).
- Support his head while he is drinking, if necessary.
- If he recovers, ask him to see a doctor.

3 Summon help

- If the victim becomes weaker or confused, place him in the recovery position (p.14 for adults and children, p.15 for babies).
- Dial 911 or call EMS.

4 Monitor victim

- Monitor the victim's breathing (p.68 for an adult, p.71 for a child or baby), pulse (p.68 for an adult, p.70 for a child or baby), and level of consciousness (p.12) every 10 minutes until help arrives.

! Important

- If the victim loses consciousness, open his airway, check his breathing, and be prepared to begin resuscitation (pp.12–20).

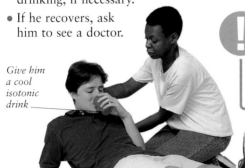

Give him a cool isotonic drink

Raise his legs

Heatstroke

If the human body is exposed to unusually high temperatures for a prolonged period, it can become dangerously overheated. The onset of heatstroke can be sudden, and the victim may lose consciousness within minutes. The aims of first-aid treatment are to move the victim to a cool place, to reduce his temperature, and to get him to a hospital quickly.

SIGNS & SYMPTOMS

- Headache and dizziness
- Hot, flushed skin
- Poor level of response
- Rapid pulse
- Raised body temperature (over 104°F/40°C)

TREATING HEATSTROKE

1 Make victim comfortable

- Move the victim to a cool place.
- Remove as much of his clothing as possible.

Lay him down in a cool place

Remove his clothes

4 Monitor victim

- Once the victim's temperature has fallen to 98.6°F (37°C) under the tongue or 97.7°F (36.5°C) beneath the armpit, replace the wet sheet (if used) with a dry one.
- Monitor the victim's condition until medical help arrives.
- If his temperature rises again, cool him down following the same procedure as before.

2 Summon help

- Dial 911 or call EMS.

3 Cool victim

- Drape a cold, wet sheet over the victim. Spray or sprinkle it with water to keep it wet. Alternatively, sponge him with cold or tepid water, or fan him with cold air.
- Keep cooling the victim until his temperature drops to 100°F (38°C) under the tongue or 99°F (37.4°C) beneath the armpit (p.68 for an adult, p.70 for a child or baby).

! Important

- If the victim loses consciousness, open his airway, check his breathing, and be prepared to begin resuscitation (pp.12–20).

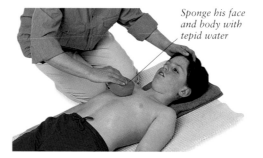

Sponge his face and body with tepid water

Fainting

Pain, fright, fatigue, hunger, emotion, or simply standing still for a long period of time have all been known to interrupt the flow of oxygen to the brain, which can cause a temporary loss of consciousness, or a faint. Your aims are to improve bloodflow to the victim's brain, to make her comfortable, and to treat any injuries that may have occurred when the victim fell. Recovery is usually rapid.

SIGNS & SYMPTOMS

- Feeling dizzy, weak, and sometimes nauseous
- Sweating
- Very pale skin
- Low pulse rate
- Brief loss of consciousness

TREATING FAINTING

1 Raise legs

- If the victim has fainted, gently raise her legs above the level of her heart to improve blood flow.
  - If she feels faint but has not fainted, ask her to lay down, and to raise her legs.
  - Support her legs with your body or with a pile of cushions, pillows, or folded blankets.

Support legs above level of heart

2 Make victim comfortable

- Loosen any restrictive clothing.
- Ensure that the victim gets plenty of fresh air. If you are indoors, open a window or fan her face.
- Keep bystanders away.
- Reassure the victim as she recovers from the faint.

3 Treat any injuries

- Look for any injuries that the victim may have sustained when she fell after fainting.
- Treat these injuries appropriately.

4 Help victim up

- When the victim feels better, help her to sit up very slowly.
- If the victim begins to feel faint again, help her to lay down.
- Raise and support her legs again, until she feels fully recovered.
- Help her to sit up again, moving very slowly and making sure that she no longer feels faint.
  - If in doubt about the victim, call her doctor. See chart p.82 Feeling faint/passing out.

! Important

- If the victim does not regain consciousness, open her airway, check her breathing, and be prepared to begin resuscitation (pp.12–20).
- Dial 911 or call EMS.

Hypothermia

The onset of hypothermia is a reaction to the cold and happens when body temperature falls below 95°F (35°C). Hypothermia may develop gradually if the victim is in a poorly heated house, or rapidly if the victim is in freezing weather or immersed in cold water. Your aims are to warm the victim gradually and to seek medical help if needed.

SIGNS & SYMPTOMS

- Shivering
- Cold, pallid skin
- Weak pulse
- Confusion and apathy
- Extreme fatigue

TREATING HYPOTHERMIA

1 Rewarm victim

- Get the victim into a shelter.
- Replace any wet clothes with warm, dry clothes and then wrap her in a survival blanket.
- If the victim is indoors, is young and healthy, and is not lethargic or confused, help her into a warm, but not hot, bath and allow her to soak.

After a bath, wrap her in warm towels

2 Warm victim in bed

- Put the victim to bed and cover her well with blankets.
- If she is still very cold, help her put on a hat and gloves.
- Give her a warm drink to sip.

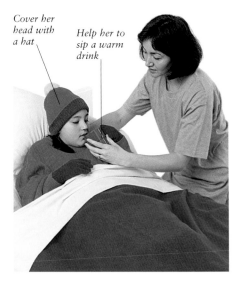

Cover her head with a hat

Help her to sip a warm drink

! Important

- Do not give the victim alcohol to drink.
- Do not give the victim a hot-water bottle or place her beside a fire or any other source of heat.
- If the victim loses consciousness, open her airway, check her breathing, and be prepared to begin resuscitation (pp.12–20).

3 Summon help

- If the victim is elderly or a baby, or if her condition worries you, call a doctor.

Frostbite

Frostbite occurs when the body reacts to freezing conditions, particularly those accompanied by a high windchill factor, by shutting down blood vessels. As a result, extremities, such as fingers and toes, may freeze and if left untreated, could eventually become gangrenous. Hypothermia (p.54) may also occur. The aims of first-aid treatment are to rewarm the frostbitten area gradually and to seek medical help.

TREATING FROSTBITE

1 Warm frozen part

- Get the victim to tuck her frozen hands into her armpits, or place the frostbitten part in your lap, between your hands to warm it.
- Move the victim out of the cold; help her if her feet are affected.
- Thaw the frostbitten part in a basin of warm water, then pat it dry.

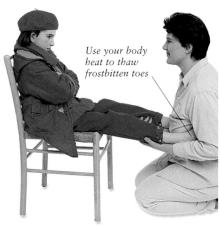

Use your body heat to thaw frostbitten toes

2 Apply dressing

- Cover the affected part with a light dressing, wrapping the dressing between frostbitten fingers and toes, and cover the part with a loose gauze bandage.
- Support the part in a raised position to reduce the chance of swelling.

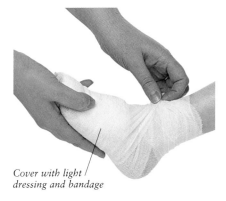

Cover with light dressing and bandage

3 Relieve pain

- As the area thaws, the skin will become hot, red, and painful.
- Give the victim the recommended dose of acetaminophen to help ease the pain.
- Take the victim to the hospital or arrange for transportation.

! Important

- Do not place a source of direct heat against the frostbitten part.
- Do not warm the frostbitten part if it may refreeze.
- Do not rub the frostbitten part.

Swallowed poisons

Poisoning can occur as a result of swallowing toxic chemicals or poisonous plants, or by overdosing on recreational or medicinal drugs. Seek immediate medical assistance and provide the emergency services with as much information as possible about the poisoning, including the type of substance that was swallowed, the amount, and when.

SIGNS & SYMPTOMS

- Pain in the abdomen or chest
- Nausea, vomiting, and diarrhea
- Breathing difficulties
- Dizziness

TREATING SWALLOWED POISONS

1 Get information

- If the victim is conscious, ask her what poison she has swallowed.
- Look around her for signs of bottles or containers.

Ask victim for details of poisoning

2 Summon help

- Dial 911 or call EMS.
- Tell the dispatcher what you think the victim has swallowed.

3 Monitor victim

- Monitor the victim's breathing (p.68 for an adult, p.71 for a child or baby), pulse (p.68 for an adult, p.70 for a child or baby), and level of consciousness (p.12) every 10 minutes until help arrives.
- Watch for signs of deterioration.
- If alcohol poisoning is a possibility, cover the victim with a blanket.

! Important

- Do not try to induce vomiting.
- Some poisons can cause anaphylactic shock. Look for warning signs (p.28).
- If the victim loses consciousness, open her airway, check her breathing, and be prepared to begin resuscitation (pp.12–20).
- If you need to give rescue breaths to a victim who has swallowed a corrosive poison, protect yourself by using a face shield (see below).

Place the shield on the victim's face, with the filter over her mouth

Snake and spider bites

A bite from a venomous snake or spider can cause severe pain and burning at the site of the wound, in addition to swelling and discoloration. Most victims of such bites recover rapidly if they receive prompt hospital treatment and are given the appropriate antivenin. The aims of first-aid treatment are to seek medical assistance quickly and to try to identify the snake or spider.

SIGNS & SYMPTOMS

- Severe pain and burning
- Pair of puncture marks (snake bite)
- Nausea and vomiting
- Sweating
- Breathing difficulties
- Irregular heartbeat

TREATING SNAKE AND SPIDER BITES

1 Keep victim still

- Lay the victim down, keeping the heart above the level of the bite.
- Keep the victim calm and still.

2 Clean wound

- Wash the wound carefully.
- Pat it dry with clean swabs or other nonfluffy material, but do not rub it.

3 Summon help

- Dial 911 or call EMS.
- If possible, give the dispatcher a description of the snake or spider that has bitten the victim.

4 Immobilize injured part

- Place a light compression bandage on the affected part to minimize blood flow. Start bandaging just above the bite and continue up the limb.
- If a leg is affected, tie both legs together with folded triangular bandages.

Bind legs together to immobilize injured leg

! Important

- Do not catch a venomous spider or snake to try to identify it.
- Do not apply a tourniquet.
- Do not cut the wound open or attempt to suck out the venom.

5 Monitor condition

- Monitor the victim's breathing (p.68 for an adult, p.71 for a child or baby), pulse (p.68 for an adult, p.70 for a child or baby), and level of consciousness (p.12) every 10 minutes until help arrives.

Animal and tick bites

Any animal bite carries a high risk of transmitting infection and should be seen by a doctor. Antibiotics or tetanus immunization may be required. Your aims are to stop the bleeding and clean the wound. Treating a tick bite involves removing the whole tick.

SIGNS & SYMPTOMS

- Puncture marks (animal)
- Pea-sized body attached to skin (tick)

TREATING ANIMAL BITES

1 Make victim safe

- Remove the victim from any danger, if possible.

2 Treat severe wound

- If the wound is serious, treat as for severe bleeding (p.31).
- Take or send the victim to the hospital for urgent treatment.

3 Treat small wound

- If the wound is superficial, wash it with soap and water and pat it dry. Cover with a dressing (p.61).
- Advise the victim to ask his or her doctor if immunization is needed.

! Important

- Do not try to capture the animal.
- Severe infections can be transmitted by animal bites. Seek medical advice in all cases.

TREATING TICK BITES

1 Remove tick

- Using a pair of fine-pointed tweezers, grasp the tick on either side of its body (including head and mouthparts).

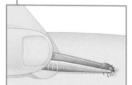

- Lever out the tick with a rocking motion.

2 Dress wound

- Wash your hands thoroughly.
- Clean the wound with antiseptic.
- Cover with an adhesive dressing.

3 Monitor victim

- Look out for a rash at the site of the bite and/or flulike symptoms days after the bite. In either case, send or take the victim to a doctor in case he or she has developed an infection. Tell the doctor that the victim was bitten by a tick.

! Important

- Do not apply a hot match, alcohol, or any other substance to the tick in an attempt to remove it.
- Ensure that you remove both the head and the body of the tick.

Insect and scorpion stings

Bee, wasp, and hornet stings are painful but are not usually life-threatening. There may be a sharp pain followed by temporary swelling, soreness, and itching. Your aims are to watch out for signs of anaphylactic shock, to remove the stinger, to dress the wound, and to reduce swelling. Scorpion stings can be life-threatening and need urgent medical attention.

SIGNS & SYMPTOMS

- Stinger stuck in skin
- Swollen red area
- Localized pain

TREATING STINGS IN THE SKIN

1 Remove sting

- If there is a stinger in the wound, gently scrape it off with your fingernail or a credit card.
- Do not grasp the venom sac with your fingers or tweezers because pressure on the sac may inject more venom into the victim.

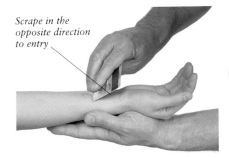

Scrape in the opposite direction to entry

2 Treat wound

- Wash the injured area with soap and water, and pat dry.
- Cover the wound area with an adhesive dressing.
- Apply a cold compress on top of the adhesive dressing to reduce pain and swelling.
- Advise the victim to seek medical help if symptoms persist.

! Important

- Dial 911 if the victim has been stung by a scorpion or shows signs of anaphylactic shock (p.28).

TREATING STINGS IN THE MOUTH

1 Reduce swelling

- In order to reduce swelling, give the victim a glass of cold water to sip or ice to suck.

Soothe sting with water

2 Summon help

- Dial 911 or call EMS.

First-aid equipment

Having the correct supplies can make a big difference in an emergency, so you should always keep a selection of essential first-aid materials at home and in your car. Store the items in a first-aid box or in a similar type of airtight container in a dry place. The box should be easily accessible in an emergency but kept away from other medicines and out of reach of children. Ideally, the box should be small and light enough for you to carry easily. Check and replenish the first-aid kit regularly so that the contents are kept up to date.

HOME FIRST-AID KIT

ADHESIVE BANDAGES
for covering small cuts and scrapes

TRIANGULAR BANDAGES
for use as a sling to support and immobilize an injured limb

CREPE ROLLER BANDAGES
for applying pressure to a wound or to support a strain or sprain

GAUZE ROLLER BANDAGES
for holding dressings in place on any part of the body

GAUZE DRESSINGS
light dressings for use directly on wounds

WOUND DRESSING
sterile dressings that combine bandage and dressing in one

Applicator

Bandage

TUBULAR BANDAGE
used with a special applicator to secure dressings on fingers or toes

TWEEZERS
for removing splinters

SCISSORS
for cutting dressings and bandages

ANTISEPTIC WIPES
for cleaning wounds

ANTISEPTIC CREAM
used on cuts and scrapes to help prevent infection

MICROPOROUS TAPE
breathable, low-tack tape for holding dressings in place

SAFETY PINS
for securing bandages and slings

CALAMINE LOTION
for treating sore and sunburned skin

FACE SHIELD
for protection from cross-infection when giving rescue breaths

DISPOSABLE GLOVES
for protection from cross-infection when touching body fluids

COLD PACK
for reducing swelling in sprains and strains

APPLYING A WOUND DRESSING

1 Apply dressing pad

- Wash your hands thoroughly and wear disposable gloves, if available.
- Choose a dressing with a pad that will cover an area 1 in (2.5 cm) beyond the edges of the wound.
- Unroll the bandage until the pad is visible, leaving a short "free" end on one side of the pad and a roll of bandage on the other.
- Place the dressing pad directly on the wound.

2 Bandage in place

- Secure the pad in place by winding the short end of the bandage once around the dressing and limb.
- Keep hold of the short end and wind the bandage roll around the dressing and limb. Continue winding the bandage until the pad is completely covered.

3 Secure bandage

- Tie the ends of the bandage together over the pad.
- Check the circulation (see below) and, if necessary, loosen the bandage and reapply.
- If blood seeps through, apply another dressing over the top. If it seeps through the second dressing, remove both and start again.

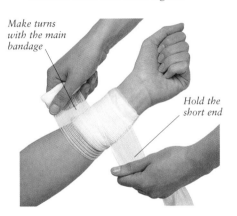

Make turns with the main bandage

Hold the short end

CHECKING CIRCULATION

1 Apply pressure

- Immediately after bandaging a limb, check the circulation in the fingers or toes beyond the bandage.
- Press on a nail or on the skin until the area turns pale, then release the pressure. The color should return immediately.

2 Loosen bandage

- If the skin color does not return immediately, the bandage is too tight and should be loosened.
- Undo a few turns of the bandage. Wait for the color to return to the skin, and reapply the bandage more loosely. Check circulation again.

3 Monitor casualty

- Every 10 minutes, check fingers or toes for signs of poor circulation such as pale, cold skin, or numbness. Loosen the bandage and reapply if necessary.

APPLYING A HAND OR FOOT BANDAGE

1 Start at wrist

- Place the end of the bandage on the underside of the wrist at the base of the thumb (or ankle for a foot bandage); secure the end by making a straight turn around the wrist.
- Bring the bandage diagonally across the back of the victim's hand in the direction of the little finger.
- Take the bandage under and across the fingers so that the upper edge touches the index finger about half way up its length.

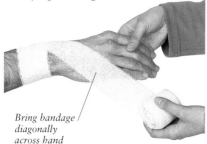

Bring bandage diagonally across hand

2 Repeat layers

- Take the bandage diagonally across the back of the hand, then around the wrist and back over the hand towards the little finger.
- Continue, covering two-thirds of the previous layer with each new turn.
- When the hand is covered, make two straight turns around the wrist (or ankle) and secure the bandage.
- Check the circulation in the fingers and toes beyond the bandage (see p.61) and loosen it if necessary.

Leave fingertips and thumb free

APPLYING A TUBULAR BANDAGE

1 Apply first layer

- Cut a length of tubular gauze bandage two-and-a-half times the length of the injured finger or toe.
- Push the gauze on to the applicator, and gently place the applicator over the finger.
- Hold the gauze in place at the base of the finger and pull the applicator off, leaving a layer of gauze behind.
- Hold the applicator just beyond the fingertip and twist it twice.

2 Apply second layer

- Push the applicator back over the injured finger, until the finger is covered with the rest of the gauze.
- Remove the applicator.

3 Secure bandage

- Secure the end of the gauze to the finger with a piece of adhesive tape, leaving a gap in one place.
- Make sure the bandage is not too tight. If the victim complains of pale cold skin, numbness, or an inability to move the finger or toe, remove the bandage and hold the dressing in place by hand.

TYING AN ARM SLING

1 Support arm

- Support the injured arm under the forearm or ask the victim to support it with his other arm.
- Pass one end of the bandage under the victim's elbow on the injured limb and pull the bandage across to the opposite shoulder, so that the longest edge is parallel with his uninjured side.

Longest edge of bandage

Support forearm

2 Form sling

- Bring the lower half of the bandage up over the forearm to meet the other end of the bandage at the shoulder on the injured side.
- Position the forearm so that the hand is slightly higher than the elbow.

Leave fingers exposed

3 Secure sling

- Tie a knot at the hollow over the victim's collarbone on the injured side of the body.
- Tuck both ends of the bandage under the knot to act as padding.

Tie knot over collarbone

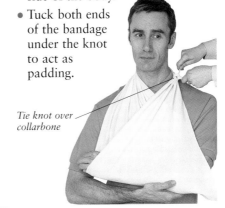

4 Secure at elbow

- Fold the point of the bandage forwards at the elbow and tuck any loose bandage underneath it.
- Secure the point of the bandage to the front of the bandage with a safety pin, or twist the corner and tuck it into the sling.
- Check the circulation in the fingers after securing the sling, and again every 10 minutes (see p.61). If necessary, remove the sling and straighten the arm.

Fold point forwards

Use safety pin to secure

2
FAMILY ILLNESS

When a family member is ill, turn to the symptoms charts in this section to find out what is wrong. From facial pain to abdominal pain, wheezing to swollen ankles, these charts provide possible reasons for the symptoms and indicate how you can help.

How to use this section

This section contains a selection of charts describing symptoms that may cause concern to family members. At the beginning of the section, there is advice on how to assess symptoms of illness, such as how to measure body temperature, take a pulse, and check breathing rates. At the end of the section, there are guidelines for looking after a sick person at home, with suggestions for which medicines to keep in the home and how to administer them.

HOW TO USE THE CHARTS

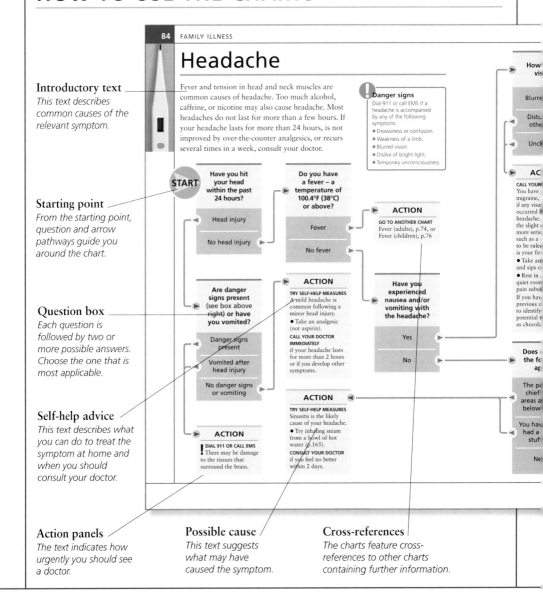

Introductory text
This text describes common causes of the relevant symptom.

Starting point
From the starting point, question and arrow pathways guide you around the chart.

Question box
Each question is followed by two or more possible answers. Choose the one that is most applicable.

Self-help advice
This text describes what you can do to treat the symptom at home and when you should consult your doctor.

Action panels
The text indicates how urgently you should see a doctor.

Possible cause
This text suggests what may have caused the symptom.

Cross-references
The charts feature cross-references to other charts containing further information.

SPECIAL BOXES

- Red danger signs and warning boxes alert you to situations in which emergency medical help may save a life. These boxes highlight advice that applies in particular medical circumstances.

- Blue information panels tell you how to gather the information you need to answer the questions in the chart.

Danger signs

an ambulance if a

Recurring attacks of vertigo

If you have been experiencing attacks of vertigo, it is very important to avoid certain activities that are potentially hazardous to you and to other people. You should not climb ladders or steep flights of stairs, operate machinery.

Checking a red rash

Safe alcohol limits

One unit of alcohol equals half a pint of beer, a small glass of wine or sherry, or one measure of hard liquor.

- The maximum recommended limit for men is 3 units a day.
- The maximum recommended limit for women is 2 units a day.

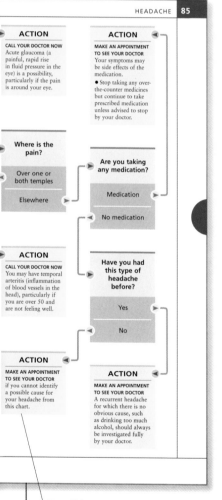

ACTION

CALL YOUR DOCTOR NOW
Acute glaucoma (a painful, rapid rise in fluid pressure in the eye) is a possibility, particularly if the pain is around your eye.

ACTION

MAKE AN APPOINTMENT TO SEE YOUR DOCTOR
Your symptoms may be side effects of the medication.
- Stop taking any over-the-counter medicines but continue to take prescribed medication unless advised to stop by your doctor.

Where is the pain?

Over one or both temples

Elsewhere

Are you taking any medication?

Medication

No medication

ACTION

CALL YOUR DOCTOR NOW
You may have temporal arteritis (inflammation of blood vessels in the head), particularly if you are over 50 and are not feeling well.

Have you had this type of headache before?

Yes

No

ACTION

MAKE AN APPOINTMENT TO SEE YOUR DOCTOR
if you cannot identify a possible cause for your headache from this chart.

ACTION

MAKE AN APPOINTMENT TO SEE YOUR DOCTOR
A recurrent headache for which there is no obvious cause, such as drinking too much alcohol, should always be investigated fully by your doctor.

Possible cause not identified
If your symptoms do not suggest a diagnosis, the chart recommends that you see a doctor.

ACTION PANELS

At the end of every pathway you will find a possible diagnosis, advice on what to do, and whether or not you need to seek medical help. There are five possible levels of attention, ranging from **DIAL 911 OR CALL EMS**, for the most serious conditions, to **TRY SELF-HELP MEASURES**, for minor complaints. It is important to note, however, that even apparently minor complaints should receive medical attention when they occur in the elderly or in people who are undergoing cancer treatment.

! DIAL 911 OR CALL EMS

Dial 911 or call EMS for the emergency services. If there is a delay in obtaining an ambulance, go to the hospital by car.

CALL YOUR DOCTOR NOW

Contact the doctor, day or night, by telephone. Dial 911 or call EMS if you fail to make contact within 1 hour.

SEE YOUR DOCTOR WITHIN 24 HOURS

It is important that the symptoms are assessed by a doctor within 24 hours of their onset.

MAKE AN APPOINTMENT TO SEE YOUR DOCTOR

The condition may require medical treatment, but a reasonable delay is unlikely to lead to problems.

TRY SELF-HELP MEASURES

For minor infections, such as a sore throat or runny nose, use self-help measures, first aid, or over-the-counter remedies to relieve discomfort. Always consult your doctor if you are unsure whether a remedy is suitable and read the manufacturer's instructions before taking medication.

Assessing symptoms (adults)

Symptoms take many forms. Some involve a new sensation; others involve a change in a normal body function. Certain symptoms can be assessed very accurately because they can be measured, for example by taking a temperature or a pulse. Others need careful and regular attention to assess whether something has changed, such as breast or testes examinations.

MEASURING BODY TEMPERATURE

1 Insert thermometer

- Place a digital thermometer in the mouth, with the tip under the tongue, and leave it until you hear it "beep", indicating that it has measured the temperature.

2 Assess result

- A result above 100.4°F (38°C) indicates a fever.

TAKING A PULSE

1 Find pulse

- Place the pads of two fingers on the inside of a person's wrist, just below the base of the thumb.
- Press firmly to feel the throbbing beat of the pulse.
- Count the number of beats per minute.

2 Assess result

- A rate of around 72 beats per minute is normal for an adult.
  - Note the quality of the pulse: if it is regular or irregular, strong or weak.

Place the pads of the fingers below the victim's thumb

CHECKING BREATHING RATE

1 Count breaths

- Watch for chest movement or place your hand on the adult's chest or back so you can feel the breaths.
- Count the number of breaths he or she takes in one minute.

2 Assess result

- The normal resting breathing rate is 12–15 breaths per minute.
- Note the quality of the person's breathing: if it is fast or slow, easy or labored.

ASSESSING WEIGHT

Check whether you are a healthy weight by using the graph (right). Trace a vertical line from your height and a horizontal line from your weight. The point at which the lines cross is your body mass index (BMI), which indicates whether or not you are within a healthy range. Being a healthy weight decreases the risk of cardiovascular disease and many other health problems.

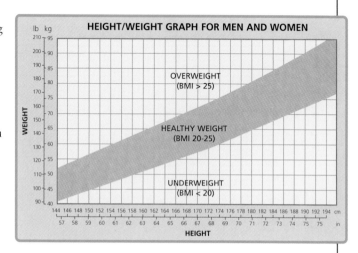

HEIGHT/WEIGHT GRAPH FOR MEN AND WOMEN

OVERWEIGHT
(BMI > 25)

HEALTHY WEIGHT
(BMI 20-25)

UNDERWEIGHT
(BMI < 20)

BREASTS: SELF-EXAMINATION

1 Examine yourself in a mirror

- The best time to check your breasts is just after your menstrual period.
- Stand in front of a mirror and look closely for dimpled skin and any changes to your nipple or to the size or shape of your breasts.

2 Feel each breast

- Lie down with one arm behind your head and firmly press each breast in small circular movements.
- Feel around the entire breast, armpit area, and nipple.
  - If you discover a lump or any changes, consult your doctor.

Feel the breast and up into the armpit

TESTES: SELF-EXAMINATION

1 Look for changes

- The best time to examine your testes is just after a bath or shower when the scrotum is relaxed.
- Check the skin of your scrotum for changes in appearance.

2 Feel for lumps

- Feel across the entire surface of each testis by rolling it slowly between fingers and thumb.
- Check for lumps and swellings.
- Consult your doctor immediately if you detect any change in appearance or texture.

Assessing symptoms
(children)

When a child is not well, temperature, pulse, and breathing rate are important symptoms to assess. To monitor your child's growth, use the height and weight charts (opposite) to assess whether he or she is within normal ranges.

MEASURING BODY TEMPERATURE

1 Insert thermometer

- Place a digital thermometer under the tongue (for a child over 7) or under the armpit and leave it until you hear it "beep," indicating that it has measured the temperature.
- Insert the tip of an aural thermometer into the ear. The reading is taken in 1 second.

2 Assess result

- For a mouth or ear reading, a result above 100.4°F (38°C) indicates a fever.
- For an armpit reading, a result above 99°F (37.4°C) indicates a fever.

Hold the digital thermometer securely in place

TAKING A PULSE

1 Find pulse

- For a baby, place two fingers on the inner side of the arm, halfway between the elbow and the armpit.
- For a child, place your fingers on the inside of the wrist, just below the base of the thumb.

2 Assess result

- Count the number of beats you can feel in one minute.
- A rate of around 140 beats per minute is normal for a baby, 120 per minute for a toddler, and 100 per minute for an older child.
- Note the quality of the pulse: if it is regular or irregular, strong or weak.

Find a pulse on the inside of the arm

CHECKING BREATHING RATE

1 Count breaths

- Place your hand on the child's chest or back so that you are able to feel the breaths.
- Count the number of breaths he or she takes in 1 minute.

Use your hand to feel how fast the baby is breathing

2 Assess result

- Compare the child's breathing rate with the maximum rate for his or her age shown in the table below.
- Note the quality of the breathing: if it is fast or slow, easy or labored.

AGE	BREATHS PER MINUTE
Under 2 months	Maximum of 60 breaths
2–11 months	Maximum of 50 breaths
1–5 years	Maximum of 40 breaths
Over 5 years	Maximum of 30 breaths

ASSESSING HEIGHT AND WEIGHT

Find your child's age on the bottom and follow a vertical line up, then find the height or weight on the left and follow a horizontal line across. Mark the point where the lines cross. The shaded band shows the normal range of growth, and the 5th, 50th, and 95th percentile lines indicate lower, middle, and upper limits respectively. If your child's measurements fall outside the band, see your doctor.

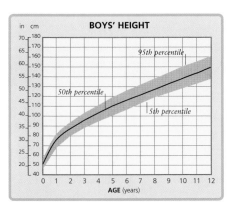

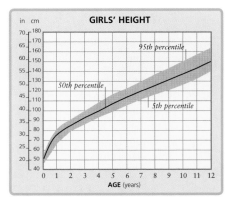

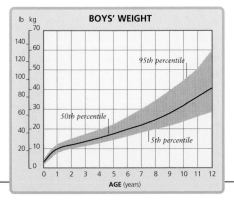

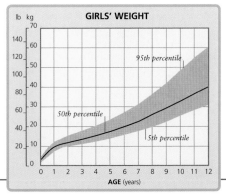

Not feeling well

There may be times when don't feel well but are unable to pinpoint a precise symptom. This feeling is commonly caused by the onset of a minor viral illness, psychological pressures, or simply an unhealthy lifestyle. You should always consult your doctor if the feeling persists because there may be a more serious underlying problem.

START

Do you have a fever – a temperature of 100.4°F (38°C) or above?

Fever

No fever

Have you lost more than 10 lb (4.5 kg) over the past 10 weeks without changing your eating habits?

Lost over 10 lb (4.5 kg)

Lost under 10 lb (4.5 kg) or gained weight

Do you have any of the following?

Feeling constantly on edge

Difficulty sleeping

Inability to concentrate or to make decisions

None of the above

Are you taking any medication?

Medication

No medication

ACTION

GO TO ANOTHER CHART
Fever (adults), p.74 or
Fever (children), p.76

ACTION

SEE YOUR DOCTOR WITHIN 24 HOURS
There are a number of possible causes for rapid weight loss, and it is important to see your doctor to rule out potentially serious conditions such as diabetes mellitus.

ACTION

MAKE AN APPOINTMENT TO SEE YOUR DOCTOR
Your symptoms may be a side effect of the medication.
● Stop taking any over-the-counter medicines but continue to take prescribed medication unless advised to stop by your doctor.

Safe alcohol limits

One unit of alcohol equals half a pint of beer, a small glass of wine or sherry, or one measure of hard liquor.
● The maximum recommended limit for men is 3 units a day.
● The maximum recommended limit for women is 2 units a day.

ACTION

MAKE AN APPOINTMENT TO SEE YOUR DOCTOR
Your symptoms may be due to an anxiety disorder or depression.
• Try physical exercise or some relaxation techniques (p.169); they may help to alleviate the symptoms.

ACTION

TRY SELF-HELP MEASURES
Body changes that occur soon after conception can make you feel unwell. Symptoms include fatigue, feeling faint, and nausea/vomiting.
• Eat frequent small meals throughout the day rather than a few larger meals. If you suffer from morning sickness, eat a snack before getting up.
• Lie down if you are feeling faint or tired.
• If you are not sure whether you are pregnant, use a home pregnancy test or consult your doctor.

ACTION

TRY SELF-HELP MEASURES
You may have a mild digestive upset as a result of infection or having eaten something that disagrees with you. Your symptoms are not likely to be dangerous, but severe diarrhea can cause dehydration, particularly in the elderly or very young.
• Avoid rich or spicy foods and drink plenty of clear fluids.
CONSULT YOUR DOCTOR
if you do not feel better within 2 days or sooner for a child.

Might you be pregnant?

Possibly pregnant

Not pregnant

Are you feeling more tired than usual?

More tired

No change

Do you regularly drink more than the recommended limit of alcohol (see box opposite)?

Within the limit

More than the limit

Do you have any of the following?

Loss of appetite

Nausea and/or vomiting

Diarrhea

None of the above

ACTION

MAKE AN APPOINTMENT TO SEE YOUR DOCTOR
if your fatigue is persistent or severe and has no obvious cause.

ACTION

MAKE AN APPOINTMENT TO SEE YOUR DOCTOR
for advice about reducing the amount of alcohol you drink. Regularly drinking too much alcohol can make you not feel well.

ACTION

MAKE AN APPOINTMENT TO SEE YOUR DOCTOR
if you cannot identify a possible cause for not feeling well from this chart.

Fever (adults)

For children under 12, see p.76 ▶

Normal temperature varies from one person to another, but if your temperature is 100.4°F (38°C) or above, you have a fever. Most fevers are due to infection, but heat exposure or certain drugs can also raise body temperature. In all cases, follow the advice for bringing down a fever (p.164).

! High temperature

If you are not feeling well, you should take your temperature every 4 hours.

- Call your doctor immediately if your temperature rises to 102°F (39°C) or above.
- Take steps to lower the fever without delay (see Bringing down a fever, p.164).

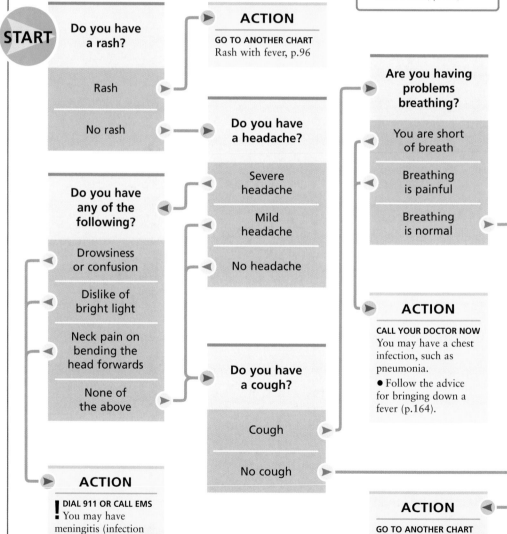

START

Do you have a rash?

- Rash
- No rash

ACTION

GO TO ANOTHER CHART
Rash with fever, p.96

Do you have a headache?

- Severe headache
- Mild headache
- No headache

Do you have any of the following?

- Drowsiness or confusion
- Dislike of bright light
- Neck pain on bending the head forwards
- None of the above

ACTION

! DIAL 911 OR CALL EMS
You may have meningitis (infection inflaming membranes around the brain).

Do you have a cough?

- Cough
- No cough

Are you having problems breathing?

- You are short of breath
- Breathing is painful
- Breathing is normal

ACTION

CALL YOUR DOCTOR NOW
You may have a chest infection, such as pneumonia.
- Follow the advice for bringing down a fever (p.164).

ACTION

GO TO ANOTHER CHART
Sore throat, p.103

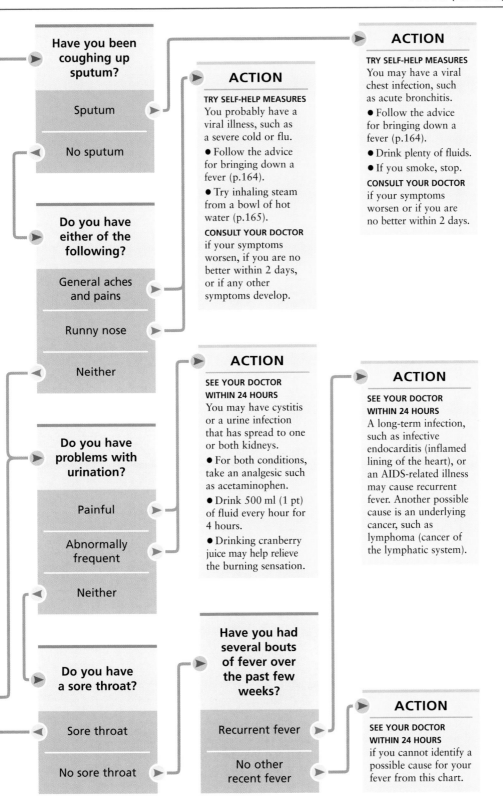

Have you been coughing up sputum?

Sputum ▶

No sputum ◀

Do you have either of the following?

General aches and pains ▶

Runny nose ▶

Neither ◀

Do you have problems with urination?

Painful ▶

Abnormally frequent ▶

Neither ◀

Do you have a sore throat?

Sore throat ◀

No sore throat ▶

Have you had several bouts of fever over the past few weeks?

Recurrent fever ▶

No other recent fever ▶

ACTION

TRY SELF-HELP MEASURES
You probably have a viral illness, such as a severe cold or flu.

● Follow the advice for bringing down a fever (p.164).

● Try inhaling steam from a bowl of hot water (p.165).

CONSULT YOUR DOCTOR
if your symptoms worsen, if you are no better within 2 days, or if any other symptoms develop.

ACTION

TRY SELF-HELP MEASURES
You may have a viral chest infection, such as acute bronchitis.

● Follow the advice for bringing down a fever (p.164).

● Drink plenty of fluids.

● If you smoke, stop.

CONSULT YOUR DOCTOR
if your symptoms worsen or if you are no better within 2 days.

ACTION

SEE YOUR DOCTOR WITHIN 24 HOURS
You may have cystitis or a urine infection that has spread to one or both kidneys.

● For both conditions, take an analgesic such as acetaminophen.

● Drink 500 ml (1 pt) of fluid every hour for 4 hours.

● Drinking cranberry juice may help relieve the burning sensation.

ACTION

SEE YOUR DOCTOR WITHIN 24 HOURS
A long-term infection, such as infective endocarditis (inflamed lining of the heart), or an AIDS-related illness may cause recurrent fever. Another possible cause is an underlying cancer, such as lymphoma (cancer of the lymphatic system).

ACTION

SEE YOUR DOCTOR WITHIN 24 HOURS
if you cannot identify a possible cause for your fever from this chart.

Fever (children)

◀ For adults and children over 12, see p.74

A fever is a temperature of 100.4°F (38°C) or above. If your child is not feeling well, you should take his or her temperature because a high fever may need urgent treatment. If a feverish child becomes unresponsive, dial 911 or call EMS. In all cases, follow the advice for bringing down a fever (p.164).

Danger signs

Dial 911 or call EMS if your child's temperature rises above 102°F (39°C) and he or she has any of the following symptoms:

- Abnormally rapid breathing (see p.71).
- Abnormal drowsiness.
- Severe headache.
- Dislike of bright light.
- Refusal to drink for more than 6 hours.

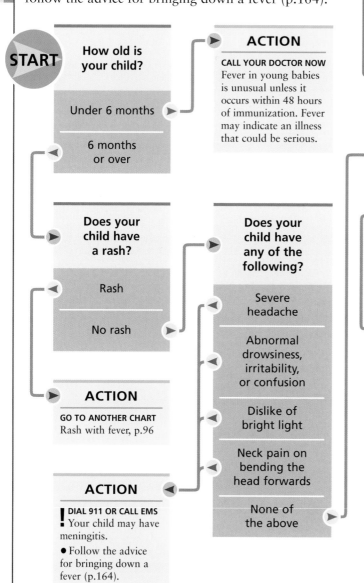

START

How old is your child?

Under 6 months

6 months or over

ACTION

CALL YOUR DOCTOR NOW
Fever in young babies is unusual unless it occurs within 48 hours of immunization. Fever may indicate an illness that could be serious.

Does your child have a rash?

Rash

No rash

ACTION

GO TO ANOTHER CHART
Rash with fever, p.96

ACTION

❗ DIAL 911 OR CALL EMS
Your child may have meningitis.

- Follow the advice for bringing down a fever (p.164).

Does your child have any of the following?

Severe headache

Abnormal drowsiness, irritability, or confusion

Dislike of bright light

Neck pain on bending the head forwards

None of the above

Is your child reluctant to move an arm or leg?

Yes

No

ACTION

CALL YOUR DOCTOR NOW
Your child could have an infection in a bone, such as osteomyelitis, or a joint infection.

ACTION

SEE YOUR DOCTOR WITHIN 24 HOURS
Your child may have acute otitis media (middle-ear infection).

- Give liquid acet-aminophen to relieve pain and reduce fever.

ACTION

! DIAL 911 OR CALL EMS Your child could have a respiratory infection, such as pneumonia.

● Give liquid acetaminophen to relieve pain and reduce fever.

Is your child's breathing abnormally noisy or rapid (see p.71)?

Abnormally rapid

Noisy

Neither

ACTION

CALL YOUR DOCTOR NOW This may be croup, in which a viral infection inflames the airways.

● Sit with your child in a steamy bathroom to ease the breathing.

Does either of the following apply?

Your child has been pulling at one ear

Your child has complained of earache

Neither

Does your child have either of the following?

Cough

Runny nose

Neither

Does your child have a sore throat?

Sore throat

No sore throat

Does your child have either of the following?

Painful urination

Diarrhea with or without vomiting

Neither

ACTION

SEE YOUR DOCTOR WITHIN 24 HOURS if you cannot identify a possible cause for your child's fever from this chart.

ACTION

TRY SELF-HELP MEASURES Your child probably has a viral illness, such as a severe cold or flu.

● Follow the advice for bringing down a fever (p.164).

● Try inhaling steam from a bowl of hot water (p.165).

CONSULT YOUR DOCTOR if your child's condition worsens, if he or she is no better within 2 days, or if he or she develops other symptoms.

ACTION

TRY SELF-HELP MEASURES Your child may have a throat infection, such as tonsillitis.

● Follow the advice for bringing down a fever (p.164).

● Follow the advice for soothing a sore throat (p.164).

CONSULT YOUR DOCTOR if your child is no better in 24 hours or if other symptoms develop.

ACTION

SEE YOUR DOCTOR WITHIN 24 HOURS Your child may have a urinary tract infection.

● Give plenty of fluids to drink.

ACTION

CALL YOUR DOCTOR NOW if your child is under 1 year. He or she may have gastroenteritis.

● Give older children plenty of clear fluids to drink.

Excessive sweating

Sweating is one of the body's cooling mechanisms. It is a normal response to heat, exercise, and stress or fear. Some people naturally sweat more than others. Wearing natural fibers, such as cotton, and using an antiperspirant often help to reduce sweating. You should consult your doctor if you sweat excessively and are unsure of the cause.

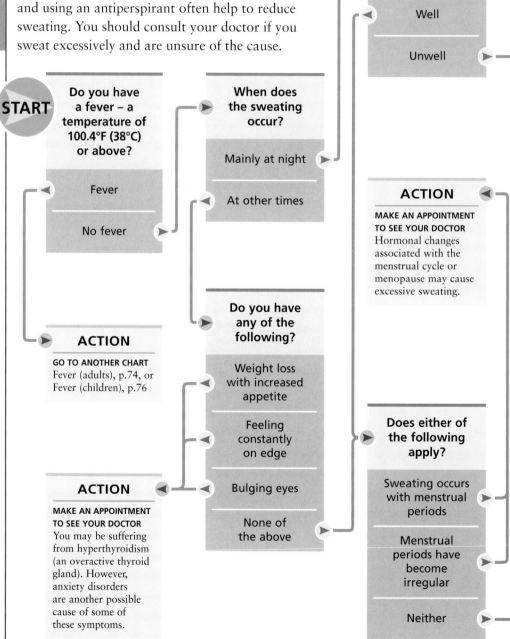

Do you feel otherwise well?

Well

Unwell

START

Do you have a fever – a temperature of 100.4°F (38°C) or above?

Fever

No fever

When does the sweating occur?

Mainly at night

At other times

ACTION

MAKE AN APPOINTMENT TO SEE YOUR DOCTOR Hormonal changes associated with the menstrual cycle or menopause may cause excessive sweating.

ACTION

GO TO ANOTHER CHART Fever (adults), p.74, or Fever (children), p.76

Do you have any of the following?

Weight loss with increased appetite

Feeling constantly on edge

Bulging eyes

None of the above

Does either of the following apply?

Sweating occurs with menstrual periods

Menstrual periods have become irregular

Neither

ACTION

MAKE AN APPOINTMENT TO SEE YOUR DOCTOR You may be suffering from hyperthyroidism (an overactive thyroid gland). However, anxiety disorders are another possible cause of some of these symptoms.

ACTION

SEE YOUR DOCTOR WITHIN 24 HOURS
You may have a chronic infection, such as tuberculosis, or a cancer, such as lymphoma (cancer of the lymphatic system).

ACTION

TRY SELF-HELP MEASURES
Being overweight can lead to excessive sweating, particularly after physical exertion.
● Adopt a sensible weight-reducing diet.
● Wash away sweat regularly and wear comfortable loose clothing made from natural fibers.
CONSULT YOUR DOCTOR if your symptoms do not improve.

ACTION

TRY SELF-HELP MEASURES
Excessive sweating of the hands and feet is a common problem.
● Wash off sweat regularly and wear socks made from natural fibers. Try to go barefoot whenever possible.
CONSULT YOUR DOCTOR if your symptoms do not improve.

Is your weight within ideal limits?

Overweight

Ideal weight

Underweight

Do you regularly drink more than the recommended limit of alcohol (see box below)?

More than the limit

Within the limit

Is the sweating limited to certain parts of the body?

Mainly hands

Mainly feet

Other parts affected

ACTION

MAKE AN APPOINTMENT TO SEE YOUR DOCTOR for advice about reducing the amount of alcohol you drink.

ACTION

SEE YOUR DOCTOR WITHIN 24 HOURS if you cannot identify a possible cause from this chart.

Are you currently taking any medication?

Medication

No medication

ACTION

MAKE AN APPOINTMENT TO SEE YOUR DOCTOR
Your symptoms may be a side effect of the medication.
● Stop taking any over-the-counter medicines but continue to take prescribed medication unless advised to stop by your doctor.

Safe alcohol limits
One unit of alcohol equals half a pint of beer, a small glass of wine or sherry, or one measure of hard liquor.
● The maximum recommended limit for men is 3 units a day.
● The maximum recommended limit for women is 2 units a day.

Lumps and swellings

Enlarged lymph nodes (glands) are often the cause of lumps and swellings under the skin, particularly in the neck, under the arms, or in the groin. These glands usually become swollen due to an infection. The swelling subsides shortly after the infection clears up. If the lumps are painful or if they are persistent but painless, you should consult your doctor.

Painless lumps or swellings

Any painless lump or swelling that does not disappear within 2 weeks should be seen by a doctor. Although in most cases the cause is not serious, a painless lump may be a sign of cancer. Early treatment can be lifesaving.

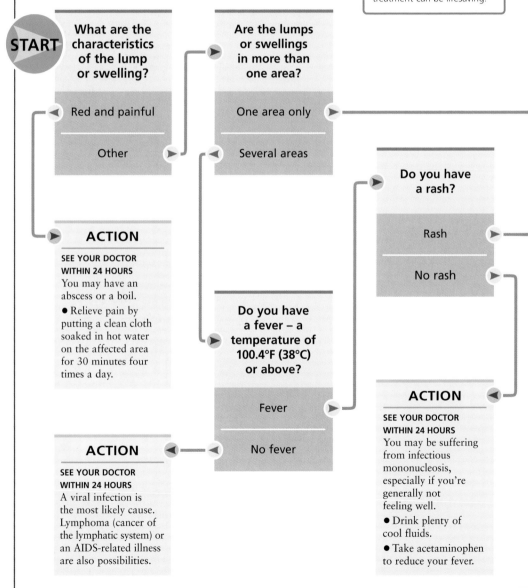

START

What are the characteristics of the lump or swelling?

Red and painful

Other

Are the lumps or swellings in more than one area?

One area only

Several areas

Do you have a rash?

Rash

No rash

Do you have a fever – a temperature of 100.4°F (38°C) or above?

Fever

No fever

ACTION

SEE YOUR DOCTOR
WITHIN 24 HOURS
You may have an abscess or a boil.
• Relieve pain by putting a clean cloth soaked in hot water on the affected area for 30 minutes four times a day.

ACTION

SEE YOUR DOCTOR
WITHIN 24 HOURS
A viral infection is the most likely cause. Lymphoma (cancer of the lymphatic system) or an AIDS-related illness are also possibilities.

ACTION

SEE YOUR DOCTOR
WITHIN 24 HOURS
You may be suffering from infectious mononucleosis, especially if you're generally not feeling well.
• Drink plenty of cool fluids.
• Take acetaminophen to reduce your fever.

ACTION

GO TO ANOTHER CHART
Testes and scrotum
problems, p.151

**Where is
the lump or
swelling?**

Testis

Groin

Breast

Sides or back
of neck

Other

**What happens
to the swelling
if you press
on it or if you
lie down?**

It disappears

It reduces
in size

No change

ACTION

MAKE AN APPOINTMENT
TO SEE YOUR DOCTOR
You may have a hernia.

ACTION

MAKE AN APPOINTMENT
TO SEE YOUR DOCTOR
Lymph nodes in the
groin often become
swollen in response
to an infection.

ACTION

GO TO ANOTHER CHART
Breast problems, p.154

**Do you have a
sore throat?**

Sore throat

No sore throat

ACTION

GO TO ANOTHER CHART
Sore throat, p.103

ACTION

SEE YOUR DOCTOR
WITHIN 24 HOURS
A number of viral
illnesses can cause
swollen glands and a
rash. Lyme disease (an
infection that causes
a rash and flulike
symptoms) is another
possibility, particularly
if you think you may
have been bitten by a
tick recently.

**Do you have a
recent injury
near the site of
the swelling?**

Injury

No injury

ACTION

TRY SELF-HELP MEASURES
An injury is likely to
cause some swelling as
a result of damage to
the tissues. An infected
wound or a rash can
also cause nearby
lymph nodes to swell.
●Make sure the
wound is clean and
protect it with a
bandage or dressing.
CONSULT YOUR DOCTOR
if there is any pain,
redness, or pus around
the wound, or if the
swelling persists after
the wound has healed.

ACTION

MAKE AN APPOINTMENT
TO SEE YOUR DOCTOR
if you cannot identify a
possible cause for your
lumps or swellings
from this chart.

Feeling faint/passing out

A sensation of dizziness or lightheadedness may be followed by passing out (loss of consciousness). The cause is usually lack of food or a reduction in blood flow to the brain. A brief episode of feeling faint without other symptoms is not a cause for alarm, but you should consult your doctor if such episodes recur or if you have passed out.

Unconsciousness

If someone remains unconscious for more than a minute or so, whatever the suspected cause, you should get emergency medical help.
- If you need to leave the person to call for help, first lay him or her in the recovery position (pp.14–15).
- Do not move the person if you suspect spinal injury.

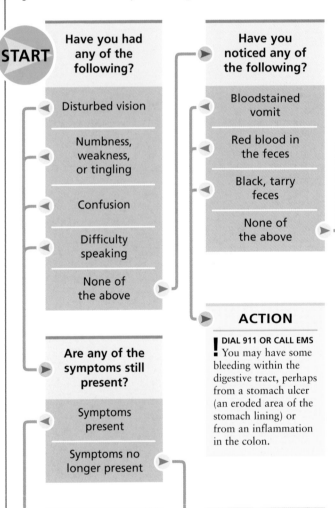

START

Have you had any of the following?

- Disturbed vision
- Numbness, weakness, or tingling
- Confusion
- Difficulty speaking
- None of the above

Are any of the symptoms still present?

- Symptoms present
- Symptoms no longer present

Have you noticed any of the following?

- Bloodstained vomit
- Red blood in the feces
- Black, tarry feces
- None of the above

Did any of the following occur when you passed out?

- You twitched uncontrollably
- You bit your tongue
- You urinated
- None of the above

ACTION

! **DIAL 911 OR CALL EMS**
You may have some bleeding within the digestive tract, perhaps from a stomach ulcer (an eroded area of the stomach lining) or from an inflammation in the colon.

ACTION

! **DIAL 911 OR CALL EMS**
You may have had a stroke.

ACTION

CALL YOUR DOCTOR NOW
You may have had a mini-stroke.

ACTION

! **DIAL 911 OR CALL EMS**
if this is your first attack. You may have had a seizure, possibly due to epilepsy.

CONSULT YOUR DOCTOR
if you have had previous similar attacks.

ACTION

TRY SELF-HELP MEASURES
Sudden shock can lead to feeling faint or even passing out.
- Rest and ask someone to stay with you until you feel better.
- Follow the first-aid advice for treating fainting (p.53)

CONSULT YOUR DOCTOR if it happens again.

Did you feel faint or pass out immediately after either of the following?

Emotional shock

Getting up suddenly

Neither

ACTION

SEE YOUR DOCTOR WITHIN 24 HOURS
if you passed out, or in the next few days even if you did not pass out. The most likely cause is a temporary drop in blood pressure due to a change in position.

ACTION

CALL YOUR DOCTOR NOW
You may have low blood pressure due to an irregular heartbeat or worsening of an existing heart condition.

Does either of the following apply?

You have diabetes

You had not eaten for several hours before passing out

Neither

Do you have any of the following?

Shortness of breath

Paler skin than normal

Inordinate fatigue

None of the above

Does either of the following apply?

You have had chest pain or you have a heart condition

You have had palpitations

Neither

ACTION

CALL YOUR DOCTOR NOW
Low blood sugar (which may be due to excessive insulin treatment) could be the cause.
- Eat or drink something sugary now.

ACTION

SEE YOUR DOCTOR WITHIN 24 HOURS
You may be anemic. This can be confirmed by a blood test.

ACTION

MAKE AN APPOINTMENT TO SEE YOUR DOCTOR
Fainting is common in early pregnancy. If you are not sure whether you are pregnant, do a home pregnancy test.

Might you be pregnant?

Possibly pregnant

Not pregnant

ACTION

CALL YOUR DOCTOR NOW
if you passed out and cannot identify a possible cause from this chart.

SEE YOUR DOCTOR WITHIN 24 HOURS
if you cannot identify a possible cause for feeling faint.

Headache

Fever and tension in head and neck muscles are common causes of headache. Too much alcohol, caffeine, or nicotine may also cause headache. Most headaches do not last for more than a few hours. If your headache lasts for more than 24 hours, is not improved by over-the-counter analgesics, or recurs several times in a week, consult your doctor.

Danger signs

Dial 911 or call EMS if a headache is accompanied by any of the following symptoms:
- Drowsiness or confusion.
- Weakness of a limb.
- Blurred vision.
- Dislike of bright light.
- Temporary unconsciousness.

START

Have you hit your head within the past 24 hours?

Head injury

No head injury

Do you have a fever – a temperature of 100.4°F (38°C) or above?

Fever

No fever

ACTION

GO TO ANOTHER CHART
Fever (adults), p.74, or Fever (children), p.76

Are danger signs present (see box above right) or have you vomited?

Danger signs present

Vomited after head injury

No danger signs or vomiting

ACTION

TRY SELF-HELP MEASURES
A mild headache is common following a minor head injury.
- Take an analgesic (not aspirin).

CALL YOUR DOCTOR IMMEDIATELY
if your headache lasts for more than 2 hours or if you develop other symptoms.

Have you experienced nausea and/or vomiting with the headache?

Yes

No

ACTION

TRY SELF-HELP MEASURES
Sinusitis is the likely cause of your headache.
- Try inhaling steam from a bowl of hot water (p.165).

CONSULT YOUR DOCTOR
if you feel no better within 2 days.

ACTION

! DIAL 911 OR CALL EMS
There may be damage to the tissues that surround the brain.

How is your vision?

Blurred vision ▶

Disturbed in other ways ◀

Unchanged ◀

ACTION

CALL YOUR DOCTOR NOW
Acute glaucoma (a painful, rapid rise in fluid pressure in the eye) is a possibility, particularly if the pain is around your eye.

ACTION

MAKE AN APPOINTMENT TO SEE YOUR DOCTOR
Your symptoms may be side effects of the medication.

● Stop taking any over-the-counter medicines but continue to take prescribed medication unless advised to stop by your doctor.

ACTION

CALL YOUR DOCTOR NOW
You have probably a migraine, particularly if any visual problems occurred before the headache. However, the slight chance of a more serious disorder, such as a stroke, needs to be ruled out if this is your first migraine.

● Take an analgesic and sips of water.

● Rest in a darkened, quiet room until the pain subsides.

If you have had any previous attacks, try to identify and avoid potential triggers, such as chocolate.

Where is the pain?

Over one or both temples ◀

Elsewhere ▶

Are you taking any medication?

Medication ▶

No medication ◀

ACTION

CALL YOUR DOCTOR NOW
You may have temporal arteritis (inflammation of blood vessels in the head), particularly if you are over 50 and are not feeling well.

Have you had this type of headache before?

Yes ▶

No ◀

Does either of the following apply?

The pain is felt chiefly in the areas above and below the eyes ◀

You have recently had a runny or stuffy nose ◀

Neither ▶

ACTION

MAKE AN APPOINTMENT TO SEE YOUR DOCTOR
if you cannot identify a possible cause for your headache from this chart.

ACTION

MAKE AN APPOINTMENT TO SEE YOUR DOCTOR
A recurrent headache for which there is no obvious cause, such as drinking too much alcohol, should always be investigated fully by your doctor.

Vertigo

The unpleasant sensation that your surroundings are moving around you is known as vertigo. It is often associated with nausea and vomiting. Healthy people may experience vertigo temporarily after a ride at an amusement park or after drinking too much alcohol. You should consult your doctor if you develop vertigo for no obvious reason.

Recurring attacks of vertigo

If you have been experiencing attacks of vertigo, it is very important to avoid certain activities that are potentially hazardous to you and others. You should not climb ladders or steep flights of stairs, operate machinery, or drive until the cause of your symptoms has been diagnosed and treated.

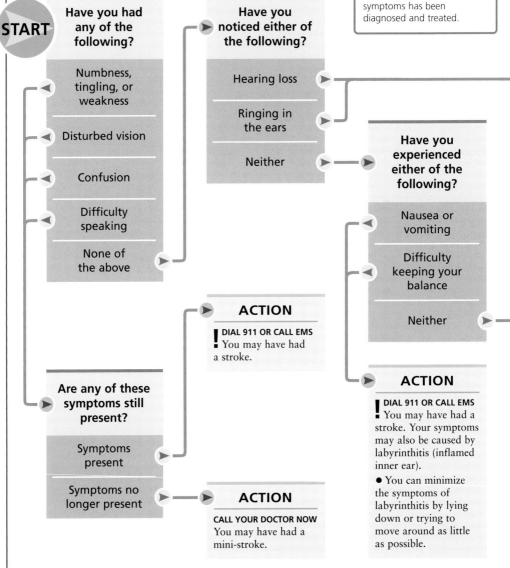

START

Have you had any of the following?

- Numbness, tingling, or weakness
- Disturbed vision
- Confusion
- Difficulty speaking
- None of the above

Have you noticed either of the following?

- Hearing loss
- Ringing in the ears
- Neither

Have you experienced either of the following?

- Nausea or vomiting
- Difficulty keeping your balance
- Neither

Are any of these symptoms still present?

- Symptoms present
- Symptoms no longer present

ACTION

! **DIAL 911 OR CALL EMS**
You may have had a stroke.

ACTION

CALL YOUR DOCTOR NOW
You may have had a mini-stroke.

ACTION

! **DIAL 911 OR CALL EMS**
You may have had a stroke. Your symptoms may also be caused by labyrinthitis (inflamed inner ear).

● You can minimize the symptoms of labyrinthitis by lying down or trying to move around as little as possible.

ACTION

**SEE YOUR DOCTOR
WITHIN 24 HOURS**
You could be suffering
from Ménière's disease
(a disorder of the inner
ear, which contains
the organs of balance
and hearing).
● Lie still in a darkened
room with your eyes
closed and avoid noise.
Acoustic neuroma
(a noncancerous tumor
of the nerve that
connects the ear to the
brain) is another,
although less likely,
possibility.

ACTION

CALL YOUR DOCTOR NOW
Your symptoms may
be a side effect of your
medication.
● Stop taking any over-
the-counter medicines
but continue to take
prescribed medication
unless advised to stop
by your doctor.

ACTION

TRY SELF-HELP MEASURES
Your symptoms are
most likely to be
caused by drinking
more alcohol than
usual or drinking on
an empty stomach.
● The effects of
alcohol should wear
off within a few hours.
● Meanwhile, drink
plenty of water.
CONSULT YOUR DOCTOR
if the sensation persists
for more than 12 hours.

Are you currently taking any medication?

Medication

No medication

Have you been drinking alcohol?

Yes

No

How old are you?

50 or over

Under 50

ACTION

**MAKE AN APPOINTMENT
TO SEE YOUR DOCTOR**
Your vertigo may be
caused by osteoarthritis
affecting the bones
and cartilage of the
upper spine (cervical
spondylosis). This can
cause pressure on the
blood vessels of the
areas of the brain that
affect balance.
● Try to avoid making
any sudden or extreme
head movements.

Does turning or raising your head bring on vertigo?

Brings on vertigo

No noticeable effect

ACTION

**SEE YOUR DOCTOR
WITHIN 24 HOURS**
if you cannot identify a
possible cause for your
vertigo from this chart.

Numbness and/or tingling

Almost everyone has experienced numbness, the loss of sensation in a part of the body, after sitting or lying in an awkward position for some time. Tingling, a prickly feeling, often occurs as sensation returns to a numb area. You should consult this chart if you experience numbness and/or tingling for which there is no obvious cause.

Danger signs

Dial 911 or call EMS if the numbness and/or tingling is accompanied by any of the following symptoms:
- Feeling faint or passing out.
- Disturbed vision.
- Confusion.
- Difficulty speaking.
- Weakness in a limb.

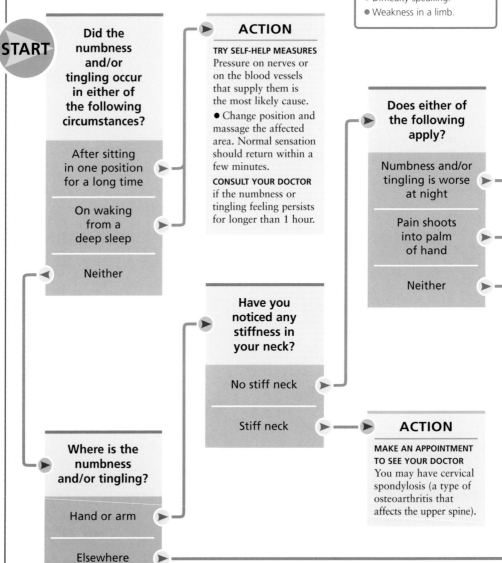

START

Did the numbness and/or tingling occur in either of the following circumstances?

- After sitting in one position for a long time
- On waking from a deep sleep
- Neither

ACTION

TRY SELF-HELP MEASURES Pressure on nerves or on the blood vessels that supply them is the most likely cause.
- Change position and massage the affected area. Normal sensation should return within a few minutes.

CONSULT YOUR DOCTOR if the numbness or tingling feeling persists for longer than 1 hour.

Does either of the following apply?

- Numbness and/or tingling is worse at night
- Pain shoots into palm of hand
- Neither

Have you noticed any stiffness in your neck?

- No stiff neck
- Stiff neck

ACTION

MAKE AN APPOINTMENT TO SEE YOUR DOCTOR You may have cervical spondylosis (a type of osteoarthritis that affects the upper spine).

Where is the numbness and/or tingling?

- Hand or arm
- Elsewhere

ACTION

MAKE AN APPOINTMENT TO SEE YOUR DOCTOR
You probably have carpal tunnel syndrome (tingling and pain in the hand and forearm due to a compressed nerve at the wrist).
● Avoid positions that worsen the symptoms.

Have you had any of the following symptoms?

Feeling faint or passing out

Disturbed vision

Confusion

Difficulty speaking

Weakness in a limb

None of the above

ACTION

! **DIAL 911 OR CALL EMS**
You may have had a stroke.

Are any of these symptoms still present?

Symptoms present

Symptoms no longer present

Are the affected areas on only one side of the body?

One side only

Both sides

Do your fingers become numb and white or blue in either of the following circumstances?

In cold weather

When using vibrating machinery

Neither

ACTION

CALL YOUR DOCTOR NOW
You may have had a mini-stroke.

ACTION

MAKE AN APPOINTMENT TO SEE YOUR DOCTOR
This type of numbness is most likely caused by hand–arm syndrome, which is associated with the long-term use of vibrating machinery.
● Avoid using vibrating machinery.
● Keep warm.
● If you smoke, stop.

ACTION

MAKE AN APPOINTMENT TO SEE YOUR DOCTOR
if you cannot identify a possible cause for your numbness and/or tingling from this chart.

ACTION

MAKE AN APPOINTMENT TO SEE YOUR DOCTOR
You may be suffering from Raynaud's phenomenon, in which there is intermittent narrowing of blood vessels in the hands or, rarely, the feet.
● Keep your hands and/or feet warm.
● If you smoke, stop.

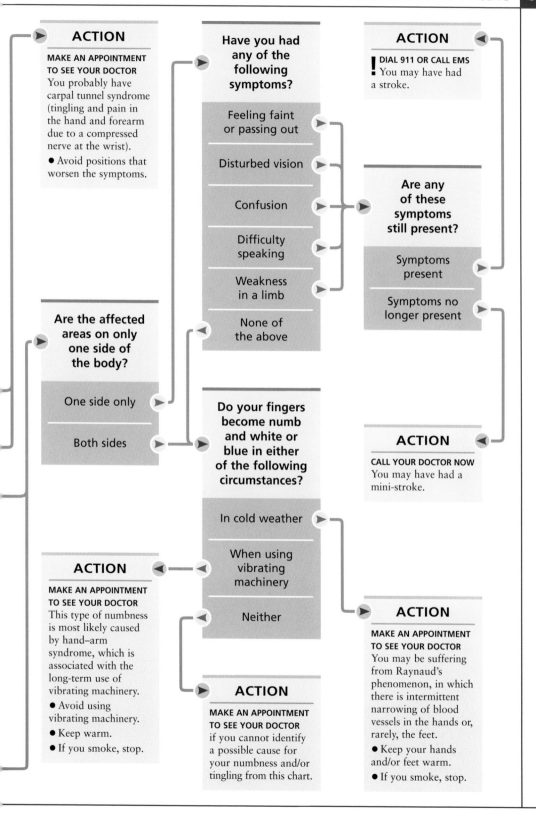

Facial pain

Pain in the face may be sharp and stabbing or dull and throbbing, and is most often caused by an inflammation of structures in the face, such as the sinuses or teeth. Facial pain is usually short-lived, but some types, such as neuralgia, may persist. Consult your doctor if the pain is persistent, unexplained, or is not relieved by analgesics.

START

Where is the pain?

- Over one or both temples
- In or around the eye
- Elsewhere

Do any of the following apply?

- Your scalp is sensitive to touch
- You don't feel well
- Pain comes on when chewing
- None of the above

ACTION

GO TO ANOTHER CHART
Eye pain or irritation, p.98

ACTION

CALL YOUR DOCTOR NOW
You may have temporal arteritis (inflammation of blood vessels around the head), especially if you are over 50.

ACTION

TRY SELF-HELP MEASURES
You probably have sinusitis, especially if you have recently had a cold and both sides of your face are affected. If only one side is affected, a dental problem, such as an abscess, is more likely.
● Take an analgesic such as acetaminophen.
● Try inhaling steam from a bowl of hot water (p.165) if you think you have sinusitis.
CONSULT YOUR DOCTOR OR DENTIST
if you do not feel better within 2 days.

ACTION

MAKE AN APPOINTMENT TO SEE YOUR DOCTOR
You may have trigeminal neuralgia (severe pain due to an irritated nerve).
● Try to avoid triggers if possible.

Which of the following describes your pain?

- Stabbing pain when touching the face or chewing
- Aching pain on chewing and/or yawning
- Dull aching around one or both cheekbones
- None of the above

ACTION

MAKE AN APPOINTMENT TO SEE YOUR DOCTOR OR DENTIST
You may have a disorder in the joint between the jaw and the skull.
● Take acetaminophen to relieve the pain.
● Hold a wrapped heating pad against the affected area.

ACTION

MAKE AN APPOINTMENT TO SEE YOUR DOCTOR
if you cannot identify a possible cause for your facial pain from this chart.

Difficulty speaking

Slurred or unclear speech and the inability to find or use words are symptoms that may have an obvious cause, such as drinking too much alcohol. But difficulty speaking can also signal a more serious condition affecting the brain's speech centers. If your speech suddenly deteriorates, consult your doctor urgently.

ACTION

! DIAL 911 OR CALL EMS
You may have had a stroke.

START

Have you had any of the following?

Are any symptoms still present?

ACTION

CALL YOUR DOCTOR NOW
You may have had a mini-stroke.

Disturbed vision

Symptoms present

Numbness, tingling, or weakness

Symptoms no longer present

ACTION

SEE YOUR DOCTOR WITHIN 24 HOURS
Your symptoms may be a side effect of medication or drugs.
● Stop taking any over-the-counter medicines but continue to take prescribed medication unless advised to stop by your doctor.

Feeling faint or passing out

ACTION

CALL YOUR DOCTOR NOW
You may have a type of facial palsy, due to damaged facial nerves.
●Take care of your eyes, which may not close fully.

Confusion

Inability to move the muscles on one side of the face

None of the above

Do any of these apply?

ACTION

MAKE AN APPOINTMENT TO SEE YOUR DOCTOR
for advice on reducing your alcohol intake.

ACTION

MAKE AN APPOINTMENT TO SEE YOUR DOCTOR
You may have glossitis (inflamed tongue).
● Rinse your mouth regularly with either a salt solution or a pain-relieving mouthwash.
● Avoid acidic and spicy foods.
● If you smoke, stop.

You have been taking drugs or medication

You have been drinking alcohol

You have a sore mouth or tongue

ACTION

SEE YOUR DOCTOR WITHIN 24 HOURS
if you cannot identify a possible cause for your speech difficulty from this chart.

None of the above

Forgetfulness or confusion

Most people are forgetful sometimes, especially if they are very busy. Absent-mindedness is also a natural part of the aging process. Confusion is the inability to think clearly and may include forgetfulness. You should consult your doctor if episodes of forgetfulness and/or confusion occur frequently or are severe enough to disrupt your life.

! Sudden onset of confusion

Call a doctor immediately if a person suddenly becomes very confused or disoriented about time or place, or seems to be seeing or hearing things that are not there.

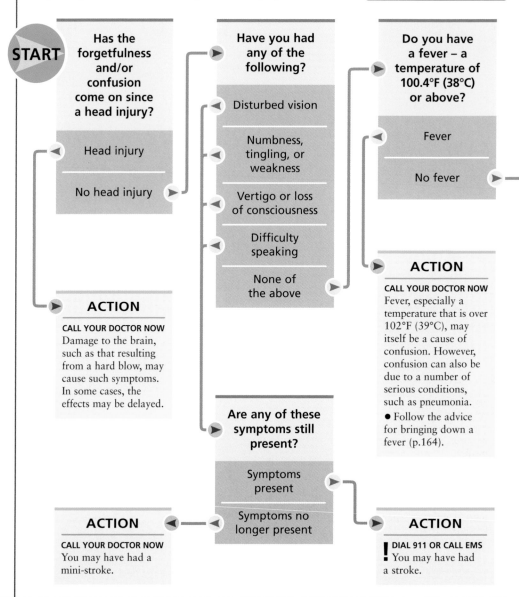

START

Has the forgetfulness and/or confusion come on since a head injury?

Head injury

No head injury

ACTION

CALL YOUR DOCTOR NOW
Damage to the brain, such as that resulting from a hard blow, may cause such symptoms. In some cases, the effects may be delayed.

Have you had any of the following?

Disturbed vision

Numbness, tingling, or weakness

Vertigo or loss of consciousness

Difficulty speaking

None of the above

Are any of these symptoms still present?

Symptoms present

Symptoms no longer present

ACTION

CALL YOUR DOCTOR NOW
You may have had a mini-stroke.

Do you have a fever – a temperature of 100.4°F (38°C) or above?

Fever

No fever

ACTION

CALL YOUR DOCTOR NOW
Fever, especially a temperature that is over 102°F (39°C), may itself be a cause of confusion. However, confusion can also be due to a number of serious conditions, such as pneumonia.
● Follow the advice for bringing down a fever (p.164).

ACTION

! DIAL 911 OR CALL EMS
You may have had a stroke.

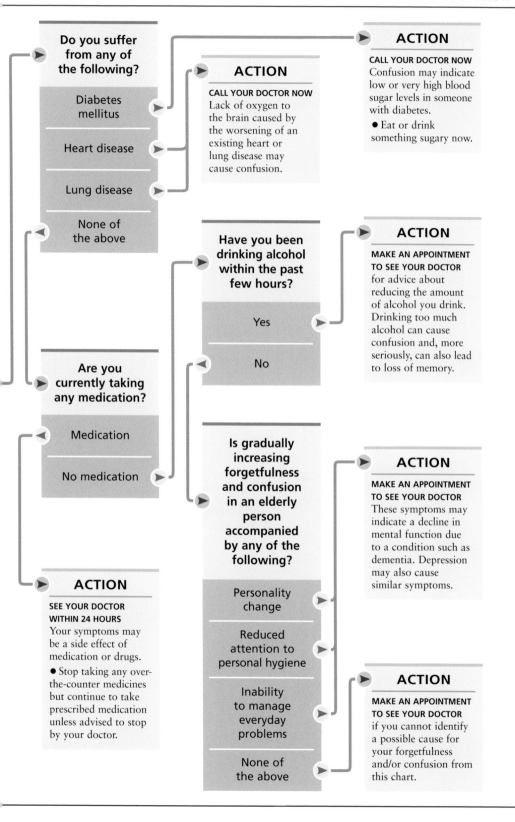

Do you suffer from any of the following?

Diabetes mellitus

Heart disease

Lung disease

None of the above

ACTION

CALL YOUR DOCTOR NOW
Lack of oxygen to the brain caused by the worsening of an existing heart or lung disease may cause confusion.

ACTION

CALL YOUR DOCTOR NOW
Confusion may indicate low or very high blood sugar levels in someone with diabetes.

● Eat or drink something sugary now.

Are you currently taking any medication?

Medication

No medication

Have you been drinking alcohol within the past few hours?

Yes

No

ACTION

MAKE AN APPOINTMENT TO SEE YOUR DOCTOR for advice about reducing the amount of alcohol you drink. Drinking too much alcohol can cause confusion and, more seriously, can also lead to loss of memory.

ACTION

SEE YOUR DOCTOR WITHIN 24 HOURS
Your symptoms may be a side effect of medication or drugs.

● Stop taking any over-the-counter medicines but continue to take prescribed medication unless advised to stop by your doctor.

Is gradually increasing forgetfulness and confusion in an elderly person accompanied by any of the following?

Personality change

Reduced attention to personal hygiene

Inability to manage everyday problems

None of the above

ACTION

MAKE AN APPOINTMENT TO SEE YOUR DOCTOR
These symptoms may indicate a decline in mental function due to a condition such as dementia. Depression may also cause similar symptoms.

ACTION

MAKE AN APPOINTMENT TO SEE YOUR DOCTOR
if you cannot identify a possible cause for your forgetfulness and/or confusion from this chart.

General skin problems

Skin problems are often caused by local infection, allergy, or irritation. They are usually not serious, although widespread skin problems may be distressing. You should consult your doctor if: a skin problem lasts more than a month or causes severe discomfort; a new lump appears, especially if it is dark-colored; or a sore fails to heal.

START

What type of skin problem do you have?

Rash

Other skin problem

Do you have a fever – a temperature of 100.4°F (38°C) or above?

Fever

No fever

ACTION
GO TO ANOTHER CHART
Rash with fever, p.96

Is the affected skin itchy?

Itchy

Not itchy

What does the area look like?

Painful, blistery rash in one area

Reddened patches covered with silvery scales

Blistery, oozing rash on or around the lips

A painful red lump with a yellow center

None of the above

Have you noticed any of the following?

Red, tender, and hot area of skin

New mole or a change in an existing mole

An open sore that has not healed after 3 weeks

None of the above

ACTION
SEE YOUR DOCTOR
WITHIN 24 HOURS
You may have cellulitis (infection of the skin and underlying tissue).

ACTION
MAKE AN APPOINTMENT TO SEE YOUR DOCTOR
You may possibly have skin cancer.

ACTION
TRY SELF-HELP MEASURES
This may be a boil.
● Apply a hot cloth for 30 mins, 4 times a day.
CONSULT YOUR DOCTOR
if the condition has not improved in 24 hours.

What does the affected skin look like?

Areas of inflamed skin with a scaly surface

One or more red bumps with a central dark spot

Intermittent red raised areas (wheals)

None of the above

What do the edges of the rash look like?

Merge into surrounding skin

Clearly defined margins

ACTION

TRY SELF-HELP MEASURES
You may have a form of eczema.

• Follow the advice for relieving itchiness (p.165).

CONSULT YOUR DOCTOR
if your rash does not improve within 1 week or if any other symptoms develop.

ACTION

MAKE AN APPOINTMENT TO SEE YOUR DOCTOR
You may have a fungal infection like ringworm.

ACTION

SEE YOUR DOCTOR WITHIN 24 HOURS
You may have Lyme disease, which is carried by ticks.

ACTION

TRY SELF-HELP MEASURES
You may have been bitten by an insect.

• Try using an antihistamine cream.

ACTION

CALL YOUR DOCTOR NOW
Your symptoms may be a side effect of the drug.

• Stop taking any over-the-counter medicines but continue to take prescribed medication unless advised to stop by your doctor.

ACTION

TRY SELF-HELP MEASURES
You may have urticaria.

• Soothe the irritation with cold compresses or calamine lotion.

• Try over-the-counter antihistamine tablets.

CALL YOUR DOCTOR NOW
if you are experiencing breathing difficulties.

Does either of the following apply?

You have a rash that spreads out from a central red spot

You have been bitten by a tick

Neither

Are you currently taking any medication?

Medication

No medication

ACTION

SEE YOUR DOCTOR WITHIN 24 HOURS
You may have shingles.

• Soothe the irritation with cold compresses or calamine lotion.

• Take an analgesic such as acetaminophen.

ACTION

MAKE AN APPOINTMENT TO SEE YOUR DOCTOR
You may have psoriasis.

ACTION

SEE YOUR DOCTOR WITHIN 24 HOURS
You may have impetigo.

• Do not touch blisters. If you have had the same problem before, it could be a cold sore.

• Use an over-the-counter antiviral cream.

ACTION

MAKE AN APPOINTMENT TO SEE YOUR DOCTOR
if you cannot identify a possible cause for your skin problem from this chart.

Rash with fever

◀ For rash without fever, see p.94

If you or your child has a temperature of 100.4°F (38°C) or above, you should check whether a rash is also present. A rash with fever is usually caused by a viral infection, most of which are not serious. However, a rash may alert you to the possibility of potentially life-threatening meningitis.

Danger signs

Dial 911 or call EMS if a rash and fever are accompanied by any of the following:
- Abnormal drowsiness.
- Seizures.
- Temperature of 102°F (39°C) or above.
- Abnormally rapid breathing (see advice on checking your child's breathing rate, p.71).
- Noisy or difficult breathing.
- Severe headache.

START

What are the features of the rash?

- Widespread itchy, blistery rash
- Rash that spreads from a central red spot
- Flat, dark red spots that do not fade when pressed
- Dull red spots or blotches that fade when pressed
- Bright red rash, particularly on the cheeks
- Pale pink rash on trunk and/or face
- None of the above

ACTION

SEE YOUR DOCTOR WITHIN 24 HOURS
You may have chickenpox, which may need treatment with an antiviral drug.
- Follow the advice for bringing down a fever (p.164).
- Apply calamine lotion to relieve the itchiness of the rash.

ACTION

SEE YOUR DOCTOR WITHIN 24 HOURS
You may have Lyme disease (an infection transmitted by ticks that causes a rash and flulike symptoms).
- Follow the advice for bringing down a fever (p.164).

ACTION

SEE YOUR DOCTOR WITHIN 24 HOURS
Fifth disease (or slapped cheek disease) due to a parvovirus infection may be the cause in a child.
- Follow the advice for bringing down a fever (p.164).

ACTION

SEE YOUR DOCTOR WITHIN 24 HOURS
You may have rubella (German measles). Roseola infantum (a viral infection that causes high fever followed by a rash of tiny pink spots) is another possibility, particularly in children under 4 years old.
- Follow the advice for bringing down a fever (p.164).
- Warn any contact you think could be pregnant.

ACTION

SEE YOUR DOCTOR WITHIN 24 HOURS
if you cannot identify a possible cause for your rash and fever from this chart.

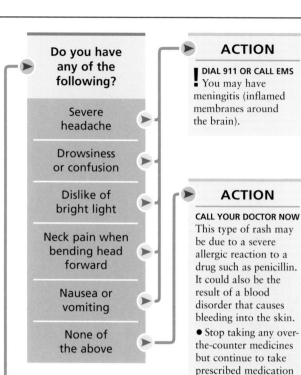

Do you have any of the following?

- Severe headache
- Drowsiness or confusion
- Dislike of bright light
- Neck pain when bending head forward
- Nausea or vomiting
- None of the above

ACTION

! DIAL 911 OR CALL EMS
You may have meningitis (inflamed membranes around the brain).

ACTION

CALL YOUR DOCTOR NOW
This type of rash may be due to a severe allergic reaction to a drug such as penicillin. It could also be the result of a blood disorder that causes bleeding into the skin.
● Stop taking any over-the-counter medicines but continue to take prescribed medication unless advised to stop by your doctor.

Checking a red rash

If you develop a dark red rash, check if it fades on pressure by pressing the side of a drinking glass onto it. If the rash is visible through the glass, it may be a form of purpura, a rash caused by bleeding from tiny blood vessels in the skin either because blood vessels are damaged or because of an abnormality in the blood. Purpura can be caused by one of several serious disorders, including meningitis, and needs prompt medical attention. Dial 911 or call EMS if you have a high fever, severe headache, or any of the other danger signs listed opposite.

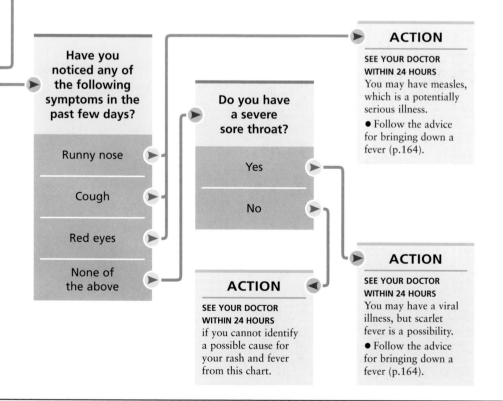

Have you noticed any of the following symptoms in the past few days?

- Runny nose
- Cough
- Red eyes
- None of the above

Do you have a severe sore throat?

- Yes
- No

ACTION

SEE YOUR DOCTOR WITHIN 24 HOURS
You may have measles, which is a potentially serious illness.
● Follow the advice for bringing down a fever (p.164).

ACTION

SEE YOUR DOCTOR WITHIN 24 HOURS
if you cannot identify a possible cause for your rash and fever from this chart.

ACTION

SEE YOUR DOCTOR WITHIN 24 HOURS
You may have a viral illness, but scarlet fever is a possibility.
● Follow the advice for bringing down a fever (p.164).

Eye pain or irritation

Injury, infection, and allergy are the most common causes of discomfort or irritation of the eye and eyelids. A painless red area in the white of the eye is likely to be a burst blood vessel and should clear up without treatment. However, you should see your doctor if your eyes are sore. Consult your doctor immediately if your vision deteriorates.

Contact lens wearers

If you wear contact lenses and experience any kind of eye pain or irritation:

- Remove your lenses without delay.
- Do not use them again until the problem has been identified and treated. If the pain is caused by grit under the lens, there is a risk that the cornea will be scratched.
- Make an appointment to see your ophthalmologist.

START

Does either of the following apply?

You have something in your eye

You have injured your eye

Neither

ACTION

TRY SELF-HELP MEASURES
A foreign object in your eye is likely to cause pain and redness.
- Follow the first-aid advice for dealing with a foreign object in the eye (p.36).

SEEK EMERGENCY HELP AT THE HOSPITAL
if a foreign object is embedded in the eye.

What is the main symptom?

Pain in and around the eye

Itching or irritation of the eyelid

Tender red lump on the eyelid

The eye feels gritty

None of the above

Has your vision deteriorated since the injury?

Yes

No

ACTION

TRY SELF-HELP MEASURES
You may have a stye (infected hair follicle) or a chalazion (infected gland in the eyelid).
- Hold a clean, warm, damp cloth on the eyelid for 20 minutes several times a day.

CONSULT YOUR DOCTOR
if your eye does not improve within 3 days.

ACTION

CALL YOUR DOCTOR NOW
Your pain may be caused by a minor eye injury.
- Follow the first-aid advice for dealing with eye wounds (p.35).

ACTION

DIAL 911 OR CALL EMS
A serious eye injury is possible. Expert help may be needed to prevent permanent damage to the eye.

Is your vision blurred?

Blurred

Not blurred

Is your eyelid turned inward or outward?

Eyelid turned inward

Eyelid turned outward

Appears normal

ACTION

MAKE AN APPOINTMENT TO SEE YOUR DOCTOR
Entropion (turning inward of the upper or lower eyelid, or both) is a possible cause of your symptoms.

ACTION

MAKE AN APPOINTMENT TO SEE YOUR DOCTOR
Ectropion (turning out of the lower eyelid) is a possible cause of your symptoms.

ACTION

CALL YOUR DOCTOR NOW
You may have acute glaucoma (painful, rapid rise in fluid pressure in the eye), which could damage vision permanently.

ACTION

SEE YOUR DOCTOR WITHIN 24 HOURS
You may have so-called cluster headaches or uveitis (inflammation of the iris), especially if the eye is red and/or watery.
• Take an analgesic such as acetaminophen to relieve symptoms.
• Rest in a quiet, darkened room.

ACTION

MAKE AN APPOINTMENT TO SEE YOUR DOCTOR
You probably have conjunctivitis (inflamed membrane covering the eye).
• Wipe the discharge away from your eye with clean, moist cotton.
• Use artificial tears, available over the counter, to relieve symptoms.

ACTION

TRY SELF-HELP MEASURES
You may have blepharitis (inflamed eyelid), especially if the skin is scaly and inflamed.
• Relieve symptoms by holding a warm, damp cloth on the eyelid.
• If you have dandruff too, using an antifungal shampoo will improve both conditions.
CONSULT YOUR DOCTOR
if self-help measures do not help.

Is there any discharge from the eye?

Watery discharge

Sticky discharge

No discharge

ACTION

MAKE AN APPOINTMENT TO SEE YOUR DOCTOR
if you cannot identify a possible cause for your eye pain or irritation from this chart.

ACTION

MAKE AN APPOINTMENT TO SEE YOUR DOCTOR
You may have keratoconjunctivitis sicca (dry eye), in which the eye fails to produce enough tears.
• Use artificial tears, available over the counter, to relieve symptoms.

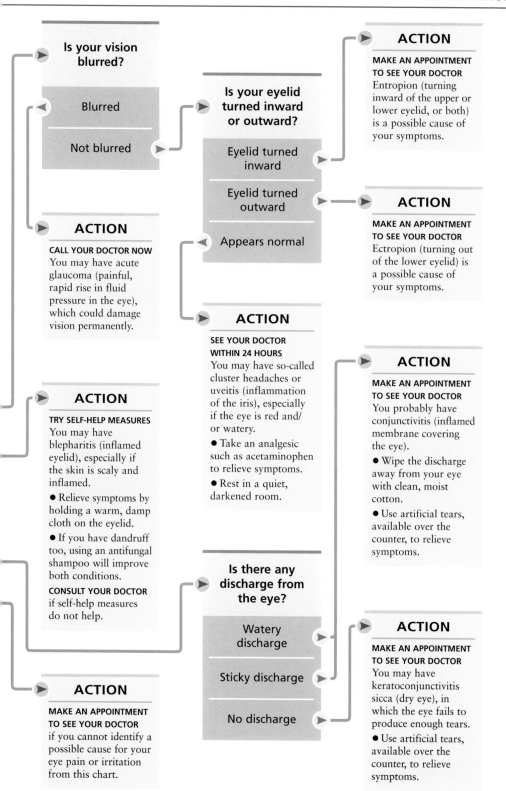

Disturbed/impaired vision

Visual disturbances might include blurred vision or seeing double. You may also see flashing lights or floating spots. These disturbances may be caused by a problem in one or both eyes or by damage to the areas in the brain that process visual information. If your vision deteriorates suddenly, you should consult your doctor immediately.

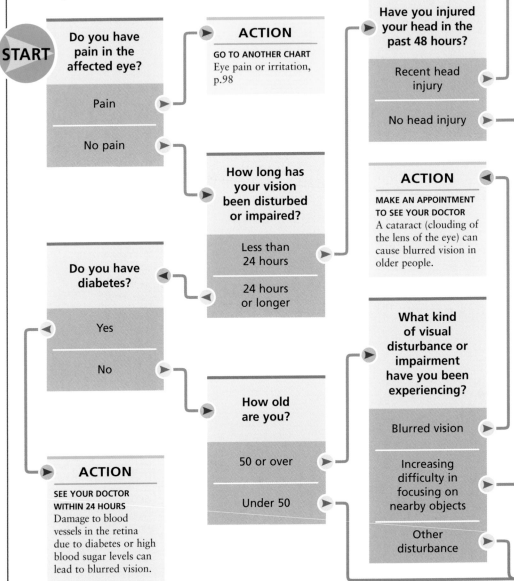

ACTION

! **DIAL 911 OR CALL EMS** You may have damaged the part of the brain that is responsible for vision.

START

Do you have pain in the affected eye?

Pain

No pain

ACTION

GO TO ANOTHER CHART Eye pain or irritation, p.98

How long has your vision been disturbed or impaired?

Less than 24 hours

24 hours or longer

Have you injured your head in the past 48 hours?

Recent head injury

No head injury

ACTION

MAKE AN APPOINTMENT TO SEE YOUR DOCTOR A cataract (clouding of the lens of the eye) can cause blurred vision in older people.

Do you have diabetes?

Yes

No

How old are you?

50 or over

Under 50

What kind of visual disturbance or impairment have you been experiencing?

Blurred vision

Increasing difficulty in focusing on nearby objects

Other disturbance

ACTION

SEE YOUR DOCTOR WITHIN 24 HOURS Damage to blood vessels in the retina due to diabetes or high blood sugar levels can lead to blurred vision.

What is the nature of your disturbed or impaired vision?

Sudden loss of all or part of the vision in one or both eyes

Blurred vision

Seeing flashing lights or floating spots

Double vision

None of the above

ACTION
! DIAL 911 OR CALL EMS
You may have blockage of a blood vessel that supplies the brain or eye. Another possibility is a detached retina, which needs prompt treatment.

ACTION
CALL YOUR DOCTOR NOW
You may have a migraine. However, the possibility of another disorder needs to be ruled out.
• Rest in a darkened quiet room until symptoms improve.
• If you also have a headache, take an analgesic such as acetaminophen.
CONSULT YOUR DOCTOR if you have had previous migraines.
• Avoid red wine, chocolate, and mature cheese – all possible migraine triggers.

ACTION
! DIAL 911 OR CALL EMS
This may be due to bleeding in the brain, such as with a stroke or subarachnoid hemorrhage (ruptured artery near the brain). Another possibility is a weakness or paralysis of the muscles that control the movement of the eyes, causing double vision.

ACTION
SEE YOUR DOCTOR WITHIN 24 HOURS
Your symptoms may be a side effect of the medication.
• Stop taking any over-the-counter medicines but continue to take prescribed medication unless advised to stop by your doctor.

ACTION
CALL YOUR DOCTOR NOW
if you cannot identify a possible cause for your disturbed or impaired vision from this chart.

ACTION
MAKE AN APPOINTMENT TO SEE YOUR OPHTHALMOLOGIST
You may be developing presbyopia (gradual loss of the eyes' ability to focus on near objects).

Are you currently taking any medication?

Medication

No medication

ACTION
SEE YOUR DOCTOR WITHIN 24 HOURS
if you cannot identify a possible cause for your disturbed or impaired vision from this chart.

Earache

Pain in one or both ears is a distressing symptom, especially for children. Earache is usually caused by an infection in the outer or middle ear. Mild discomfort, however, may be due to wax blockage. Consult your doctor if you suffer from earache, particularly if it is persistent. A severe or recurrent middle-ear infection may damage hearing.

START

Does pulling the earlobe make the pain worse?

- Increases pain
- Pain is no worse

ACTION

MAKE AN APPOINTMENT TO SEE YOUR DOCTOR
Your earache is probably due to otitis externa (infection of the outer ear) or a boil in the ear canal.
- Take an analgesic such as acetaminophen.

ACTION

SEE YOUR DOCTOR WITHIN 24 HOURS
You may have otitis media (middle-ear infection) with a perforated eardrum; otitis externa (outer-ear infection) is another possibility.
- Take an analgesic such as acetaminophen.

ACTION

MAKE AN APPOINTMENT TO SEE YOUR DOCTOR
if the discomfort persists for longer than 24 hours. Barotrauma (ear damage or pain caused by pressure changes) may be the cause of your pain.

Is there a discharge from the affected ear?

- Discharge
- No discharge

Did the pain start during or immediately after an airplane flight?

- During or immediately after flight
- Unrelated to air travel

ACTION

TRY SELF-HELP MEASURES
A cold may often be accompanied by mild earache. Persistent or severe earache is likely to be due to otitis media (middle-ear infection).
- Take a decongestant to relieve stuffiness and an analgesic, such as acetaminophen, to relieve discomfort.

CONSULT YOUR DOCTOR
if the pain is severe or if it persists for longer than 2 days.

Do you have a runny or stuffy nose?

- Yes
- No

ACTION

SEE YOUR DOCTOR WITHIN 24 HOURS
if you cannot identify a possible cause for your earache from this chart.

Sore throat

A raw or rough feeling in the throat is a symptom that most people have from time to time. A sore throat is often the first sign of a common cold and is also a feature of other viral infections. You can treat a sore throat yourself at home unless you also have other, more serious symptoms. However, if your sore throat persists or is severe, consult your doctor.

ACTION

MAKE AN APPOINTMENT TO SEE YOUR DOCTOR
You may be suffering from infectious mononucleosis.

START

Do you have a fever – a temperature of 100.4°F (38°C) or above?

Fever

No fever

Do you have swelling in your groin and/or armpits ?

Yes

No

Do you have any of these?

General aches and pains

Runny nose

Headache

Cough

None of the above

ACTION

MAKE AN APPOINTMENT TO SEE YOUR DOCTOR
You may have either tonsillitis or pharyngitis (inflamed throat).
• Follow the advice for soothing a sore throat (p.164).

ACTION

TRY SELF-HELP MEASURES
Activities such as smoking or breathing smoke, shouting, and loud singing are likely to cause throat irritation.
• Follow the advice for soothing a sore throat (p.164).

CONSULT YOUR DOCTOR
if your symptoms worsen, change, or are no better in 2 days.

ACTION

TRY SELF-HELP MEASURES
You probably have a severe cold or flu.
• Follow the advice for bringing down a fever (p.164).

CONSULT YOUR DOCTOR
if your symptoms worsen, change, or are no better after 2 days.

Before the onset of your sore throat, had you been doing any of these?

Smoking heavily or breathing smoke

Shouting or singing loudly

None of the above

ACTION

TRY SELF-HELP MEASURES
You may have a cold.
• Follow the advice for soothing a sore throat (p.164).

CONSULT YOUR DOCTOR
if you are no better within 2 days.

Hoarseness or loss of voice

The sudden onset of hoarseness or huskiness of the voice is a common symptom of upper respiratory tract infections that involve the larynx or vocal cords. Such infections are almost always caused by viruses. Hoarseness and loss of voice that develop gradually are most commonly caused by overuse of the voice, smoking, or, rarely, cancer of the larynx.

! Persistent change in the voice

It is important to seek medical advice if you develop hoarseness or any other voice change that lasts for more than 2 weeks, since the slight possibility of cancer of the larynx needs to be ruled out.

START

How long ago did the hoarseness or loss of voice develop?

- Over a week ago
- Within the past week

Do you use your voice a lot; for example, are you a singer or teacher?

- Normal voice use
- Regular loud voice use

ACTION

MAKE AN APPOINTMENT TO SEE YOUR DOCTOR Regular overuse of your voice can lead to chronic laryngitis or vocal cord nodules (small, noncancerous lumps found on the vocal cords).

- If you smoke, stop.
- Try inhaling steam from a bowl of hot water (p.165) to relieve your hoarseness.
- Rest your voice as much as possible.

Have you had any of the following symptoms in the past week?

- Runny nose and/or sneezing
- Cough
- Sore throat
- None of the above

ACTION

TRY SELF-HELP MEASURES You probably have acute viral laryngitis.

- If you smoke, stop.
- Try inhaling steam from a bowl of hot water (p.165) to relieve your hoarseness.
- Rest your voice as much as possible.

CONSULT YOUR DOCTOR if you do not feel better within 2 days or if any other symptoms develop.

Before the onset of hoarseness, had you been using your voice more than usual?

- More voice use than usual
- Normal voice use

Do you smoke, or have you smoked in the past?

Yes

No

ACTION

MAKE AN APPOINTMENT TO SEE YOUR DOCTOR
Heavy smoking over a long period of time can result in laryngitis.
- If you smoke, stop.
- Rest your voice as much as possible.
Another possibility is cancer of the larynx, which is more common in regular smokers.

ACTION

MAKE AN APPOINTMENT TO SEE YOUR DOCTOR
Hypothyroidism (underactivity of the thyroid gland) can cause a husky voice.

ACTION

TRY SELF-HELP MEASURES
Excessive use of the voice can inflame the vocal cords.
- If you smoke, stop.
- Try inhaling steam from a bowl of hot water (p.165) to relieve your hoarseness.
- Rest your voice as much as possible.
CONSULT YOUR DOCTOR
if your voice is no better within 2 days or if any other symptoms develop.

ACTION

CALL YOUR DOCTOR NOW
Breathing in dust, fumes, or smoke can inflame the airways.

Do you have any of the following?

Fatigue

Increased skin dryness or roughness

Feeling the cold more than you used to

Unexplained weight gain

General hair thinning

None of the above

Did either of the following apply before the onset of hoarseness?

You inhaled dust, chemical fumes, or smoke from a fire

You spent time in a smoky atmosphere

Neither

ACTION

TRY SELF-HELP MEASURES
Being in a smoky atmosphere can inflame the vocal cords.
- If you smoke, stop.
- Try inhaling steam from a bowl of hot water (p.165) to relieve your hoarseness.
- Rest your voice as much as possible.
CONSULT YOUR DOCTOR
if your voice is no better within 2 days or if any other symptoms develop.

ACTION

MAKE AN APPOINTMENT TO SEE YOUR DOCTOR
if you cannot identify a possible cause for your hoarseness or loss of voice from this chart.

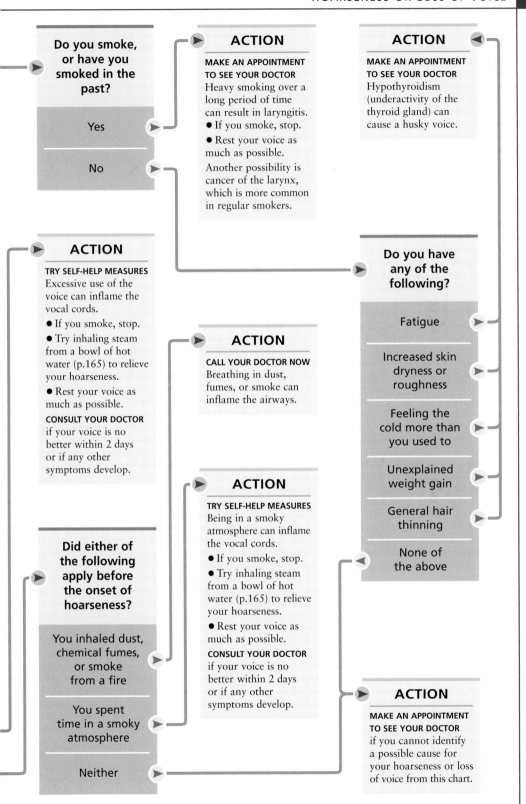

Coughing (adults)

For children under 12, see p.108 ▶

A natural defence mechanism, coughing is the body's way of clearing the airways of inhaled particles or secretions. Persistent coughing may be due to infection or inflammation in the lungs or to the effects of irritants such as tobacco smoke. Persistent coughing should be investigated by your doctor.

! Coughing up blood

If you cough up sputum that contains streaks of blood on one occasion only, the most likely cause is a small tear in the lining of the windpipe; if you feel well, you need not be concerned. However, if you have more than one such episode, there may be a more serious cause; you should see a doctor without delay.

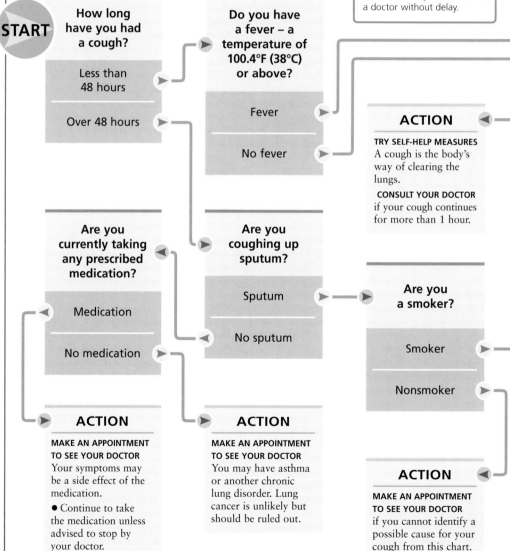

START

How long have you had a cough?

- Less than 48 hours ▶
- Over 48 hours ▶

Do you have a fever – a temperature of 100.4°F (38°C) or above?

- Fever ▶
- No fever ▶

ACTION

TRY SELF-HELP MEASURES A cough is the body's way of clearing the lungs.

CONSULT YOUR DOCTOR if your cough continues for more than 1 hour.

Are you currently taking any prescribed medication?

- Medication ◀
- No medication ▶

Are you coughing up sputum?

- Sputum ▶
- No sputum ◀

Are you a smoker?

- Smoker ▶
- Nonsmoker ▶

ACTION

MAKE AN APPOINTMENT TO SEE YOUR DOCTOR Your symptoms may be a side effect of the medication.

● Continue to take the medication unless advised to stop by your doctor.

ACTION

MAKE AN APPOINTMENT TO SEE YOUR DOCTOR You may have asthma or another chronic lung disorder. Lung cancer is unlikely but should be ruled out.

ACTION

MAKE AN APPOINTMENT TO SEE YOUR DOCTOR if you cannot identify a possible cause for your cough from this chart.

Do you have either of the following?

Pain on breathing

Shortness of breath

Neither

ACTION

CALL YOUR DOCTOR NOW
You may have pneumonia.
● Take acetaminophen to help reduce your fever and pain.

Have you coughed up sputum?

Sputum

No sputum

ACTION

TRY SELF-HELP MEASURES
You may have acute bronchitis.
● Take acetaminophen to reduce your fever and chest pain.
● Drink plenty of fluids.
● If you smoke, stop.
CONSULT YOUR DOCTOR
if your symptoms worsen or if you are no better within 2 days.

ACTION

TRY SELF-HELP MEASURES
You may have a viral illness such as a severe cold or flu.
● Follow the advice for bringing down a fever (p.164).
● Try inhaling steam from a bowl of hot water (p.165) to relieve your symptoms.
MAKE AN APPOINTMENT TO SEE YOUR DOCTOR
if you are no better in 2 days or if other symptoms develop.

Have you inhaled any of these in the last few hours?

Particle of food

Tobacco smoke

Dust, fumes, or smoke from a fire

None of the above

ACTION

CALL YOUR DOCTOR NOW
Inflammation of the airways can result from breathing in any of these substances.

Do you have either of the following?

Runny nose

Sore throat

Neither

ACTION

TRY SELF-HELP MEASURES
Smoke can irritate the lungs.
● Move into a well-ventilated area.

ACTION

MAKE AN APPOINTMENT TO SEE YOUR DOCTOR
You may have chronic lung damage from smoking or possibly lung cancer.
● Stop smoking.

ACTION

MAKE AN APPOINTMENT TO SEE YOUR DOCTOR
Asthma or possibly heart failure may be the cause of your symptoms.
● If you smoke, stop.

ACTION

TRY SELF-HELP MEASURES
You probably have a viral infection, such as a cold.
● Try inhaling steam from a bowl of hot water (p.165) to relieve your symptoms.
MAKE AN APPOINTMENT TO SEE YOUR DOCTOR
if you are no better in 2 days or if other symptoms develop.

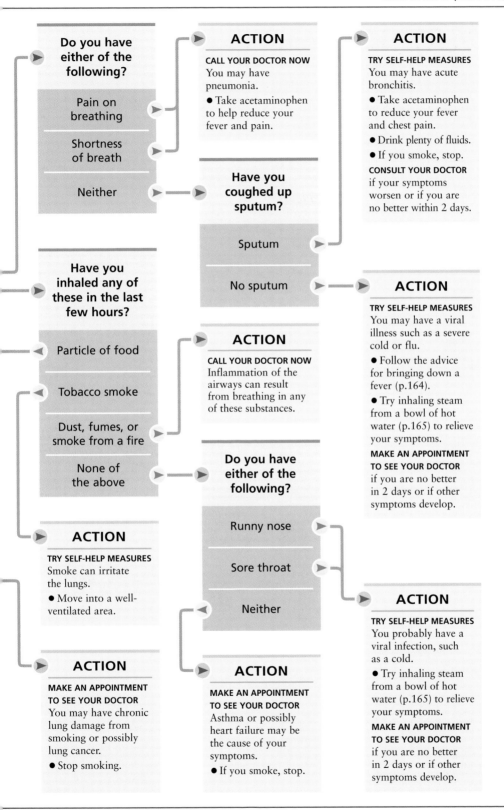

Coughing (children)

◀ **For adults and children over 12, see p.106**

Coughing is a normal reaction to irritation in the throat or lungs. Most coughs are due to minor infections of the nose and/or throat, but a sudden onset of coughing may be caused by choking. Coughing is unusual in babies less than 6 months old and may indicate a serious lung infection.

! Danger signs

Dial 911 or call EMS if your child is coughing and has any of the following symptoms:
- Blue-tinged lips or tongue.
- Abnormal drowsiness.
- Inability to produce sounds.
- Inability to drink.
- Excessively rapid breathing.

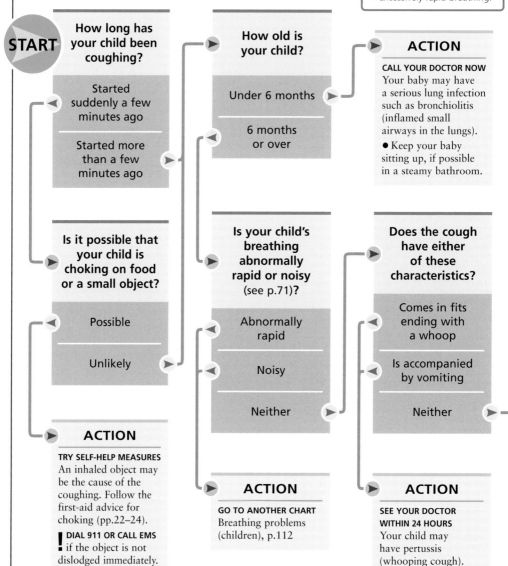

START

How long has your child been coughing?

- Started suddenly a few minutes ago
- Started more than a few minutes ago

How old is your child?

- Under 6 months
- 6 months or over

ACTION

CALL YOUR DOCTOR NOW
Your baby may have a serious lung infection such as bronchiolitis (inflamed small airways in the lungs).
- Keep your baby sitting up, if possible in a steamy bathroom.

Is it possible that your child is choking on food or a small object?

- Possible
- Unlikely

Is your child's breathing abnormally rapid or noisy (see p.71)?

- Abnormally rapid
- Noisy
- Neither

Does the cough have either of these characteristics?

- Comes in fits ending with a whoop
- Is accompanied by vomiting
- Neither

ACTION

TRY SELF-HELP MEASURES
An inhaled object may be the cause of the coughing. Follow the first-aid advice for choking (pp.22–24).

▮ DIAL 911 OR CALL EMS if the object is not dislodged immediately.

ACTION

GO TO ANOTHER CHART
Breathing problems (children), p.112

ACTION

SEE YOUR DOCTOR WITHIN 24 HOURS
Your child may have pertussis (whooping cough).

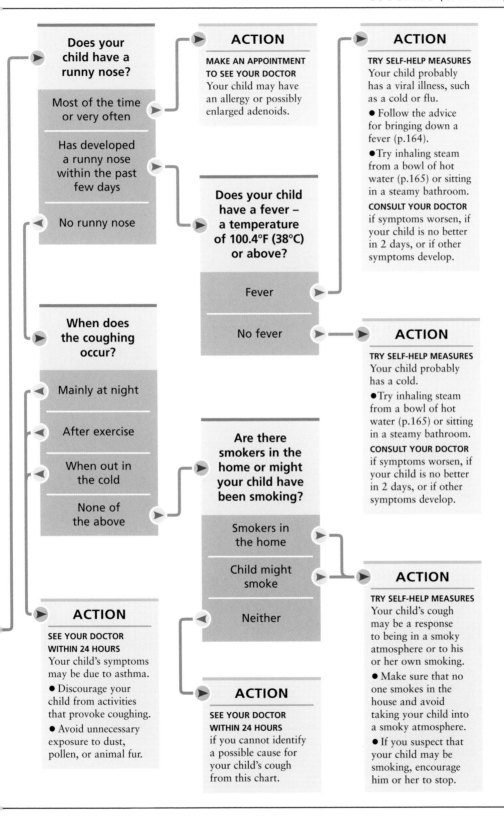

Does your child have a runny nose?

Most of the time or very often ▶

Has developed a runny nose within the past few days ▶

No runny nose ◀

When does the coughing occur?

Mainly at night ◀

After exercise ◀

When out in the cold ◀

None of the above ▶

Does your child have a fever – a temperature of 100.4°F (38°C) or above?

Fever ▶

No fever ▶

Are there smokers in the home or might your child have been smoking?

Smokers in the home ▶

Child might smoke ▶

Neither ◀

ACTION

MAKE AN APPOINTMENT TO SEE YOUR DOCTOR
Your child may have an allergy or possibly enlarged adenoids.

ACTION

TRY SELF-HELP MEASURES
Your child probably has a viral illness, such as a cold or flu.
● Follow the advice for bringing down a fever (p.164).
●Try inhaling steam from a bowl of hot water (p.165) or sitting in a steamy bathroom.
CONSULT YOUR DOCTOR
if symptoms worsen, if your child is no better in 2 days, or if other symptoms develop.

ACTION

TRY SELF-HELP MEASURES
Your child probably has a cold.
●Try inhaling steam from a bowl of hot water (p.165) or sitting in a steamy bathroom.
CONSULT YOUR DOCTOR
if symptoms worsen, if your child is no better in 2 days, or if other symptoms develop.

ACTION

TRY SELF-HELP MEASURES
Your child's cough may be a response to being in a smoky atmosphere or to his or her own smoking.
● Make sure that no one smokes in the house and avoid taking your child into a smoky atmosphere.
● If you suspect that your child may be smoking, encourage him or her to stop.

ACTION

SEE YOUR DOCTOR
WITHIN 24 HOURS
Your child's symptoms may be due to asthma.
● Discourage your child from activities that provoke coughing.
● Avoid unnecessary exposure to dust, pollen, or animal fur.

ACTION

SEE YOUR DOCTOR
WITHIN 24 HOURS
if you cannot identify a possible cause for your child's cough from this chart.

Shortness of breath (adults)

For children under 12, see p.112 ►

Feeling short of breath is to be expected after strenuous exercise. Breathing should return to normal after resting. If you are short of breath at rest or following normal activities, such as getting dressed, you should consult your doctor because your symptom may be due to a serious heart or lung disorder.

! Danger signs

Dial 911 or call EMS if either you or someone you are with has one or both of the following symptoms:
- Sudden and severe shortness of breath.
- Blue-tinged lips.

While waiting for medical help, loosen any restricting clothing and help the person sit upright.

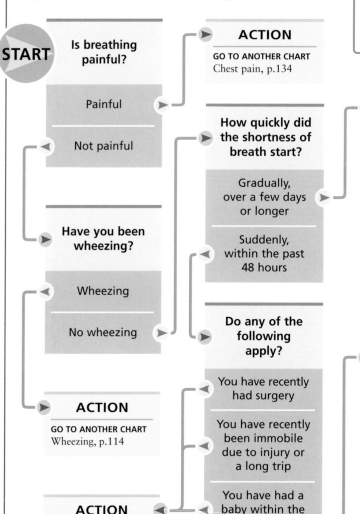

START

Is breathing painful?

Painful ►

Not painful ◄

Have you been wheezing?

Wheezing ◄

No wheezing ►

► **ACTION**

GO TO ANOTHER CHART
Chest pain, p.134

How quickly did the shortness of breath start?

Gradually, over a few days or longer ►

Suddenly, within the past 48 hours ◄

Do any of the following apply?

You have recently had surgery ◄

You have recently been immobile due to injury or a long trip ◄

You have had a baby within the past 2 weeks ◄

None of the above ►

► **ACTION**

GO TO ANOTHER CHART
Wheezing, p.114

ACTION ◄

! DIAL 911 OR CALL EMS
You may have a pulmonary embolism (blood clot in the lung).

Do you have either of the following?

Swollen ankles ►

Cough with sputum on most days ►

Neither ►

Do you have any of the following?

Waking at night feeling breathless ►

Frothy pink or white sputum ►

Temperature of 100.4°F (38°C) or above ►

None of the above ►

ACTION

SEE YOUR DOCTOR WITHIN 24 HOURS
You may have chronic heart failure, which causes fluid to gather in the lungs and tissues.
- If you smoke, stop.
- Avoid strenuous exercise and stressful situations.

ACTION

MAKE AN APPOINTMENT TO SEE YOUR DOCTOR
You may have lung disease caused by inhaling damaging dusts or gases.

ACTION

MAKE AN APPOINTMENT TO SEE YOUR DOCTOR
You may have inflammation of the lungs due to an allergy.

ACTION

MAKE AN APPOINTMENT TO SEE YOUR DOCTOR
You may have chronic bronchitis or lung damage from smoking.
- If you smoke, stop.
- Avoid exposure to smoke, pollution, dust, dampness, and cold.
- Exercise lightly.

Do you have, or have you ever had, regular exposure to or contact with the following?

Dust or fumes

Grain crops, caged birds, or animals

Neither

ACTION

SEE YOUR DOCTOR WITHIN 24 HOURS
You may be anemic, but a blood test will be needed to confirm the diagnosis.
- Get plenty of rest.

ACTION

CALL YOUR DOCTOR NOW
You may have fluid on the lungs (pulmonary edema) caused by acute heart failure.

Did the shortness of breath start straight after a stressful event?

Yes

No

Do you have any of the following?

Faintness or fainting

Paler skin than normal

Undue fatigue

None of the above

ACTION

CALL YOUR DOCTOR NOW
You may have a lung infection, such as pneumonia, especially if you also have a cough.
- Take acetaminophen to reduce fever.

ACTION

CALL YOUR DOCTOR NOW
You may have had a panic attack, but this needs to be confirmed by a doctor.
- If you have had such attacks before, breathing into a bag may relieve symptoms (p.168).

ACTION

SEE YOUR DOCTOR WITHIN 24 HOURS
if you cannot identify a possible cause for your shortness of breath from this chart.

Breathing problems (children)

◀ For adults and children over 12, see p.110

Noisy or rapid breathing and shortness of breath indicate breathing problems. Such problems may not be obvious in children, who may simply avoid exertion. A child with severe difficulty breathing needs urgent hospital treatment. Breathing problems that occur suddenly also need immediate attention.

Danger signs

Dial 911 or call EMS if your child's breathing rate is excessively rapid (see advice on checking your child's breathing rate, p.71) and if breathing problems are accompanied by any of the following symptoms:

● Blue-tinged lips or tongue.
● Abnormal drowsiness.
● Inability to swallow, talk, or produce sounds.

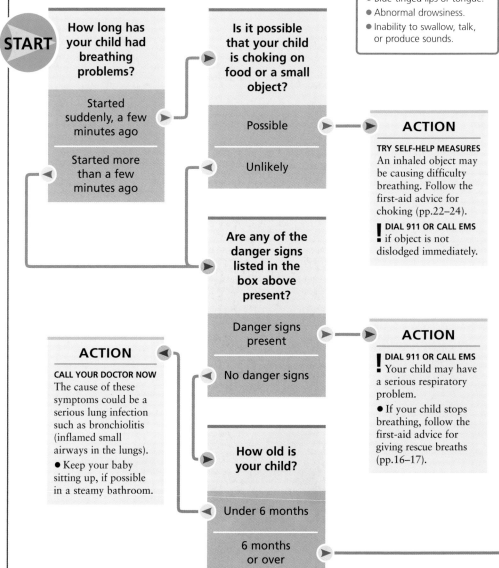

START

How long has your child had breathing problems?

Started suddenly, a few minutes ago

Started more than a few minutes ago

Is it possible that your child is choking on food or a small object?

Possible

Unlikely

ACTION

TRY SELF-HELP MEASURES
An inhaled object may be causing difficulty breathing. Follow the first-aid advice for choking (pp.22–24).

! DIAL 911 OR CALL EMS if object is not dislodged immediately.

Are any of the danger signs listed in the box above present?

Danger signs present

No danger signs

ACTION

CALL YOUR DOCTOR NOW
The cause of these symptoms could be a serious lung infection such as bronchiolitis (inflamed small airways in the lungs).
● Keep your baby sitting up, if possible in a steamy bathroom.

ACTION

! DIAL 911 OR CALL EMS
Your child may have a serious respiratory problem.
● If your child stops breathing, follow the first-aid advice for giving rescue breaths (pp.16–17).

How old is your child?

Under 6 months

6 months or over

Does your child have any of the following?

Noisy breathing

Barking cough

Shortness of breath

None of the above

Does your child have a fever – a temperature of 100.4°F (38°C) or above?

Fever

No fever

Does your child suffer from repeated episodes of any of the following?

Wheezing

Coughing at night

Coughing after exercise

Coughing after going out in the cold

None of the above

ACTION

CALL YOUR DOCTOR NOW
These symptoms may be due to croup (inflammation of the windpipe).
● Sit with your child in a steamy bathroom to relieve breathing difficulties.
● Encourage your child to drink plenty of fluids.
● Ensure that your child sits quietly and avoids exertion.

ACTION

SEE YOUR DOCTOR WITHIN 24 HOURS
Your child may have developed asthma.
● Keep your child rested and warm.
● Minimize contact with any possible triggers, such as dust, pollen, or animal fur.
● Avoid exposing your child to smoke.
● Avoid using perfume and air fresheners.

ACTION

CALL YOUR DOCTOR NOW
Your child may have a lung infection, such as pneumonia. Another possible cause is bronchiolitis (inflamed small airways in the lungs), particularly in young children.
● Give your child liquid acetaminophen to reduce fever.
● Offer frequent drinks.
● Increase the humidity in your child's room by putting a bowl of water near a radiator.

ACTION

SEE YOUR DOCTOR WITHIN 24 HOURS
if you cannot identify a possible cause for the breathing problems from this chart.

Wheezing

◀ For children under 12, see p.112
A whistling or rasping sound on exhaling occurs
when the air passages become narrowed. The most
common causes are inflammation due to infection,
asthma, or inhaled dust. In rare cases, a narrowing
of the airways may be due to a tumor. If you have
persistent wheezing, you should see your doctor.

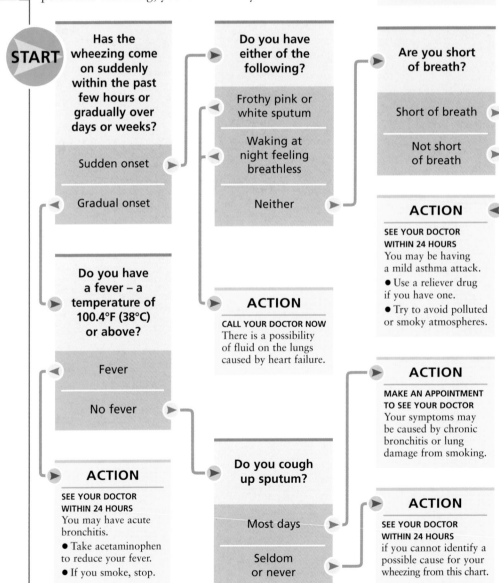

ACTION

CALL YOUR DOCTOR NOW
You could be having
an asthma attack.
● If you have a reliever
inhaler, use it now.
● Stay calm and sit in
a comfortable position.

START

Has the wheezing come on suddenly within the past few hours or gradually over days or weeks?

Sudden onset

Gradual onset

Do you have either of the following?

Frothy pink or white sputum

Waking at night feeling breathless

Neither

Are you short of breath?

Short of breath

Not short of breath

ACTION

SEE YOUR DOCTOR WITHIN 24 HOURS
You may be having
a mild asthma attack.
● Use a reliever drug
if you have one.
● Try to avoid polluted
or smoky atmospheres.

Do you have a fever – a temperature of 100.4°F (38°C) or above?

Fever

No fever

ACTION

CALL YOUR DOCTOR NOW
There is a possibility
of fluid on the lungs
caused by heart failure.

ACTION

MAKE AN APPOINTMENT TO SEE YOUR DOCTOR
Your symptoms may
be caused by chronic
bronchitis or lung
damage from smoking.

ACTION

SEE YOUR DOCTOR WITHIN 24 HOURS
You may have acute
bronchitis.
● Take acetaminophen
to reduce your fever.
● If you smoke, stop.

Do you cough up sputum?

Most days

Seldom or never

ACTION

SEE YOUR DOCTOR WITHIN 24 HOURS
if you cannot identify a
possible cause for your
wheezing from this chart.

Difficulty swallowing

Any difficulty swallowing is usually the result of a sore throat due to infection. Self-treatment should ease the soreness and allow normal swallowing. However, persistent difficulty swallowing may be due to a disorder of the stomach or esophagus, the tube connecting the throat to the stomach, and should be investigated by your doctor.

START

Is your throat sore?

Sore

Not sore

Is it possible that you have swallowed something sharp, such as a fish bone?

Possible

Unlikely

ACTION

GO TO ANOTHER CHART
Sore throat, p.103

ACTION

CALL YOUR DOCTOR NOW
Something may have either scratched your throat or become lodged in it.

Which of the following applies?

Food seems to stick high up in the chest

You have a feeling of something being stuck in the throat

Neither

ACTION

MAKE AN APPOINTMENT TO SEE YOUR DOCTOR
Anxiety disorders may be a cause of this type of difficulty swallowing.

ACTION

MAKE AN APPOINTMENT TO SEE YOUR DOCTOR
if you cannot identify a possible cause for your difficulty swallowing from this chart.

Do you get a burning pain in the center of the chest in either of these situations?

When you bend forward

When you lie down

Neither

ACTION

MAKE AN APPOINTMENT TO SEE YOUR DOCTOR
You probably have an inflamed esophagus due to acid reflux.

Does either of the following apply?

The difficulty swallowing is getting worse

You have lost weight

Neither

ACTION

SEE YOUR DOCTOR WITHIN 24 HOURS
You may have a narrowed esophagus caused by acid reflux, but cancer of the esophagus is possible.

Vomiting (adults)

For children under 12, see p.118 ▷
Irritation or inflammation of the digestive tract is the most common cause of vomiting. But vomiting may also be triggered by conditions affecting the brain or by an inner-ear disorder, or it can be a side effect of medication. If you suffer from frequent episodes of vomiting, you should consult your doctor.

Danger signs

Dial 911 or call EMS if your vomit contains blood, which may appear in any of the following forms:
● Bright red streaks.
● Black material that resembles coffee grounds.
● Blood clots.

START

Have you suffered from other episodes of vomiting?

Previous episodes

Single episode

Do you have pain in the abdomen?

Severe pain

Mild pain

No pain

ACTION

CALL YOUR DOCTOR NOW
You could have a serious abdominal condition, such as appendicitis.

ACTION

CALL YOUR DOCTOR NOW
You may have acute glaucoma (a painful, rapid rise in fluid pressure in the eye), especially if your vision is also blurred.

Do you have pain in or around an eye?

Eye pain

No eye pain

ACTION

! DIAL 911 OR CALL EMS
You may have had a stroke. Your symptoms may also be caused by labyrinthitis (inflamed inner ear).

● You can minimize the symptoms of labyrinthitis by lying down or moving as little as possible.

ACTION

MAKE AN APPOINTMENT TO SEE YOUR DOCTOR
You may have a digestive tract disorder.

Do you have a headache?

Headache

No headache

Do you have any of the following?

Temperature of 100.4°F (38°C) or above

Diarrhea

Dizziness

None of the above

Vomiting and medications

If you are taking any oral medication, including oral contraceptives, an episode of vomiting may reduce the effectiveness of the drug because your body cannot absorb the active ingredients. If you use oral contraceptives, you will need to use an additional form of contraception such as condoms for some time after the vomiting has stopped. Follow the instructions provided with the oral contraceptives or consult your doctor if you are not sure what to do. You should also see your doctor if you are taking any other prescribed medicine and have been vomiting.

Have you eaten or drunk any of the following?

An unusually large or rich meal

A large amount of alcohol

Food that may have been contaminated

None of the above

ACTION

TRY SELF-HELP MEASURES
You probably have gastritis (inflammation of the stomach lining).

● Take over-the-counter antacids to neutralize the acid in the stomach.

● Eat small meals at regular intervals.

● Stop drinking alcohol until you are better.

● If you smoke, stop.

CONSULT YOUR DOCTOR
if you are no better in 2 days or if other symptoms develop.

ACTION

GO TO ANOTHER CHART
Headache, p.84

ACTION

TRY SELF-HELP MEASURES
You may have food poisoning.

● Follow the advice for preventing dehydration (p.165).

CONSULT YOUR DOCTOR
if you are no better in 2 days or if other symptoms develop.

Are you taking any medication?

Medication

No medication

ACTION

TRY SELF-HELP MEASURES
You may have a case of gastroenteritis.

● Follow the advice for preventing dehydration (p.165).

CONSULT YOUR DOCTOR
if you are no better in 2 days or if other symptoms develop.

ACTION

SEE YOUR DOCTOR WITHIN 24 HOURS
Your symptoms may be a side effect of the medication.

● Stop taking any over-the-counter medicines but continue to take prescribed medication unless advised to stop by your doctor.

ACTION

SEE YOUR DOCTOR WITHIN 24 HOURS
if you cannot identify a possible cause for your vomiting from this chart.

Vomiting (children)

◀ **For adults and children over 12, see p.116**

Children vomit as a result of many illnesses, including ear infections and urinary and digestive tract disorders. Anxiety or excitement may also cause vomiting. Rarely, vomiting may be due to an infection or injury to the brain. If vomiting is persistent, consult your child's doctor urgently.

❗ Danger signs

Dial 911 or call EMS if your child's vomiting is accompanied by any of the following symptoms:
- Greenish yellow vomit.
- Abdominal pain for 4 hours.
- Flat, dark-red or purple spots on skin that do not fade when pressed.
- Refusal to drink or feed (in babies) for over 6 hours.
- Abnormal drowsiness.
- Sunken eyes.
- Dry tongue.
- Not urinating during the day for 3 hours (if child is under 1 year old) or 6 hours (in an older child).
- Black or bloodstained feces.

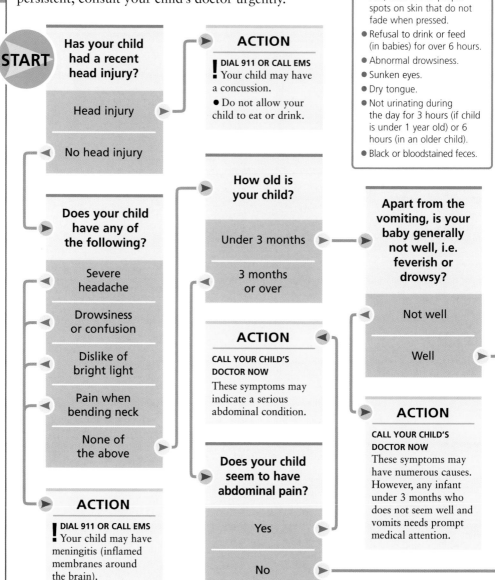

START

Has your child had a recent head injury?

Head injury ▶

No head injury ◀

ACTION

❗ **DIAL 911 OR CALL EMS**
Your child may have a concussion.

- Do not allow your child to eat or drink.

Does your child have any of the following?

Severe headache ◀

Drowsiness or confusion ◀

Dislike of bright light ◀

Pain when bending neck ◀

None of the above ▶

ACTION

❗ **DIAL 911 OR CALL EMS**
Your child may have meningitis (inflamed membranes around the brain).

How old is your child?

Under 3 months ▶

3 months or over ◀

ACTION

CALL YOUR CHILD'S DOCTOR NOW
These symptoms may indicate a serious abdominal condition.

Does your child seem to have abdominal pain?

Yes ▶

No ▶

Apart from the vomiting, is your baby generally not well, i.e. feverish or drowsy?

Not well ◀

Well ▶

ACTION

CALL YOUR CHILD'S DOCTOR NOW
These symptoms may have numerous causes. However, any infant under 3 months who does not seem well and vomits needs prompt medical attention.

What are the characteristics of the vomiting?

Frequent and effortless after feeding

Forceful after several feedings

Occasional, not associated with feeding

ACTION

BRING YOUR CHILD TO THE DOCTOR WITHIN 24 HOURS This type of vomiting in an infant may be the result of a digestive tract problem, such as pyloric stenosis, in which the stomach outlet becomes abnormally narrowed.

ACTION

TRY SELF-HELP MEASURES This type of vomiting is rarely serious and has several possible causes.
●Always burp your baby after feeding.
CONSULT YOUR CHILD'S DOCTOR if your infant does not seem well or is failing to gain weight.

ACTION

TRY SELF-HELP MEASURES Babies often vomit for no particular reason. It is no cause for concern if the baby seems well and is gaining weight.
● Be sure to burp your baby after each feeding.
CONSULT YOUR CHILD'S DOCTOR if your baby seems sick or vomits frequently.

Does your child have diarrhea?

Diarrhea

No diarrhea

ACTION

CALL YOUR CHILD'S DOCTOR NOW if your child is under 6 months old. He may have a case of gastroenteritis.
● Make sure older children drink plenty of clear fluids.
CONSULT YOUR CHILD'S DOCTOR if your child is no better within 24 hours or if any other symptoms develop.

Does your child have any of the following?

Pain when urinating

Renewed bedwetting or daytime "accidents"

Temperature of 100.4°F (38°C) or above

None of the above

ACTION

CALL YOUR CHILD'S DOCTOR NOW Your child may have a lung infection such as pertussis, bronchiolitis, or pneumonia.

ACTION

BRING YOUR CHILD TO THE DOCTOR WITHIN 24 HOURS He may have a urinary tract infection.
● Give plenty of fluids to drink.

ACTION

BRING YOUR CHILD TO THE DOCTOR WITHIN 24 HOURS Your child may have an infection such as acute otitis media (an infection of the middle ear) or a urinary tract infection.
● Give liquid acetaminophen to relieve pain and fever.

Did vomiting follow violent coughing?

Followed coughing

No coughing

ACTION

BRING YOUR CHILD TO THE DOCTOR WITHIN 24 HOURS if you cannot identify a cause for your child's vomiting from this chart.

Abdominal pain (adults)

For children under 12, see p.124 ▶

Mild abdominal pain is often due to a stomach or bowel upset that will clear up without treatment. However, severe or persistent abdominal pain, especially if it is accompanied by other symptoms, may indicate a more serious problem that should be investigated by your doctor.

Danger signs

Dial 911 or call EMS if you have severe abdominal pain that lasts for longer than 4 hours and is associated with any of the following additional symptoms:
● Vomiting.
● Fever.
● Swollen or tender abdomen.
● Feeling faint, drowsy, or confused.
● Blood in the urine or feces.

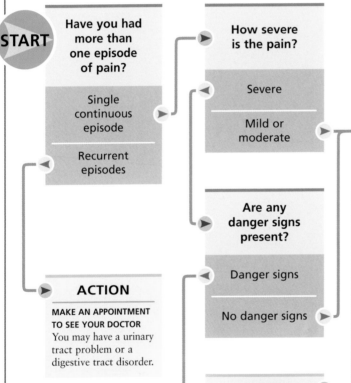

START

Have you had more than one episode of pain?

Single continuous episode

Recurrent episodes

How severe is the pain?

Severe

Mild or moderate

Are any danger signs present?

Danger signs

No danger signs

Do you have diarrhea?

Diarrhea

No diarrhea

ACTION

MAKE AN APPOINTMENT TO SEE YOUR DOCTOR
You may have a urinary tract problem or a digestive tract disorder.

ACTION

❗ DIAL 911 OR CALL EMS
You may have a serious abdominal condition, such as appendicitis.

ACTION

TRY SELF-HELP MEASURES
You may have a case of gastroenteritis.
● Drink plenty of clear fluids or over-the-counter rehydration solutions to prevent dehydration.

CONSULT YOUR DOCTOR
if you are no better in 2 days or if other symptoms develop.

ACTION

SEE YOUR DOCTOR WITHIN 24 HOURS
You may have gallstones, especially if you have suffered from nausea and vomiting following a fatty meal.
● Take an analgesic such as acetaminophen to relieve symptoms.
● Avoid eating foods that are high in fat.

ACTION

CALL YOUR DOCTOR NOW
You may have kidney stones, especially if you have been vomiting.
● Drink plenty of fluids to flush the stones into the urine.
● Save any urine you pass, particularly if you pass a stone.
● Take acetaminophen to relieve discomfort.

What kind of pain have you been experiencing?

Pain that starts in the back and may move to the groin

Pain in the center of the upper abdomen

Pain in the upper right abdomen that may spread to the back

Pain mainly below the waist

None of the above

Do any of the following apply?

Pain is related to eating

Pain is relieved by antacids

Pain comes on when lying or bending over

None of the above

ACTION

MAKE AN APPOINTMENT TO SEE YOUR DOCTOR
You may have nonulcer dyspepsia (a recurrent and persistent form of indigestion) or gastroesophageal reflux, in which acid from the stomach is regurgitated into the esophagus.
● Eat small meals at regular intervals.
● Avoid eating shortly before going to bed.
● Reduce your intake of alcohol, coffee, and tea.
● If you smoke, stop.

ACTION

GO TO ANOTHER CHART
Chest pain, p.134

Do you have either of the following?

Pain when urinating

Urinating more often than usual

Neither

ACTION

SEE YOUR DOCTOR WITHIN 24 HOURS
You may have cystitis or a urine infection that has spread to one or both kidneys.
● For both conditions, take an analgesic such as acetaminophen.
● Drink 1 pint (500 ml) of fluid every hour for 4 hours.
● Drinking cranberry juice may relieve the burning sensation.

ACTION

SEE YOUR DOCTOR WITHIN 24 HOURS
if you cannot identify a possible cause for your abdominal pain from this chart.

Are you female or male?

Female

Male

ACTION

GO TO ANOTHER CHART
Abdominal pain (women), p.122

Abdominal pain (women)

◀ First refer to abdominal pain, p.120

Several disorders specific to women can cause discomfort or pain in the lower abdomen. Many of these conditions are related to the reproductive tract (ovaries, uterus, or fallopian tubes) or to pregnancy. Abdominal pain that occurs during pregnancy should always be taken seriously.

❗ Abdominal pain during pregnancy

Intermittent, mild abdominal pains are common throughout pregnancy due to stretching of the muscles and ligaments of the abdomen. Abdominal pain that occurs in early pregnancy can be due to complications, such as miscarriage or an ectopic pregnancy. In later pregnancy, pain is most commonly caused by the onset of labor. Rarely, partial separation of the placenta from the wall of the uterus may occur.

● If you develop severe pain, call your doctor at once.

START

Do you have pain when you urinate?

- Yes
- No

ACTION

SEE YOUR DOCTOR WITHIN 24 HOURS
You may have cystitis.

● Take an analgesic such as acetaminophen.

● Drink 1 pint (500 ml) of fluid every hour for 4 hours.

● Drinking cranberry juice may help relieve the burning sensation.

Are you pregnant?

- More than 14 weeks pregnant
- Less than 14 weeks pregnant
- Do not think so

Have you had sexual intercourse in the past 3 months?

- Yes
- No

ACTION

CALL YOUR DOCTOR NOW
You could be having a late miscarriage or placental abruption (separation of the placenta from the wall of the uterus).

● Rest in bed until you receive medical advice.

ACTION

CALL YOUR DOCTOR NOW
Pain at this stage may indicate a threatened miscarriage or an ectopic pregnancy.

● Rest in bed until you receive medical advice.

Did your last menstrual period occur at the time you expected?

- On time
- Missed or late

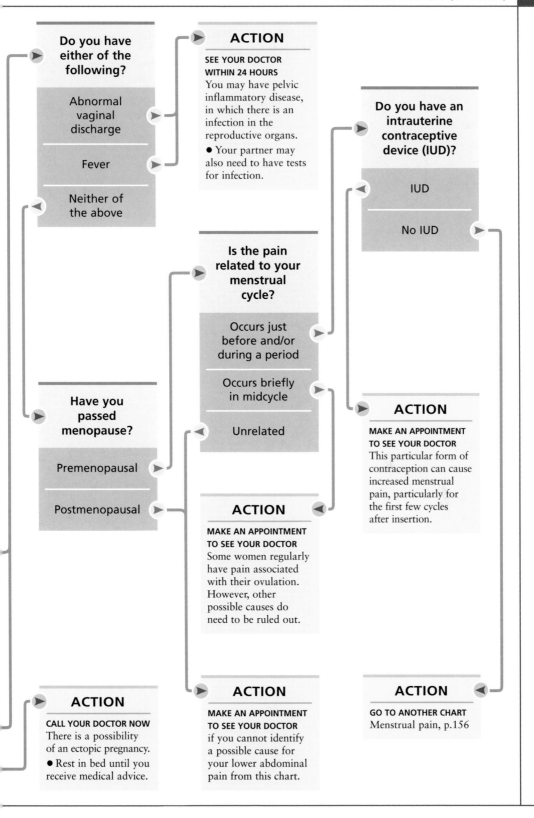

Do you have either of the following?

Abnormal vaginal discharge

Fever

Neither of the above

ACTION

SEE YOUR DOCTOR WITHIN 24 HOURS
You may have pelvic inflammatory disease, in which there is an infection in the reproductive organs.
● Your partner may also need to have tests for infection.

Do you have an intrauterine contraceptive device (IUD)?

IUD

No IUD

Is the pain related to your menstrual cycle?

Occurs just before and/or during a period

Occurs briefly in midcycle

Unrelated

Have you passed menopause?

Premenopausal

Postmenopausal

ACTION

MAKE AN APPOINTMENT TO SEE YOUR DOCTOR
This particular form of contraception can cause increased menstrual pain, particularly for the first few cycles after insertion.

ACTION

MAKE AN APPOINTMENT TO SEE YOUR DOCTOR
Some women regularly have pain associated with their ovulation. However, other possible causes do need to be ruled out.

ACTION

CALL YOUR DOCTOR NOW
There is a possibility of an ectopic pregnancy.
● Rest in bed until you receive medical advice.

ACTION

MAKE AN APPOINTMENT TO SEE YOUR DOCTOR
if you cannot identify a possible cause for your lower abdominal pain from this chart.

ACTION

GO TO ANOTHER CHART
Menstrual pain, p.156

Abdominal pain (children)

◀ For adults and children over 12, see p.120

Many children suffer from abdominal pain at some time, and some children have recurrent episodes. Usually, the cause is not serious, and the pain subsides in a few hours without treatment. In rare cases, abdominal pain is a symptom of a serious disorder that requires prompt medical attention.

! Danger signs

Dial 911 or call an ambulance if your child's abdominal pain is accompanied by any of the following symptoms:
- Greenish yellow vomit.
- Pain in the groin or scrotum.
- Blood in the feces.
- Pain has been continuous for more than 4 hours.

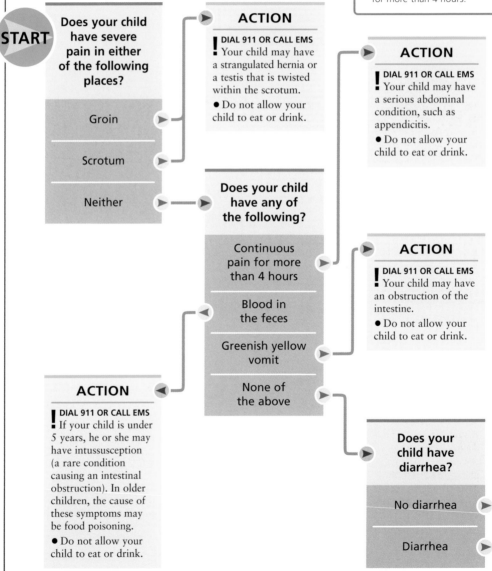

START

Does your child have severe pain in either of the following places?

Groin ▶

Scrotum ▶

Neither ▶

▶ ACTION

! DIAL 911 OR CALL EMS Your child may have a strangulated hernia or a testis that is twisted within the scrotum.
- Do not allow your child to eat or drink.

Does your child have any of the following?

Continuous pain for more than 4 hours ▶

Blood in the feces

Greenish yellow vomit ▶

None of the above ▶

▶ ACTION

! DIAL 911 OR CALL EMS Your child may have a serious abdominal condition, such as appendicitis.
- Do not allow your child to eat or drink.

▶ ACTION

! DIAL 911 OR CALL EMS Your child may have an obstruction of the intestine.
- Do not allow your child to eat or drink.

ACTION

! DIAL 911 OR CALL EMS If your child is under 5 years, he or she may have intussusception (a rare condition causing an intestinal obstruction). In older children, the cause of these symptoms may be food poisoning.
- Do not allow your child to eat or drink.

Does your child have diarrhea?

No diarrhea ▶

Diarrhea ▶

Has pain been relieved by either of the following?

Vomiting

Passing gas or stools

Neither

Does your child have any of the following?

Sore throat

Cough

Runny nose

None of the above

ACTION

MAKE AN APPOINTMENT TO SEE YOUR DOCTOR
Recurrent abdominal pain in children can sometimes be related to anxiety.

ACTION

TRY SELF-HELP MEASURES
Young children often have abdominal pain in association with a cold or flu.
• Give your child liquid acetaminophen to relieve pain.
• Inhaling steam from a bowl of hot water (p.165) may help.

┃ DIAL 911 OR CALL EMS
▪ if your child develops danger signs (see box opposite).

Does your child have any of the following?

Pain when urinating

Temperature of 100.4°F (38°C) or above

Renewed bedwetting or daytime "accidents"

None of the above

Has your child suffered from similar bouts of abdominal pain over the past few weeks?

Previous abdominal pain

No previous pain

ACTION

SEE YOUR DOCTOR WITHIN 24 HOURS
if you cannot identify a possible cause for your child's abdominal pain from this chart.

ACTION

CALL YOUR DOCTOR NOW
if your child is under 1 year. He or she may have gastroenteritis.
• Give older children plenty of clear fluids to drink.

CONSULT YOUR DOCTOR
if an older child is no better within 24 hours or if other symptoms develop.

ACTION

SEE YOUR DOCTOR WITHIN 24 HOURS
Your child may have a urinary tract infection.
• Give your child plenty of clear fluids to drink.

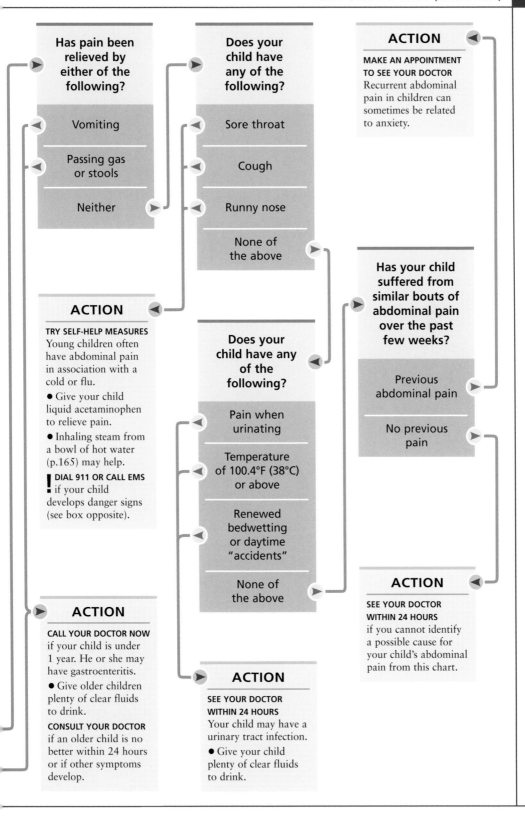

Swollen abdomen

Enlargement of the abdomen is usually due to weight gain or poor muscle tone from lack of exercise. A swollen abdomen may also result from a disorder of either the digestive system or the urinary system. If you have abdominal swelling that has come on rapidly, you should consult your doctor irrespective of any other symptoms you may have.

ACTION

GO TO ANOTHER CHART
Abdominal pain (adults), p.120, or Abdominal pain (children), p.124

START

How long has your abdomen been swollen?

Less than 24 hours

Longer than 24 hours

Do you have abdominal pain?

Severe pain

Mild pain

No pain

ACTION

MAKE AN APPOINTMENT TO SEE YOUR DOCTOR
You may be suffering from excessive gas or constipation, possibly due to irritable bowel syndrome.

Is the pain relieved by passing gas or having a bowel movement?

Relieved

Unrelieved

ACTION

TRY SELF-HELP MEASURES
A swollen abdomen may be the the first sign of an unsuspected pregnancy, especially if you have been using contraception or if your menstrual periods tend to be irregular.
• If you think that you might be pregnant, perform a home pregnancy test.

Do any of the following apply?

Your ankles are swollen

You could be pregnant

You have difficulty urinating

You urinate only small volumes

None of the above

ACTION

GO TO ANOTHER CHART
Swollen ankles, p.148

ACTION

SEE YOUR DOCTOR
WITHIN 24 HOURS
The swelling could be due to an abnormally full bladder caused by a blockage at the bladder outlet.

ACTION

MAKE AN APPOINTMENT TO SEE YOUR DOCTOR
if you cannot identify a possible cause for your abdominal swelling from this chart.

Anal and rectal problems

The anus is the opening of the lower large intestine (rectum) to the outside. Discomfort during bowel movements may be due to a disorder of the rectum, the anus, or the skin around the anus. Rectal or anal bleeding is often due to hemorrhoids but can also be an early symptom of cancer. Consult your doctor if you have any bleeding or persistent discomfort.

START

Have you noticed bleeding from the anus?

Bleeding

No bleeding

ACTION

SEE YOUR DOCTOR WITHIN 24 HOURS
Although hemorrhoids are a likely cause, there is a slight possibility of cancer of the colon, rectum, or anus that needs to be excluded.

Do you have either of the following?

Pain in or around the anus or rectum

Sore area in the crease above the anus

Neither

ACTION

SEE YOUR DOCTOR WITHIN 24 HOURS
You may have a pilonidal sinus (small pit at the top of this crease, which can result in an abscess).
● Soak the affected area in warm water.

Do you have itching around the anus?

Itching

No itching

Do you have small, irregular, fleshy lumps around the anus?

Yes

No

ACTION

MAKE AN APPOINTMENT TO SEE YOUR DOCTOR
You may have a pinworm infestation.

Do you have either of the following?

White "threads" in your feces

Itching is worse in bed at night

Neither

ACTION

TRY SELF-HELP MEASURES
You may have hemorrhoids, but itching can also occur for no obvious reason.
● Try using an over-the-counter hemorrhoid preparation to relieve the itching.
CONSULT YOUR DOCTOR if the itching continues for more than 3 days.

ACTION

MAKE AN APPOINTMENT TO SEE YOUR DOCTOR
It is possible that you have genital warts.

ACTION

MAKE AN APPOINTMENT TO SEE YOUR DOCTOR
if you cannot identify a possible cause for your anal or rectal problem from this chart.

Diarrhea (adults)

For children under 12 years, see p.130 ➤
Diarrhea is the frequent passing of abnormally loose
or watery feces, and is usually a result of infection.
However, persistent diarrhea may be caused by a
serious gastrointestinal disorder. You should consult
your doctor if diarrhea continues for more than
2 days or if it recurs.

Dehydration

A person with bad diarrhea
can become dehydrated if
fluids are not replaced quickly
enough. The symptoms of
dehydration include confusion
or drowsiness, a dry mouth,
loss of elasticity in the skin,
and failure to urinate for
several hours. Elderly people
are particularly at risk. Follow
the advice for preventing
dehydration on p.165, but
seek urgent medical help if a
person has severe symptoms.

START

Have you noticed blood in your feces?

Blood

No blood

Have you had several bouts of diarrhea over the past few weeks?

Yes

No

Has the diarrhea been alternating with bouts of constipation?

Constipation and diarrhea

Diarrhea alone

ACTION

**SEE YOUR DOCTOR
WITHIN 24 HOURS**
You may have an
intestinal infection,
such as amebiasis,
or ulcerative colitis
(ulceration of the
rectum and colon).
However, the slight
possibility of cancer
of the colon or rectum
needs to be excluded.

ACTION

**MAKE AN APPOINTMENT
TO SEE YOUR DOCTOR**
You probably have
irritable bowel
syndrome, especially
if you have suffered
abdominal pain and
excessive gas.
However, the slight
possibility of cancer of
the colon or rectum
needs to be excluded.
• Avoid large meals,
spicy, fried, and fatty
foods, and milk
products.
• Cut down on coffee,
tea, soda, and beer.

ACTION

TRY SELF-HELP MEASURES
You may have food
poisoning.
• Follow the advice
for preventing
dehydration (p.165).
CONSULT YOUR DOCTOR
if you are no better in
2 days or if any other
symptoms develop.

Have you recently consumed food or water that may have been contaminated?

Possible

Unlikely

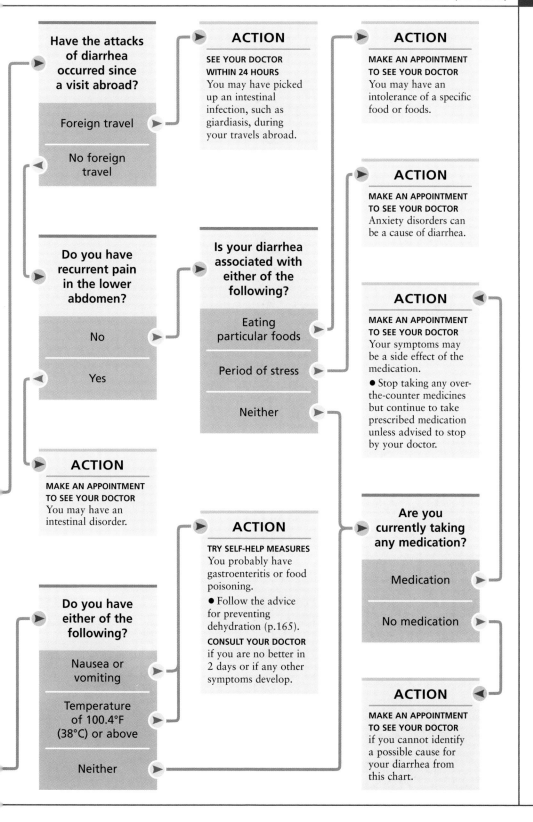

Have the attacks of diarrhea occurred since a visit abroad?

Foreign travel ►

No foreign travel

ACTION

SEE YOUR DOCTOR WITHIN 24 HOURS
You may have picked up an intestinal infection, such as giardiasis, during your travels abroad.

ACTION

MAKE AN APPOINTMENT TO SEE YOUR DOCTOR
You may have an intolerance of a specific food or foods.

Do you have recurrent pain in the lower abdomen?

No ►

Yes

Is your diarrhea associated with either of the following?

Eating particular foods ►

Period of stress ►

Neither ►

ACTION

MAKE AN APPOINTMENT TO SEE YOUR DOCTOR
Anxiety disorders can be a cause of diarrhea.

ACTION ◄

MAKE AN APPOINTMENT TO SEE YOUR DOCTOR
Your symptoms may be a side effect of the medication.
● Stop taking any over-the-counter medicines but continue to take prescribed medication unless advised to stop by your doctor.

ACTION

MAKE AN APPOINTMENT TO SEE YOUR DOCTOR
You may have an intestinal disorder.

ACTION

TRY SELF-HELP MEASURES
You probably have gastroenteritis or food poisoning.
● Follow the advice for preventing dehydration (p.165).
CONSULT YOUR DOCTOR if you are no better in 2 days or if any other symptoms develop.

Are you currently taking any medication?

Medication ►

No medication ►

Do you have either of the following?

Nausea or vomiting ►

Temperature of 100.4°F (38°C) or above ►

Neither ►

ACTION ◄

MAKE AN APPOINTMENT TO SEE YOUR DOCTOR
if you cannot identify a possible cause for your diarrhea from this chart.

Diarrhea (children)

◀ For adults and children over 12, see p.128

Diarrhea is the abnormally frequent passage of loose or watery feces. Breast-fed babies may pass loose feces several times a day, and this is normal. If your child has diarrhea, he or she should drink plenty of clear fluids to avoid dehydration. If symptoms do not improve, consult your doctor.

Danger signs

Dial 911 or call EMS if your child also has any of the following symptoms:
- Abnormal drowsiness.
- Severe abdominal pain or abdominal pain that lasts for 4 hours or more.
- No urination during the day for 3 hours (if under 1 year) or 6 hours (in an older child).
- Refusal to drink or feed (in babies) for over 6 hours.
- Blood in the feces.

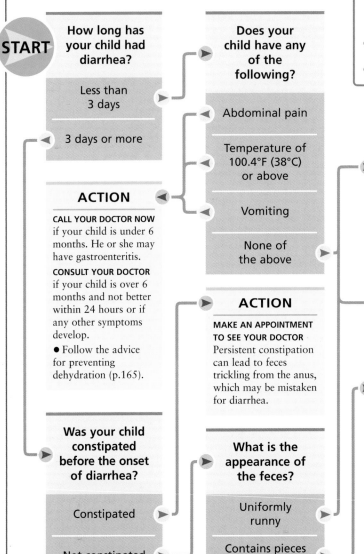

START

How long has your child had diarrhea?

Less than 3 days

3 days or more

Does your child have any of the following?

Abdominal pain

Temperature of 100.4°F (38°C) or above

Vomiting

None of the above

Is your child currently taking any medication?

Medication

No medication

ACTION

CALL YOUR DOCTOR NOW if your child is under 6 months. He or she may have gastroenteritis.

CONSULT YOUR DOCTOR if your child is over 6 months and not better within 24 hours or if any other symptoms develop.
- Follow the advice for preventing dehydration (p.165).

ACTION

MAKE AN APPOINTMENT TO SEE YOUR DOCTOR Persistent constipation can lead to feces trickling from the anus, which may be mistaken for diarrhea.

Is your child gaining weight and growing at a normal rate (see growth charts, p.71)?

Yes

No

Was your child constipated before the onset of diarrhea?

Constipated

Not constipated

What is the appearance of the feces?

Uniformly runny

Contains pieces of food

ACTION

SEE YOUR DOCTOR WITHIN 24 HOURS
Your child's symptoms may be a side effect of the drug.
● Stop giving any over-the-counter medicines but continue to give prescribed medication unless advised to stop by your doctor.

How old is your child?

Under 12 months

12 months to 3 years

Over 3 years

ACTION

TRY SELF-HELP MEASURES
Young children often fail to chew and digest food properly, which can lead to so-called "toddler's diarrhea."
● Follow the advice for preventing dehydration (p.165).
CONSULT YOUR DOCTOR
if symptoms persist or if your child develops other symptoms.

ACTION

MAKE AN APPOINTMENT TO SEE YOUR DOCTOR
It is possible that your child has a condition affecting the digestive tract, such as food intolerance or celiac disease (gluten allergy).

Was your baby given any of the following before the onset of diarrhea?

Unfamiliar foods

Sugary foods or sweetened drinks

Neither

ACTION

SEE YOUR DOCTOR WITHIN 24 HOURS
if you cannot identify a possible cause for your child's diarrhea from this chart.

Is your child experiencing unusual stress, anxiety, or excitement?

Stress or anxiety

Excitement

Neither

ACTION

SEE YOUR DOCTOR WITHIN 24 HOURS
if you cannot identify a possible cause for your child's diarrhea from this chart.

ACTION

TRY SELF-HELP MEASURES
Foods that are new to your baby may cause digestive upsets.
● Withhold the food that seems to be causing the trouble for at least 1 week.
CONSULT YOUR DOCTOR
if your baby is no better in 24 hours or if he or she develops other symptoms.

ACTION

TRY SELF-HELP MEASURES
Sugar in food and drink can cause diarrhea in babies.
● Avoid giving your baby sweetened foods and drinks.
CONSULT YOUR DOCTOR
if your baby is no better in 24 hours or if he or she develops other symptoms.

ACTION

TRY SELF-HELP MEASURES
Psychological stress or unusual excitement can cause diarrhea in children. The symptoms will normally stop as soon as the cause has disappeared.
CONSULT YOUR DOCTOR
if there is a long-term cause of anxiety in your child's life or if he or she develops other symptoms.

Constipation

Some people have a bowel movement once or twice a day; others do so less frequently. If you have fewer bowel movements than usual or if your feces are small and hard, you are constipated. The cause is often a lack of fluid or fiber-rich foods in the diet. If constipation occurs suddenly or persists despite a change in your diet, consult your doctor.

Blood in the feces

Blood can appear in the feces as red streaks or in larger amounts. It can also make the stools look black. Small amounts of blood in the feces are usually caused by minor anal problems, such as hemorrhoids, but you should always consult your doctor if you notice blood in the feces because it is vital that other causes, such as colorectal cancer, are excluded.

START

How long have you suffered from constipation?

For a few weeks or less

For several months or years

Does either of the following apply?

You regularly ignore the urge to defecate

You regularly use stimulant laxatives

Neither

Do you have pain in your rectum or anus when you defecate?

Pain

No pain

ACTION

MAKE AN APPOINTMENT TO SEE YOUR DOCTOR
Pain on defecation can cause or worsen constipation. You may have hemorrhoids or an anal fissure (tear in the lining of the anus).

ACTION

TRY SELF-HELP MEASURES
Your bowel reflexes may have become sluggish as a result of being ignored.
● Include more fiber-rich foods in your diet.
● Increase your daily fluid intake.
CONSULT YOUR DOCTOR
if your symptoms have not improved within 2 weeks.

ACTION

MAKE AN APPOINTMENT TO SEE YOUR DOCTOR
Regular use of stimulant laxatives, such as senna, can seriously disrupt the normal functioning of the bowels.

Do you have intermittent bouts of cramping pain in the lower abdomen?

Pain

No pain

ACTION

TRY SELF-HELP MEASURES
Your constipation is probably due to a lack of fiber or fluid in your diet and possibly to lack of exercise.
● Include more fiber-rich foods in your diet.
● Avoid eating too much processed food.
● Increase your daily fluid intake.
● Do not ignore the urge to defecate.
CONSULT YOUR DOCTOR
if your symptoms have not improved within 2 weeks.

ACTION

MAKE AN APPOINTMENT TO SEE YOUR DOCTOR
Irritable bowel syndrome is a possible cause, especially if your constipation alternates with bouts of diarrhea. However, other causes, such as cancer of the colon, rectum, or anus, may need to be ruled out.

Do you have any of the following?

Fatigue

Increased dryness or roughness of the skin

Feeling the cold more than you used to

Unexplained weight gain

General hair thinning

None of the above

ACTION

MAKE AN APPOINTMENT TO SEE YOUR DOCTOR
Hypothyroidism (underactivity of the thyroid gland, which causes many body functions to slow down) is a possibility.

Are you taking any medication?

Medication

No medication

Do any of the following apply?

You are pregnant

You have been drinking less fluid than usual

You have changed your diet

None of the above

ACTION

TRY SELF-HELP MEASURES
Lack of fluid in the bowel as a result of an inadequate fluid intake or excessive fluid loss can cause constipation.
● Drink plenty of fluids, especially if the weather is hot.
CONSULT YOUR DOCTOR
if your symptoms have not improved within 2 weeks.

ACTION

MAKE AN APPOINTMENT TO SEE YOUR DOCTOR
if you cannot identify a possible cause for your constipation from this chart.

ACTION

MAKE AN APPOINTMENT TO SEE YOUR DOCTOR
Your symptoms may be a side effect of the medication.
● Stop taking any over-the-counter medicines but continue to take prescribed medication unless advised to stop by your doctor.

ACTION

TRY SELF-HELP MEASURES
Constipation is quite common in pregnancy.
● Include more fiber-rich foods in your diet.
● Avoid eating too much processed food.
● Increase your daily fluid intake, but avoid caffeine and alcohol.
● Do not ignore the urge to defecate.
CONSULT YOUR DOCTOR
if your symptoms have not improved within 2 weeks.

ACTION

TRY SELF-HELP MEASURES
A change in your regular diet, especially when traveling, can make you constipated.
● Include more fiber-rich foods in your diet.
● Avoid eating too much processed food.
● Increase your daily fluid intake.
● Do not ignore the urge to defecate.
CONSULT YOUR DOCTOR
if your symptoms have not improved within 2 weeks.

Chest pain

Pain in the chest, or any discomfort felt in the front or back of the ribcage, is most often due to minor disorders such as muscle strain or indigestion. However, you should dial 911 or call EMS if you have a crushing pain in the center or left side of your chest, if you are also short of breath or feel faint, or if the pain is unlike any pain you have had before.

ACTION

! **DIAL 911 OR CALL EMS**
You may have a blood clot in the lung.

START

What kind of pain are you experiencing?

Crushing

Spreading from the center of the chest to the neck, arms, or jaw

Neither of the above

Are you short of breath?

Short of breath

Not short of breath

Do any of the following apply?

You have recently had surgery

You have recently been immobile due to injury or illness

You have had a baby within the past 2 weeks

None of the above

Does the pain subside after you rest for a few minutes?

Pain subsides

Pain persists

ACTION

CALL YOUR DOCTOR NOW
Recurrent chest pain could be an indication of angina, especially if pain in the chest occurs with exertion and disappears with rest.

Is pain related to breathing?

Related to breathing

Not related to breathing

ACTION

! **DIAL 911 OR CALL EMS**
You may be having a heart attack.

• While waiting, chew half an aspirin, unless you are allergic to it.

Have you had this pain before?

Previous episodes of this kind of pain

Never before

ACTION

! **DIAL 911 OR CALL EMS**
You may be having a heart attack.

• While waiting, chew half an aspirin, unless you are allergic to it.

Do you have a fever – a temperature of 100.4°F (38°C) or above?

Fever

No fever

ACTION

CALL YOUR DOCTOR NOW
You may have a chest infection, such as pneumonia.
● Take an analgesic such as acetaminophen to reduce fever and chest pain.
● Drink lots of fluid.

ACTION

CALL YOUR DOCTOR NOW
You may have a partially collapsed lung.

Does either of the following apply?

You have had a chest injury

You have been exercising

Neither

ACTION

TRY SELF-HELP MEASURES
You have probably strained and/or bruised a muscle.
● Take an analgesic such as acetaminophen and rest for 24 hours.
CONSULT YOUR DOCTOR
if the pain has not improved after this time.

Is the chest sore to touch?

Sore to touch

Not sore to touch

ACTION

SEE YOUR DOCTOR WITHIN 24 HOURS
You may have a lung infection or pleurisy.
● Take an analgesic such as acetaminophen to relieve pain and fever.
● If you have a fever, drink lots of fluid.

ACTION

MAKE AN APPOINTMENT TO SEE YOUR DOCTOR
if you cannot identify a possible cause for your chest pain from this chart.

Does the pain have any of the following features?

Related to eating or to particular foods

Relieved by antacids

Brought on by bending or lying down

None of the above

ACTION

MAKE AN APPOINTMENT TO SEE YOUR DOCTOR
You may have recurrent indigestion or heartburn caused by acid reflux.

ACTION

! DIAL 911 OR CALL EMS
You may be having a heart attack.
● While waiting, chew half an aspirin, unless you are allergic to it.

Palpitations

Abnormally fast or irregular heartbeats, or palpitations, are often caused by anxiety or by stimulants, such as caffeine and nicotine. Palpitations may also occur as a side effect of medication or because of a heart disorder. Call your doctor immediately if palpitations are frequent or persistent or if you have other symptoms.

START

Do you have any of the following?

- Shortness of breath
- Chest discomfort
- Feeling faint or passing out
- None of the above

ACTION

! DIAL 911 OR CALL EMS
You may have a serious arrhythmia (abnormal heart rate or rhythm) due to an underlying heart disorder.

ACTION

SEE YOUR DOCTOR WITHIN 24 HOURS
Your symptoms may be a side effect of the medication.

● Stop taking any over-the-counter medicines but continue to take prescribed medication unless advised to stop by your doctor.

Do you have any of the following?

- Weight loss with increased appetite
- Feeling on edge
- Increased sweating
- Bulging eyes
- None of the above

Do any of the following apply?

- You have had a lot of coffee, tea, or soda
- You have been smoking more than usual
- You are taking medications
- None of the above

ACTION

MAKE AN APPOINTMENT TO SEE YOUR DOCTOR
You may have hyperthyroidism (an overactive thyroid gland) or you might be suffering from anxiety.

ACTION

TRY SELF-HELP MEASURES
These symptoms may be due to anxiety.

● Try some relaxation exercises (p.169).

CONSULT YOUR DOCTOR if your symptoms continue for 2 days.

ACTION

TRY SELF-HELP MEASURES
● Avoid caffeine and nicotine because these can disturb your heart rhythm.

CONSULT YOUR DOCTOR if your symptoms continue for 2 days.

Have you been feeling tense or stressed?

- Feeling under stress
- No increase in stress

ACTION

MAKE AN APPOINTMENT TO SEE YOUR DOCTOR
if you cannot identify a possible cause for your palpitations from this chart.

Poor bladder control

If urinating is painful, see p.138 ▷
Inability to control urination may result in leakage of urine or difficulty urinating. These symptoms may be due to a bladder, nerve, or muscle disorder. In men, an enlarged prostate gland is a common cause. Urinary tract infections can also cause leakage of urine, especially in elderly people.

! **Inability to urinate**
Inability to urinate, even though the bladder is full, is a serious symptom. It may be the result of an obstruction or damage to nerves that supply the bladder, or it may be a side effect of certain drugs. You should call your doctor immediately.

START

Are you female or male?

Female ▷

Male ◁

ACTION
MAKE AN APPOINTMENT TO SEE YOUR DOCTOR
You may be suffering from an irritable bladder.

Do you have either of the following?

A strong urge to urinate with little urine passed ▷

Leakage of urine when you cough, sneeze, or run ◁

Neither ▷

ACTION
MAKE AN APPOINTMENT TO SEE YOUR DOCTOR
You may have an enlarged prostate gland, especially if you are over 55, or a narrowing of the urethra (tube that empties the bladder).

ACTION
MAKE AN APPOINTMENT TO SEE YOUR DOCTOR
Some drugs, particularly those that act on urine production or on the nervous system, can affect bladder control.
● Stop taking any over-the-counter medicines but continue to take prescribed medication unless advised to stop by your doctor.

Are you currently taking any medication?

Medication ▷

No medication ▷

ACTION
TRY SELF-HELP MEASURES
You probably have stress incontinence.
● Try Kegel exercises: contract, hold, and relax pelvic floor muscles 10 times, several times a day to strengthen them.
CONSULT YOUR DOCTOR
if the condition does not improve in 1 month.

Do you have either of the following?

Difficulty starting to urinate ▷

Weak urinary stream ▷

Neither ▷

ACTION
MAKE AN APPOINTMENT TO SEE YOUR DOCTOR
if you cannot identify a possible cause for your poor bladder control from this chart.

Painful urination

Pain or discomfort while urinating is usually caused by inflammation of the urinary tract, often due to infection. Frequent painless urination can be due to diabetes or kidney problems and should be investigated by your doctor. Discolored urine can accompany this type of pain but may not indicate disease (see Checking the appearance of urine, right).

Checking the appearance of urine

The appearance of urine varies considerably. For example, urine is often darker in the morning than later in the day. Some drugs and foods may also cause a temporary color change in the urine. Beets, for example, may turn the urine red. A change in your urine can indicate a disorder. Very dark urine may be a sign of liver disease, such as acute hepatitis, while red or cloudy urine may be due to bleeding or an infection in the kidney or bladder.

• If you are not sure about the cause of a change in the appearance of your urine, consult your doctor.

START

Do you have either of the following?

Pain in the back just above the waist

A temperature of 100.4°F (38°C) or above

Neither

ACTION

CALL YOUR DOCTOR NOW
You may have pyelonephritis (infection of the kidneys).
• Take an analgesic such as acetaminophen.

Have you felt the need to urinate more frequently than usual?

Increased frequency

No increased frequency

Do you have any of the following?

Lower abdominal pain

Blood in the urine

Cloudy urine

None of the above

ACTION

SEE YOUR DOCTOR WITHIN 24 HOURS
You may have cystitis.
• Take an analgesic such as acetaminophen.
• Drink 1 pint (500 ml) of fluid every hour for 4 hours.
• Drinking cranberry juice may help relieve the burning sensation.

Are you female or male?

Female

Male

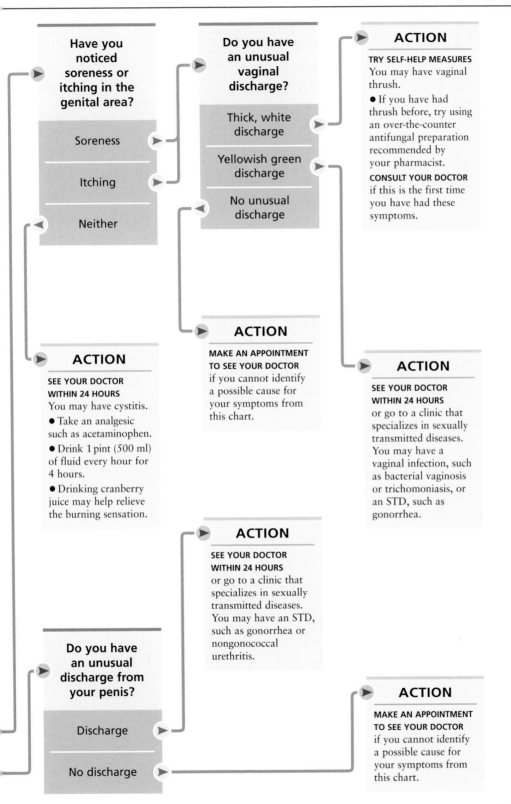

Have you noticed soreness or itching in the genital area?

Soreness

Itching

Neither

Do you have an unusual vaginal discharge?

Thick, white discharge

Yellowish green discharge

No unusual discharge

ACTION

TRY SELF-HELP MEASURES
You may have vaginal thrush.

● If you have had thrush before, try using an over-the-counter antifungal preparation recommended by your pharmacist.

CONSULT YOUR DOCTOR
if this is the first time you have had these symptoms.

ACTION

SEE YOUR DOCTOR WITHIN 24 HOURS
You may have cystitis.

● Take an analgesic such as acetaminophen.
● Drink 1 pint (500 ml) of fluid every hour for 4 hours.
● Drinking cranberry juice may help relieve the burning sensation.

ACTION

MAKE AN APPOINTMENT TO SEE YOUR DOCTOR
if you cannot identify a possible cause for your symptoms from this chart.

ACTION

SEE YOUR DOCTOR WITHIN 24 HOURS
or go to a clinic that specializes in sexually transmitted diseases. You may have a vaginal infection, such as bacterial vaginosis or trichomoniasis, or an STD, such as gonorrhea.

ACTION

SEE YOUR DOCTOR WITHIN 24 HOURS
or go to a clinic that specializes in sexually transmitted diseases. You may have an STD, such as gonorrhea or nongonococcal urethritis.

Do you have an unusual discharge from your penis?

Discharge

No discharge

ACTION

MAKE AN APPOINTMENT TO SEE YOUR DOCTOR
if you cannot identify a possible cause for your symptoms from this chart.

Back pain

Mild back pain is usually caused by poor posture, sudden movement, or lifting heavy objects, all of which may strain the back. Back pain is also common in pregnancy. Persistent or severe back pain may be the result of a more serious problem. You should consult your doctor if pain is severe or does not improve after 48 hours.

Danger signs
Dial 911 or call EMS if you have back pain that is associated with one of the following symptoms:
- Difficulty controlling your bladder.
- Difficulty controlling your bowels.
- Sudden pain above waist with shortness of breath.
- Difficulty moving.

START

Did the pain in your back come on after either of the following?

An injury or fall

A sudden, awkward movement

Neither

Do you have either of the following?

Pain in the back just above the waist

A temperature of 100.4°F (38°C) or above

Neither

Did the pain occur after any of the following?

Lifting a heavy weight

A coughing fit

Strenuous or unusual physical activity

None of the above

ACTION

CALL YOUR DOCTOR NOW
You may have pyelonephritis (infection of the kidneys).
- Take an analgesic such as acetaminophen.

Have you noticed either of the following?

Difficulty moving a leg

Numbness or tingling in a leg

Neither of the above

ACTION

CALL YOUR DOCTOR NOW
You may have pinched a nerve in your back or damaged your spine.

ACTION

TRY SELF-HELP MEASURES
You have probably strained a back muscle and/or bruised your back by overstretching a muscle.
- Rest and take analgesic such as acetaminophen.
- Place a covered hot-water bottle or heat pad against your back for additional relief.

CONSULT YOUR DOCTOR
if you are no better within 24 hours.

Does either of the following apply?

Pain makes any movement difficult ▶

Pain shoots from the spine down the back of the leg ▶

Neither ◀

ACTION

SEE YOUR DOCTOR WITHIN 24 HOURS
You may have fractured a vertebra as a result of osteoporosis or have sciatica, caused by a slipped disk.

ACTION

MAKE AN APPOINTMENT TO SEE YOUR DOCTOR
You may have osteoarthritis.

ACTION

MAKE AN APPOINTMENT TO SEE YOUR DOCTOR
You may have ankylosing spondylitis (a form of arthritis affecting the back of the pelvis and the vertebrae of the spine), especially if you are male.

How old are you?

45 or over ▶

Under 45 ▶

ACTION

TRY SELF-HELP MEASURES
You have probably strained some of the muscles or sprained some of the ligaments in your back.
● Take an analgesic such as acetaminophen.
● Place a covered hot-water bottle or a heat pad against your back to ease the pain.
CONSULT YOUR DOCTOR if you do not feel any better in 2 or 3 days or if any other symptoms develop.

ACTION

SEE YOUR DOCTOR WITHIN 24 HOURS
You may have fractured a vertebra as a result of osteoporosis.

ACTION

CALL YOUR DOCTOR NOW
New back pain or a worsening of existing back pain may indicate the start of labor.

Are you in the last 3 months of pregnancy?

Pregnant ▶

Not pregnant ▶

Have you been suffering from increasing pain and stiffness for several months?

Yes ▶

No ▶

Does either of the following apply?

You are over 60 ▶

You have recently been immobile due to illness or injury ▶

Neither ▶

ACTION

MAKE AN APPOINTMENT TO SEE YOUR DOCTOR if you cannot identify a possible cause for your back pain from this chart.

Neck pain or stiffness

Pain and/or stiffness in the neck is usually due to a minor problem that does not require treatment, such as a muscle strain or a ligament sprain. However, if the pain occurs with fever, meningitis is a possibility. Neck pain or stiffness becomes more common as people grow older; and may then be due to a disorder of the neck bones and joints.

! Danger signs

Dial 911 or call EMS if you have neck pain associated with any of the following:
- Difficulty controlling your bladder.
- Difficulty controlling your bowels.
- Severe headache.
- Drowsiness or confusion.
- Dislike of bright light.

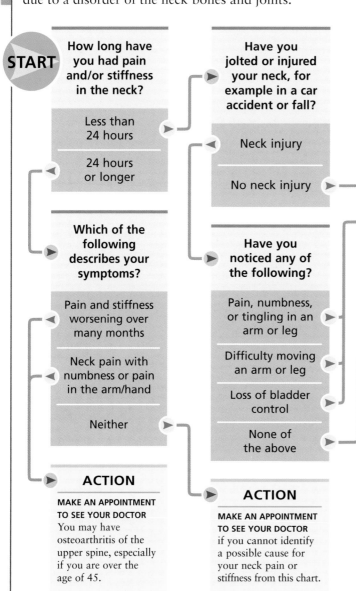

START

How long have you had pain and/or stiffness in the neck?

- Less than 24 hours
- 24 hours or longer

Which of the following describes your symptoms?

- Pain and stiffness worsening over many months
- Neck pain with numbness or pain in the arm/hand
- Neither

Have you jolted or injured your neck, for example in a car accident or fall?

- Neck injury
- No neck injury

Have you noticed any of the following?

- Pain, numbness, or tingling in an arm or leg
- Difficulty moving an arm or leg
- Loss of bladder control
- None of the above

ACTION

! DIAL 911 OR CALL EMS
You may have damaged your spine.
- Follow the first-aid advice for spinal injuries (p.46).

ACTION

TRY SELF-HELP MEASURES
Your neck is probably strained and/or bruised from overstretching a muscle.
- Take an analgesic such as acetaminophen and rest lying down.
- A heat pad or covered hot-water bottle placed against your neck may provide additional pain relief.

CONSULT YOUR DOCTOR if you are no better in 24 hours.

ACTION

MAKE AN APPOINTMENT TO SEE YOUR DOCTOR
You may have osteoarthritis of the upper spine, especially if you are over the age of 45.

ACTION

MAKE AN APPOINTMENT TO SEE YOUR DOCTOR
if you cannot identify a possible cause for your neck pain or stiffness from this chart.

Do you have any of the following?

Temperature of 100.4°F (38°C) or above

Severe headache

Drowsiness or confusion

Dislike of bright light

Nausea or vomiting

None of the above

ACTION

! **DIAL 911 OR CALL EMS**
You may have meningitis (infection inflaming membranes around the brain).

Does either of the following apply?

Pain is severe enough to prevent movement

Pain shoots down one arm from the neck

Neither

Can you feel any tenderness or swelling at the sides or the back of the neck?

Yes

No

ACTION

GO TO ANOTHER CHART
Lumps and swellings, p.80

ACTION

SEE YOUR DOCTOR WITHIN 24 HOURS
Your neck pain may be due to pressure on a nerve as a result of a slipped disk or osteoarthritis of the upper spine.

ACTION

TRY SELF-HELP MEASURES
You may have strained your neck over-stretching a muscle.
● Rest your neck as much as possible by lying down.
● Take a nonsteroidal anti-inflammatory drug, such as ibuprofen, to ease the pain.
● Keeping your neck warm with a heating pad or covered hot-water bottle may help.
CONSULT YOUR DOCTOR if you are no better in 3 days.

Did either of the following apply in the 24 hours before the onset of pain?

You exercised unusually strenuously

You sat or slept in an awkward position

Neither

ACTION

MAKE AN APPOINTMENT TO SEE YOUR DOCTOR if you cannot identify a possible cause for your neck pain or stiffness from this chart.

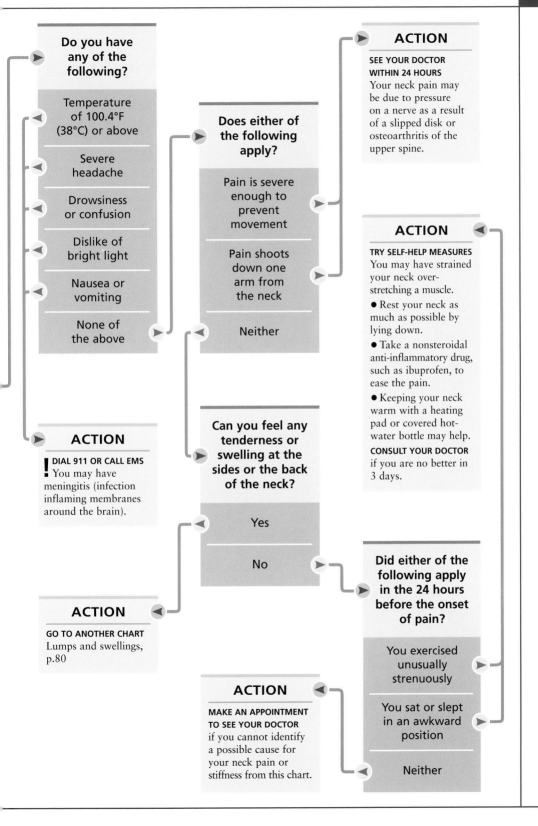

Arm or hand pain

If you have joint pain, see p.146 ▶

Pain in the arm or hand is often caused by injury or a problem in the neck or shoulder. Rarely, pain in the arm is due to a heart attack or a serious neck disorder. Consult your doctor if the pain is severe, recurrent, or persistent.

START ▶

Did the pain start during or soon after either of the following?

- An injury or fall
- Repetitive arm or hand movements ▶
- Neither ▶

Is the pain associated with any of the following?

- Chest tightness ▶
- Shortness of breath ▶
- Nausea, sweating, or feeling faint ▶
- None of the above ◀

What are the features of the pain?

- Localized in upper arms or shoulders ▶
- Extends from the wrist into the palm and lower arm ◀
- Shoots down the length of the arm ▶
- None of the above ▶

▶ **ACTION**

MAKE AN APPOINTMENT TO SEE YOUR DOCTOR
You may have repetitive strain injury.
● Take an analgesic such as acetaminophen.

▶ **ACTION**

! DIAL 911 OR CALL EMS
You may be having a heart attack.
● While waiting, chew half an aspirin, unless you are allergic to it.

▶ **ACTION**

MAKE AN APPOINTMENT TO SEE YOUR DOCTOR
You may have inflammation of a tendon or polymyalgia, in which muscles become inflamed, particularly if you are over 60 years old.

▶ **ACTION**

SEE YOUR DOCTOR WITHIN 24 HOURS
You may have a pinched nerve in your neck.

▶ **ACTION**

MAKE AN APPOINTMENT TO SEE YOUR DOCTOR
if you cannot identify a possible cause for your arm or hand pain from this chart.

▶ **ACTION**

CALL YOUR DOCTOR NOW
if you are in severe pain. You may have either fractured a bone or damaged a muscle.
● Follow the first-aid advice for a broken arm (p.44).
TRY SELF-HELP MEASURES
if not in severe pain.
● Follow the first-aid advice for sprains and strains (p.47).

▶ **ACTION** ◀

MAKE AN APPOINTMENT TO SEE YOUR DOCTOR
You may have a compressed nerve in the wrist (carpal tunnel syndrome).

Leg pain

If you have joint pain, see p.146 ➤

Leg pain due to a strained muscle or torn ligament usually goes away without treatment. Pain may also result from a problem in the lower back or in the blood vessels in the leg. If your leg is also swollen, hot, or red, see your doctor at once.

START ➤

Did the pain start during or soon after either of the following?

An injury or fall

Unusual exercise ➤

Neither ➤

➤ **ACTION**

TRY SELF-HELP MEASURES
You may have strained a muscle.
● Follow the first-aid advice for sprains and strains (p.47).

➤ **What are the features of the pain?**

Affects a small area that is also red and hot ➤

Sudden tightening of calf muscles ➤

Constant pain in the calf, which may be swollen ◄

Shooting pain down the back of the leg ◄

Heavy, aching legs ➤

None of the above ➤

➤ **ACTION**

CALL YOUR DOCTOR NOW
if you are in severe pain. You may have either fractured a bone or damaged a muscle.
● Follow the first-aid advice for a broken leg (p.45).
TRY SELF-HELP MEASURES
if not in severe pain.
● Follow the first-aid advice for sprains and strains (p.47).

ACTION ◄

CALL YOUR DOCTOR NOW
You may have deep vein thrombosis (blood clot in a vein in your leg).

➤ **ACTION**

MAKE AN APPOINTMENT TO SEE YOUR DOCTOR
You may have sciatica.

➤ **ACTION**

SEE YOUR DOCTOR WITHIN 24 HOURS
Your symptoms may be caused by cellulitis (infection of the skin and underlying tissue) or superficial thrombophlebitis (inflamed surface vein).

➤ **ACTION**

MAKE AN APPOINTMENT TO SEE YOUR DOCTOR
You may have a muscle cramp, but, if the pain occurs with exercise and disappears with rest, you may have claudication due to narrowing of the blood vessels in the leg.

ACTION ◄

MAKE AN APPOINTMENT TO SEE YOUR DOCTOR
Varicose veins are a possible cause.

Does sitting down with your feet up relieve the pain?

Yes ➤

No ◄

➤ **ACTION**

MAKE AN APPOINTMENT TO SEE YOUR DOCTOR
if you cannot identify a possible cause for your leg pain from this chart.

Joint pain

If your ankle is swollen painlessly, see p.148 ▶
Pain in a joint may be caused by injury or strain and often disappears without a cause being found. Gout or a joint infection can cause a joint to become red, hot, and swollen. Joint pain may also be a reaction to an infection or due to arthritis. Consult your doctor if pain is severe or persistent.

START

Have you injured the joint?

Injury

No injury ▶

Does either of the following apply?

You cannot move the joint ▶

The joint appears misshapen or swollen ▶

Neither

ACTION

TRY SELF-HELP MEASURES
You have probably strained a ligament around the joint.
● Follow the first-aid advice for sprains and strains (p.47).
CONSULT YOUR DOCTOR
if the joint is no better in 24 hours.

Do you have either of the following?

Hot joint(s) ▶

Red joint(s) ▶

Neither ▶

ACTION

CALL YOUR DOCTOR NOW
You may have fractured a bone, strained or torn a muscle, or torn a ligament.
● Follow the first-aid advice for a broken arm or leg (pp.44–45).

ACTION

MAKE AN APPOINTMENT TO SEE YOUR DOCTOR
You may have osteoarthritis.
● Take an analgesic such as acetaminophen.
● Put a covered hot-water bottle or heating pad on the joint.

How many joints are affected?

One joint

More than one ▶

ACTION

CALL YOUR DOCTOR NOW
You may have septic arthritis (infected joint) or gout.
● Rest the painful joint.
● Take ibuprofen at the recommended intervals.
● Drink lots of fluid.

Does moving the joint affect the pain?

Considerably worsens it ▶

Slightly worsens it or no change

Did the pain come on gradually over months or years?

Yes

No ▶

Have you recently had either of the following?

An infection with a rash

An infection without a rash

Neither

ACTION

SEE YOUR DOCTOR WITHIN 24 HOURS
You may have rheumatoid arthritis.
● Take an analgesic such as ibuprofen.

Which joint or joints are affected?

Shoulder

Hip

Neck

Other joint(s)

ACTION

GO TO ANOTHER CHART
Neck pain or stiffness, p.142

ACTION

SEE YOUR DOCTOR WITHIN 24 HOURS
Certain bacterial infections of the intestines and genital tract can lead to reactive arthritis (short-term inflammation of the joint).

ACTION

MAKE AN APPOINTMENT TO SEE YOUR DOCTOR
You may have a frozen shoulder.
● Take an analgesic such as acetaminophen to ease the pain.
● Rest your shoulder.

ACTION

TRY SELF-HELP MEASURES
Your symptoms are probably a result of overuse, although recent viral illness may also be the cause.
● Rest the painful joint(s).
● Take an analgesic such as acetaminophen to ease the pain.
CONSULT YOUR DOCTOR
if your condition is no better in 2 days.

ACTION

SEE YOUR DOCTOR WITHIN 24 HOURS
Some viral illnesses, such as rubella (German measles), can cause joint pain, but if you have been bitten by a tick, an infection such as Lyme disease could be the cause of the pain.

Is the problem in a child under 12?

Under 12

12 or over

ACTION

SEE YOUR DOCTOR WITHIN 24 HOURS
Most childhood hip problems are not serious, but some need prompt treatment to prevent lasting damage to the joint.

ACTION

MAKE AN APPOINTMENT TO SEE YOUR DOCTOR
if you cannot identify a possible cause for your joint pain from this chart.

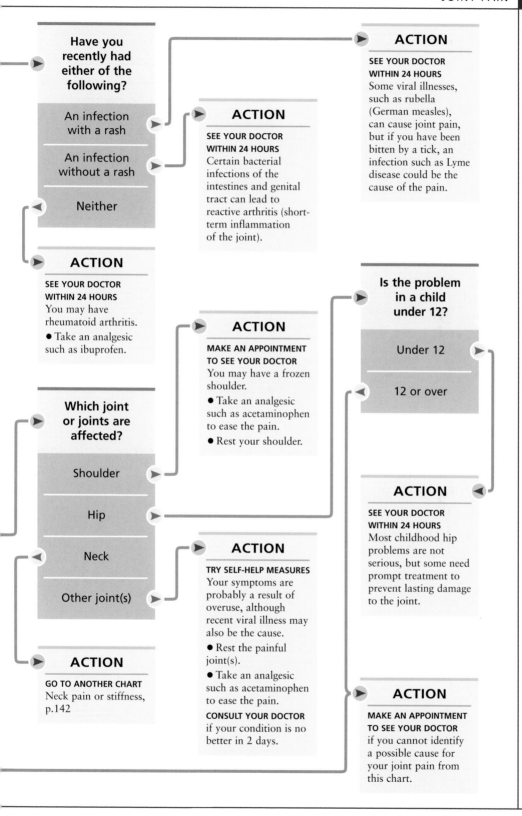

Swollen ankles

◄ If you have a painful swollen ankle, see p.146

Slight, painless swelling of the ankles is most often caused by fluid accumulating in the tissues after long periods of sitting or standing still, but it may be due to heart, liver, or kidney disorders. Ankle swelling is common during pregnancy. If swelling persists or if you have other symptoms, consult your doctor.

Are you pregnant?

Pregnant ►

Not pregnant ►

START

Are both ankles affected?

Both ankles ►

One ankle

Is the calf of the affected leg either of the following?

Swollen

Tender

Neither ►

ACTION

CALL YOUR DOCTOR NOW
You may have deep vein thrombosis (blood clot in a vein in your leg).

Have you been suffering from increased shortness of breath?

Shortness of breath

No shortness of breath ►

ACTION

SEE YOUR DOCTOR WITHIN 24 HOURS
You may be suffering from heart failure, in which fluid accumulates around the body. Other possible causes are a liver or kidney problem.

Have you injured your ankle within the past few weeks?

Recent injury ►

No recent injury ►

ACTION

TRY SELF-HELP MEASURES
Swelling can persist or recur for several weeks following an injury.
● If the injury occurred within the past 2 days, follow the first-aid advice for sprains and strains (p.47).
● For a less recently sustained injury, try resting the limb for 48 hours.
CONSULT YOUR DOCTOR
if swelling persists despite rest or if the ankle is painful, tender, or inflamed.

Does either of the following apply?

Your face or fingers are swollen

You have gained over 5 lb (2.3 kg) in the past week

Neither

ACTION

CALL YOUR DOCTOR NOW Retaining excessive amounts of fluid may be a symptom of pre-eclampsia, which, if severe, can be serious.

ACTION

TRY SELF-HELP MEASURES Swollen ankles are common during pregnancy, particularly in the last 3 months.
- Avoid standing still for long periods.
- Put your feet up whenever possible.

CONSULT YOUR DOCTOR if your face and/or fingers become swollen or if you start to put on weight rapidly.

ACTION

TRY SELF-HELP MEASURES You may have varicose veins, which can cause fluid to accumulate in the ankles.
- Avoid standing still for long periods.
- Walk as much as possible.
- When sitting down, try to keep your feet raised above hip level.
- Wear support hose.

CONSULT YOUR DOCTOR if the swelling worsens or if other symptoms develop.

Did your ankles become swollen during either of the following?

A long train, car, or bus trip

Airplane flight

Neither

ACTION

TRY SELF-HELP MEASURES Hours of inactivity will lead to accumulation of fluid in the ankles and increases the risk of developing a blood clot.
- Clear excess fluid by taking a brisk walk.
- Avoid sitting or standing still for long periods.
- When seated, keep your legs raised.

ACTION

MAKE AN APPOINTMENT TO SEE YOUR DOCTOR Your symptom may be a side effect of the drug.
- Stop taking any over-the-counter medicines but continue to take prescribed medication unless advised to stop by your doctor.

Are you currently taking any medication?

Medication

No medication

Do you have prominent veins in one or both legs affected by swelling?

Prominent veins

No prominent veins

ACTION

MAKE AN APPOINTMENT TO SEE YOUR DOCTOR if you cannot identify a possible cause for your swollen ankles from this chart.

Erectile dysfunction

Occasional incidences of erectile dysfunction, or failure to have or maintain an erection, are not that uncommon. Difficulties are usually caused by factors such as stress, fatigue, anxiety, or alcohol. Physical causes are not common. If erectile dysfunction occurs frequently, consult your doctor for advice. Safe and effective treatments are available.

Nonmedical advice

Treatment from a nonmedical source could result in the incorrect diagnosis being made or the wrong treatment given. It is important that you consult a doctor, who can rule out any medical cause of your erection problems, before having any form of treatment.

START

Are you interested in sex?

Yes

No

How often do you fail to achieve or maintain an erection?

Only occasionally

Frequently

ACTION

MAKE AN APPOINTMENT TO SEE YOUR DOCTOR
Certain illnesses, such as diabetes, can lead to erectile problems. Some drugs, including those prescribed for high blood pressure and antidepressants, can also have an effect on sexual performance.

ACTION

CONSULT YOUR DOCTOR
if you are concerned about any problems with your sexual performance. Most men have occasional erection problems, most likely due to anxiety – for example at the beginning of a new sexual relationship – or due to factors such as fatigue or drinking too much alcohol.

ACTION

MAKE AN APPOINTMENT TO SEE YOUR DOCTOR
Lack of interest in sex is likely to reduce your ability to achieve an erection.

Are you currently receiving treatment for an illness?

Treatment

No treatment

ACTION

MAKE AN APPOINTMENT TO SEE YOUR DOCTOR
Anxiety about your sexual performance is the most likely explanation for your problem. A physical cause is unlikely.

Do you wake up with an erection?

Sometimes

Never

ACTION

MAKE AN APPOINTMENT TO SEE YOUR DOCTOR
if you cannot identify a possible cause for your erection problem from this chart.

Testes/scrotum problems

Check regularly for lumps or swellings in the testes, the sperm-producing organs, and the scrotum, the sac containing the testes (see Testes: self-examination, p.69). The cause may be minor, but there is a possibility of cancer of the testis, which is easily treated if diagnosed early. Painful swelling in the genital area requires immediate medical attention.

START

What is the nature of your symptoms?

- Pain and swelling
- Painless enlargement in or near testis
- Generalized painless swelling of the scrotum
- None of the above

Does the problem affect one or both testes?

- One
- Both

ACTION

! **DIAL 911 OR CALL EMS** You may have torsion, or twisting, of the testis, especially if the pain is severe, which can result in permanent damage if not treated promptly. A less serious possible cause is inflammation of the epididymis (sperm-carrying tube), especially if you also have a fever.

ACTION

CALL YOUR DOCTOR NOW Internal damage to the testes is a possibility.

Have you had an injury in the genital area within the past 48 hours?

- Injury
- No injury

ACTION

MAKE AN APPOINTMENT TO SEE YOUR DOCTOR You may have one of the following disorders of the scrotum: an accumulation of fluid, a hernia, or varicose veins. However, the slight possibility of cancer of the testis needs to be ruled out.

ACTION

MAKE AN APPOINTMENT TO SEE YOUR DOCTOR You probably have a cyst in the epididymis (sperm-carrying tube in the scrotum). However, the slight possibility of cancer of the testis needs to be ruled out.

ACTION

MAKE AN APPOINTMENT TO SEE YOUR DOCTOR if you cannot identify a possible cause for your testes or scrotum problem from this chart.

ACTION

SEE YOUR DOCTOR WITHIN 24 HOURS You may have an infection of the testes or epididymides (sperm-carrying tubes). The cause could be a viral infection, such as mumps, or a sexually transmitted disease.

Penis problems

◀ If you have erectile dysfunction, see p.150

Pain or soreness of the penis that is not related to injury is often due to infection in the urinary tract or skin of the penis. Inflammation may be caused by friction during sexual intercourse. You should consult your doctor if there is any change in the appearance of the skin of the penis.

Blood in the semen
Blood-streaked semen is usually caused by leakage from small blood vessels in the testes or epididymis. A single episode is unlikely to be a cause for concern, but, if it recurs, you should consult your doctor. It is also important to consult your doctor if you notice a blood-stained discharge that is not related to ejaculation or if you notice blood in your urine.

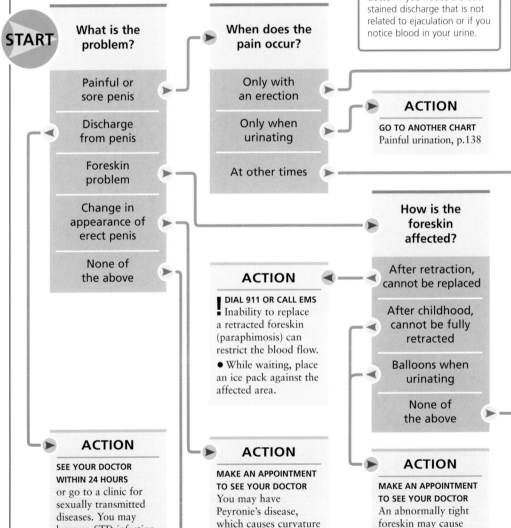

START

What is the problem?
- Painful or sore penis
- Discharge from penis
- Foreskin problem
- Change in appearance of erect penis
- None of the above

When does the pain occur?
- Only with an erection
- Only when urinating
- At other times

ACTION
GO TO ANOTHER CHART
Painful urination, p.138

How is the foreskin affected?
- After retraction, cannot be replaced
- After childhood, cannot be fully retracted
- Balloons when urinating
- None of the above

ACTION
! DIAL 911 OR CALL EMS
Inability to replace a retracted foreskin (paraphimosis) can restrict the blood flow.
• While waiting, place an ice pack against the affected area.

ACTION
SEE YOUR DOCTOR
WITHIN 24 HOURS
or go to a clinic for sexually transmitted diseases. You may have an STD infection such as gonorrhea.

ACTION
MAKE AN APPOINTMENT
TO SEE YOUR DOCTOR
You may have Peyronie's disease, which causes curvature of the erect penis.

ACTION
MAKE AN APPOINTMENT
TO SEE YOUR DOCTOR
An abnormally tight foreskin may cause these problems.

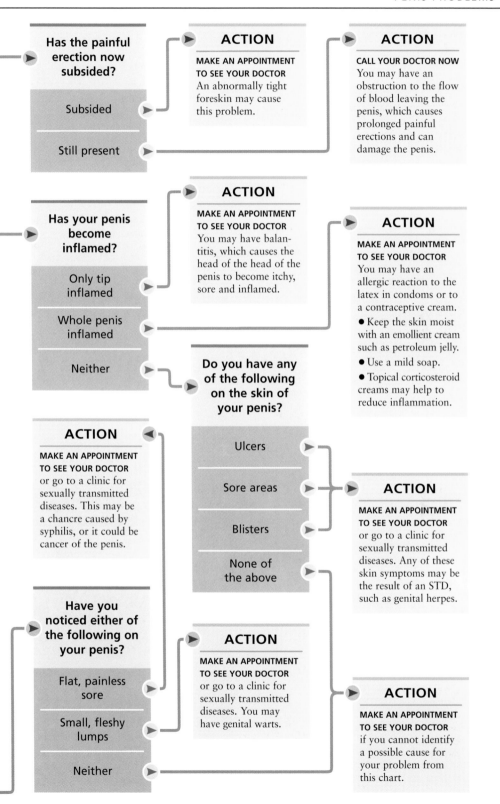

Has the painful erection now subsided?

Subsided ▶

Still present ▶

ACTION

MAKE AN APPOINTMENT TO SEE YOUR DOCTOR
An abnormally tight foreskin may cause this problem.

ACTION

CALL YOUR DOCTOR NOW
You may have an obstruction to the flow of blood leaving the penis, which causes prolonged painful erections and can damage the penis.

Has your penis become inflamed?

Only tip inflamed ▶

Whole penis inflamed ▶

Neither ▶

ACTION

MAKE AN APPOINTMENT TO SEE YOUR DOCTOR
You may have balan-titis, which causes the head of the head of the penis to become itchy, sore and inflamed.

ACTION

MAKE AN APPOINTMENT TO SEE YOUR DOCTOR
You may have an allergic reaction to the latex in condoms or to a contraceptive cream.
● Keep the skin moist with an emollient cream such as petroleum jelly.
● Use a mild soap.
● Topical corticosteroid creams may help to reduce inflammation.

Do you have any of the following on the skin of your penis?

Ulcers ▶

Sore areas ▶

Blisters ▶

None of the above ▶

ACTION

MAKE AN APPOINTMENT TO SEE YOUR DOCTOR
or go to a clinic for sexually transmitted diseases. This may be a chancre caused by syphilis, or it could be cancer of the penis.

ACTION

MAKE AN APPOINTMENT TO SEE YOUR DOCTOR
or go to a clinic for sexually transmitted diseases. Any of these skin symptoms may be the result of an STD, such as genital herpes.

Have you noticed either of the following on your penis?

Flat, painless sore ▶

Small, fleshy lumps ▶

Neither ▶

ACTION

MAKE AN APPOINTMENT TO SEE YOUR DOCTOR
or go to a clinic for sexually transmitted diseases. You may have genital warts.

ACTION

MAKE AN APPOINTMENT TO SEE YOUR DOCTOR
if you cannot identify a possible cause for your problem from this chart.

Breast problems

It is important to familiarize yourself with the normal look and feel of your breasts so that you are able to detect any changes in them (see Breasts: self-examination, p.69). Most breast problems are not serious, but consult your doctor if you notice any changes. Minor conditions clearly related to breast-feeding usually respond well to simple treatments.

START

Are you breastfeeding a baby?
- Breastfeeding
- Not breastfeeding

Where is the problem?
- In the breast
- On the nipple

What is the nature of your symptoms?
- Small, hard lump in breast
- Swollen, hard, and tender breasts
- Redness of part or all of one breast
- None of the above

ACTION

MAKE AN APPOINTMENT TO SEE YOUR DOCTOR if you cannot identify a possible cause for your breast problem from this chart.

What is the nature of your breast problem?
- Single lump in the breast
- A nipple has changed in appearance
- Discharge from the nipple
- Breasts feel tender
- Breasts feel lumpy and hard
- None of the above

ACTION

MAKE AN APPOINTMENT TO SEE YOUR DOCTOR These symptoms may be caused by minor problems that are easily treatable or that need no treatment. However, such changes must be investigated promptly to rule out the chance of breast cancer.

ACTION

MAKE AN APPOINTMENT TO SEE YOUR DOCTOR Discharge from the nipple may be caused by a local infection or a hormonal problem. However, the possibility of breast cancer needs to be ruled out.

How is your nipple affected?
- Tender only when feeding
- Tender and painful all the time

ACTION

MAKE AN APPOINTMENT TO SEE YOUR DOCTOR if you cannot identify a possible cause for your breast problem from this chart.

ACTION

MAKE AN APPOINTMENT TO SEE YOUR DOCTOR if the lump has not disappeared within a week or if the breast becomes painful or red. The lump may be caused by a blocked milk duct.

ACTION

SEE YOUR DOCTOR WITHIN 24 HOURS You may have mastitis (a breast infection causing inflammation) or even a breast abscess, particularly if you are also not feeling well.

- Continue to breastfeed from both of your breasts.

ACTION

TRY SELF-HELP MEASURES Overfull breasts are common, especially when you first start breastfeeding and your milk supply has not yet adjusted to your baby's needs.

- Continue to breastfeed your baby at regular intervals.
- Take an analgesic such as acetaminophen.
- Place a heating pad or covered hot-water bottle on the affected breast(s).

CONSULT YOUR DOCTOR or breastfeeding adviser if you are concerned.

ACTION

TRY SELF-HELP MEASURES This problem may be a result of your baby not latching on to your nipple properly.

- Make sure that your baby takes the nipple and the surrounding area into his or her mouth properly.

CONSULT YOUR DOCTOR or breastfeeding adviser if you are still having problems when you use the correct feeding technique.

ACTION

TRY SELF-HELP MEASURES Your symptoms may be due to cracked nipples, usually caused by your baby not latching on properly.

- Keep your nipples dry between feedings and use moisturizing cream.

CONSULT YOUR DOCTOR or breastfeeding adviser if the problem persists or makes breastfeeding difficult.

Does either of the following apply?

You are due to menstruate within 10 days

You might be pregnant

Neither

ACTION

MAKE AN APPOINTMENT TO SEE YOUR DOCTOR if you are concerned. The problem may simply be the result of hormonal changes associated with the menstrual cycle that can lead to premenstrual breast tenderness.

ACTION

MAKE AN APPOINTMENT TO SEE YOUR DOCTOR Breast tenderness is common during pregnancy. If you are not sure whether you are pregnant, perform a home pregnancy test.

ACTION

MAKE AN APPOINTMENT TO SEE YOUR DOCTOR if you cannot identify a possible cause for your breast problem from this chart.

Menstrual period pain

Many women experience mild cramping pain in the lower abdomen during menstruation. This pain is considered normal unless it interferes with everyday activities; it can usually be relieved by an analgesic. If you regularly have severe pain or if your periods become unusually painful, consult your doctor to rule out the possibility of infection or disorder.

START

Are your menstrual periods more painful than usual?

No worse than usual

Worse than usual

Have you had an unusual vaginal discharge between periods?

No discharge

Discharge

ACTION

TRY SELF-HELP MEASURES
Some pain experienced during your menstrual period is quite normal.
• Take an analgesic such as ibuprofen.
MAKE AN APPOINTMENT TO SEE YOUR DOCTOR
if pain interferes with normal activities.

Have you had any of the following?

Lower abdominal pain between menstrual periods

Lower back pain between periods

Fever

None of the above

ACTION

SEE YOUR DOCTOR WITHIN 24 HOURS
You could have pelvic inflammatory disease, which causes infection in the reproductive organs.

ACTION

MAKE AN APPOINTMENT TO SEE YOUR DOCTOR
if you cannot identify a possible cause for your menstrual pain from this chart.

ACTION

MAKE AN APPOINTMENT TO SEE YOUR DOCTOR
An increase in menstrual pain is a side effect of some IUDs.

Do you have an intrauterine contraceptive device (IUD)?

IUD

No IUD

Have your menstrual periods become heavier or longer?

Heavier

Longer

Neither

ACTION

MAKE AN APPOINTMENT TO SEE YOUR DOCTOR
You may have fibroids (noncancerous tumors in the uterus) or endometriosis. This is a condition in which the tissue that usually lines the uterus becomes attached to other organs in the abdomen and bleeds during menstruation.

Heavy menstrual periods

If you bleed between periods, see p.158 ▶
Some women lose more blood than others during their menstrual periods. If normal sanitary protection is not sufficient, if bleeding lasts longer than 5 days, or if you notice that you are passing blood clots, the bleeding is probably excessive. If you are concerned about heavy menstrual periods, consult your doctor.

START

Are your menstrual periods heavier or longer than usual?

About the same

Heavier or longer

Do you have an intrauterine contraceptive device (IUD)?

IUD

No IUD

ACTION

MAKE AN APPOINTMENT TO SEE YOUR DOCTOR
Some IUDs can cause menstrual periods to be heavier than normal.

ACTION

MAKE AN APPOINTMENT TO SEE YOUR DOCTOR
Heavy, painful periods may be an indication that you have fibroids (noncancerous tumors in the uterus) or endometriosis, which causes the tissue that usually lines the uterus to become attached to other organs in the abdomen and bleed during menstruation.

Have you had a single heavy menstrual period that was later than usual?

Yes

No

ACTION

MAKE AN APPOINTMENT TO SEE YOUR DOCTOR
Some women regularly have heavy menstrual periods, sometimes accompanied by pain in the lower abdomen. However, the loss of significant quantities of iron through heavy bleeding could make you susceptible to iron-deficiency anemia.

ACTION

MAKE AN APPOINTMENT TO SEE YOUR DOCTOR
if you are concerned about the cause of your late period. Late periods may be heavier than usual. However, if you are sexually active there is a possibility that you have had an early miscarriage.

Are your menstrual periods more painful than usual?

More painful

The same or less painful

ACTION

MAKE AN APPOINTMENT TO SEE YOUR DOCTOR
if you cannot identify a possible cause for your heavy menstrual periods from this chart.

Abnormal vaginal bleeding

Vaginal bleeding is considered abnormal if it occurs outside the normal menstrual cycle, during pregnancy, or after menopause. Although there is often a simple explanation, you should always see your doctor if you have any abnormal vaginal bleeding. If you are pregnant and you notice bleeding, you should consult your doctor immediately.

! Bleeding in pregnancy
If you have any vaginal bleeding during pregnancy, you should contact your doctor immediately. If the bleeding is heavy, dial 911 or call EMS. Although some causes of bleeding are not serious, it is important to rule out miscarriage or problems such as a low-lying placenta or partial separation of the placenta from the wall of the uterus.

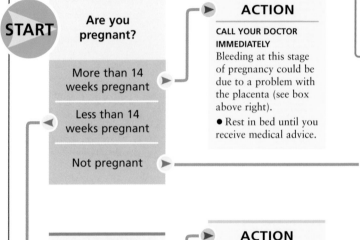

START

Are you pregnant?

More than 14 weeks pregnant

Less than 14 weeks pregnant

Not pregnant

ACTION
CALL YOUR DOCTOR IMMEDIATELY
Bleeding at this stage of pregnancy could be due to a problem with the placenta (see box above right).
• Rest in bed until you receive medical advice.

Is the bleeding similar to that of a normal period?

Like a period

Different

Do you have unusual pain in the lower back or abdomen?

Lower back pain

Abdominal pain

Neither

ACTION
CALL YOUR DOCTOR IMMEDIATELY
You may be having a miscarriage or you could have an ectopic pregnancy.
• Rest in bed until you receive medical advice.

ACTION
CALL YOUR DOCTOR IMMEDIATELY
Bleeding at this stage of pregnancy could be the first sign of a threatened miscarriage.
• Rest in bed until you receive medical advice.

How long has it been since your last menstrual period?

Less than 6 months

More than 6 months

Does either of the following apply?

You have only recently started having periods ▶

You are over 40 ◀

Neither ▶ ▶

ACTION

MAKE AN APPOINTMENT TO SEE YOUR DOCTOR if you are concerned. Irregular periods are fairly common in the first year or so of menstruation.

ACTION

MAKE AN APPOINTMENT TO SEE YOUR DOCTOR if you are concerned or if your pattern does not return to normal within three menstrual cycles. Having an occasional irregular period is unlikely to indicate a serious problem if the period was normal in all other respects.

ACTION

MAKE AN APPOINTMENT TO SEE YOUR DOCTOR if you are concerned. Your menstrual periods may become irregular as you approach menopause.

❗ Hormonal contraceptives

In the first few menstrual cycles after starting hormonal contraception or changing to a different type of oral contraception, spotting is fairly common. If abnormal bleeding persists or develops when you have had no previous problems, you should consult your doctor. He or she may examine you and change the dosage or type of hormonal contraceptive.

Have you had sex in the past 3 months?

Had sex ▶ ▶

Not had sex ▶

Have you noticed bleeding within a few hours of having sex?

Bleeding after having sex ▶

Bleeding unrelated to having sex ▶

ACTION

MAKE AN APPOINTMENT TO SEE YOUR DOCTOR You may have a cervical abnormality, such as cervical erosion (which causes fragile tissue that has a tendency to bleed to form on the surface of the cervix), the development of precancerous cells, or cancer of the cervix.

ACTION

MAKE AN APPOINTMENT TO SEE YOUR DOCTOR Bleeding after menopause may be due to a minor problem affecting the vagina or cervix, such as cervical erosion (in which the cervix becomes covered with delicate tissue, which has a tendency to bleed). However, the possibility of cancer of the uterus needs to be ruled out.

ACTION

MAKE AN APPOINTMENT TO SEE YOUR DOCTOR if you cannot identify a possible cause for your abnormal bleeding from this chart.

ACTION

CALL YOUR DOCTOR NOW Bleeding, especially if accompanied by pain in the lower abdomen, may be the first sign of an ectopic pregnancy or of an impending miscarriage, even if you were not aware of being pregnant.

Vaginal discharge

◄ **If the discharge contains blood, see p.158**

A thin, clear or whitish discharge from the vagina is normal. This discharge will vary in consistency and quantity with the stage of the menstrual cycle, during sexual arousal, and during pregnancy. An abnormal discharge is usually caused by infection and should be investigated by your doctor.

ACTION ◄

CONSULT YOUR DOCTOR
if you are concerned or if you develop genital irritation. These forms of contraception sometimes cause an increase in normal vaginal secretions.

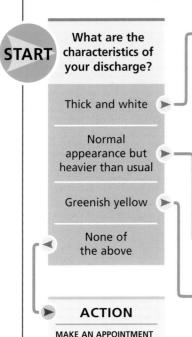

START

What are the characteristics of your discharge?

- Thick and white ►
- Normal appearance but heavier than usual ►
- Greenish yellow ►
- None of the above

► **ACTION**

TRY SELF-HELP MEASURES
You may have thrush, particularly if you also have genital irritation.
- If you have had these symptoms before, try an over-the-counter product recommended by a pharmacist.

CONSULT YOUR DOCTOR
if this is the first time you have had these symptoms.

► **Do any of the following apply?**

- You are taking oral contraceptives ►
- You have an IUD ►
- You are pregnant ◄
- None of the above ►

► **Do you have either of the following?**

- Fever ►
- Lower abdominal pain ►
- Neither ◄

► **ACTION**

MAKE AN APPOINTMENT TO SEE YOUR DOCTOR
if you cannot identify a possible cause for your discharge from this chart.

► **ACTION**

MAKE AN APPOINTMENT TO SEE YOUR DOCTOR
if you are concerned or if you develop genital irritation. Increased vaginal secretion is normal in pregnancy.

ACTION ◄

MAKE AN APPOINTMENT TO SEE YOUR DOCTOR
or go to a clinic that specializes in sexually transmitted diseases. You may have a vaginal infection such as bacterial vaginosis.

ACTION ◄

SEE YOUR DOCTOR WITHIN 24 HOURS
You could have pelvic inflammatory disease (an infection of the reproductive organs).

ACTION ◄

MAKE AN APPOINTMENT TO SEE YOUR DOCTOR
Cervical erosion, which causes fragile tissue to form on the surface of the cervix, may be the cause of your discharge.

Genital irritation (women)

Itching and/or soreness in the genital area are symptoms of genital irritation, which is often caused by chemicals in toiletries or detergents. Avoid these products and the irritation should clear up. Genital irritation may also be due to infection, but often there is no obvious cause. If the irritation is persistent, consult your doctor.

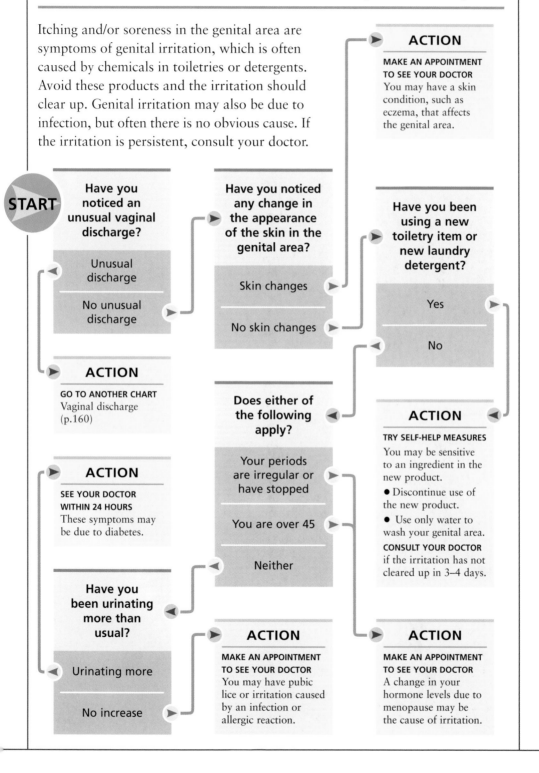

ACTION

MAKE AN APPOINTMENT TO SEE YOUR DOCTOR
You may have a skin condition, such as eczema, that affects the genital area.

START

Have you noticed an unusual vaginal discharge?

Unusual discharge

No unusual discharge

ACTION

GO TO ANOTHER CHART
Vaginal discharge (p.160)

ACTION

SEE YOUR DOCTOR
WITHIN 24 HOURS
These symptoms may be due to diabetes.

Have you been urinating more than usual?

Urinating more

No increase

Have you noticed any change in the appearance of the skin in the genital area?

Skin changes

No skin changes

Does either of the following apply?

Your periods are irregular or have stopped

You are over 45

Neither

ACTION

MAKE AN APPOINTMENT TO SEE YOUR DOCTOR
You may have pubic lice or irritation caused by an infection or allergic reaction.

Have you been using a new toiletry item or new laundry detergent?

Yes

No

ACTION

TRY SELF-HELP MEASURES
You may be sensitive to an ingredient in the new product.
● Discontinue use of the new product.
● Use only water to wash your genital area.
CONSULT YOUR DOCTOR
if the irritation has not cleared up in 3–4 days.

ACTION

MAKE AN APPOINTMENT TO SEE YOUR DOCTOR
A change in your hormone levels due to menopause may be the cause of irritation.

Home medicine chest

It is a good idea to keep a small supply of instruments and medicines at home for everyday aches and pains and first-aid emergencies. Many people now take complementary remedies as well as traditional medicines; recommendations for both are given here. All supplies should be kept in their original containers with the manufacturer's instructions and stored in a locked cabinet out of children's reach.

CONVENTIONAL MEDICINES

DIGITAL THERMOMETER
Use this type of thermometer for taking a temperature by mouth or armpit

PAIN RELIEF FOR ADULTS
Acetaminophen, aspirin, and ibuprofen give relief from pain and inflammation

PAIN RELIEF FOR CHILDREN
Liquid acetaminophen or liquid ibuprofen provide relief from pain, fever, and inflammation

AURAL THERMOMETER
These are used in the ear and are ideal for young children

1% HYDROCORTISONE CREAM
Use this cream to soothe itchy or inflamed skin

ORAL SYRINGE
A syringe or dropper is convenient for giving liquid medicines to young children

ANTACID MEDICATION
Liquid or tablet antacids can help relieve the symptoms of indigestion and heartburn

SUNSCREEN
Creams and oils protect skin from sun damage

COLD REMEDIES
Decongestants and lozenges can relieve cold symptoms

COUGH REMEDIES
Use cough mixtures or lozenges to soothe dry or chesty coughs

ALLERGY MEDICATION
Antihistamines help control hay fever, allergic conjunctivitis, and bites

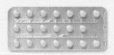

ORAL REHYDRATION DRINK
This fruit-flavoured drink prevents dehydration

MOTION SICKNESS PILLS
Taking these pills prior to travel can help prevent motion sickness

LAXATIVE
Pills help relieve constipation

COMPLEMENTARY REMEDIES

GARLIC
Garlic is a herbal remedy that wards off infection and maintains a healthy heart and circulation

ECHINACEA
Use this herb to protect against infection and to relieve the symptoms of colds, coughs, and flu

CHAMOMILE
This homeopathic remedy soothes teething pains and treats stress, nausea, and vomiting

LAVENDER OIL
This aromatherapy oil eases headaches and aids relaxation

ALLIUM
This is a standard homeopathic remedy for hay fever

ARNICA CREAM
This homeopathic remedy aids the healing of bruises and sprains

VALERIAN
This herbal remedy aids relaxation and induces sleep

GRAPHITES
This homeopathic remedy is used to relieve eczema and dermatitis

NUX VOMICA
This homeopathic remedy treats indigestion and upset stomachs

USING CONVENTIONAL MEDICINES

- Never give your own prescribed medicines to another person, even if you think that his or her symptoms are similar to yours.

- Do not use any medicine that is past its sell-by date or that shows signs of deterioration. Dispose of out-of-date medicine by flushing it down the toilet or returning it to the pharmacist.

- Complete the whole course of any prescribed medication, even if your symptoms have disappeared.

- Do not stop taking a prescription medicine unless advised to do so by your doctor.

- Never give a child more than the stated children's dose of a medicine, and do not give a child even a small amount of a drug that is intended only for adults, unless advised to do so by a doctor.

- Tell your doctor if you have taken or are taking any homeopathic or herbal remedies.

USING COMPLEMENTARY REMEDIES

- Take homeopathic pilules no less than 30 minutes before or after food, and avoid drinking coffee and eating strongly flavored foods during a course of medication.

- Ensure that only the person taking the homeopathic remedy touches it; otherwise, it may lose its potency.

- Keep the remedies away from any other medications and strong smells.

- Take herbal remedies for short periods only, because the effects of long-term use are not yet known.

- Avoid complementary medicines if you are pregnant or breastfeeding.

- Some remedies may interact with conventional medicines; consult your doctor before taking them.

- If you have any doubts, consult a homeopath or herbalist for advice.

Caring for a sick person

When looking after a sick person at home, whether a child or an adult, your main concerns will be to ensure that he or she is comfortable and drinking plenty of fluids, that you provide the correct medication at the right time, and that any new or worsening symptoms are dealt with correctly. A sick child or baby can be more demanding, but loving, patient care is one of the best aids to recovery.

BRINGING DOWN A FEVER

1 Check temperature

- A fever is a body temperature that is above 100.4°F (38°C). See pp.68 and 70 for advice on the different ways of measuring a temperature.
- If you or your child develops a fever, look at the charts on pp.74 and 76 to check whether medical help is required or whether the cause can be treated at home.

2 Relieve fever

- Drink plenty of cool fluids.
- Reduce temperature and relieve discomfort with an over-the-counter analgesic such as acetaminophen.
- Give babies over 3 months of age and children under 12 years liquid acetaminophen (not aspirin).
- Cool young children by removing most of their clothing, wiping them with a washcloth moistened with tepid water, and fanning them, but do not let them get too cold.
  - Children under 5 years old are susceptible to febrile seizures (p.43) if they have a high fever and should be watched very closely.

Use fan to keep room cool

Provide cool fluids

Wipe skin with tepid washcloth

Remove clothing and bedclothes

SOOTHING A SORE THROAT

- Rest your voice by speaking as little as possible.
- Drink plenty of fluids, especially hot or very cold drinks.
- Eat ice cream and icicles; they help ease a tickly throat.
- Take analgesics, such as acetaminophen or ibuprofen, in the correct doses.

- Suck throat lozenges containing a local anesthetic (these are suitable only for adults).
- Gargle warm salt water (half a teaspoon of salt in a glass of water).
- Install a humidifier or place bowls of water near radiators to keep the air moist.

RELIEVING ITCHINESS

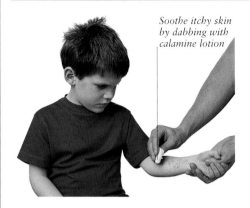

Soothe itchy skin by dabbing with calamine lotion

- For itchiness caused by dry skin, moisturize the skin by applying emollients, such as aqueous cream and petroleum jelly, after washing and bathing.
- To soothe severe itching caused by chicken pox, apply calamine lotion to the spots.
- For severe itching, apply topical corticosteroids sparingly to the area. Always follow the manufacturer's instructions with corticosteroids.

PREVENTING DEHYDRATION

- If you have a fever or are suffering from vomiting and diarrhea, drink plenty of fluids every 1–2 hours, such as diluted orange juice, weak sweetened tea, or an over-the-counter rehydration solution, which contains essential minerals and glucose.
- Do not give milk to adults, children, or bottle-fed babies if they are suffering from diarrhea or vomiting.
- If a breastfed baby is affected, continue to breastfeed and offer the baby extra fluids.

Give fruit-flavored rehydrating fluids to drink

RELIEVING A BLOCKED NOSE

- Fill a bowl or basin with hot water and lean over it with a towel pulled over your head. Breathe deeply.
- Alternative methods are to rub a vapor ointment on the chest or to use decongestant capsules that are filled with menthol and other strong-smelling oils.

> **! Important**
> - Do not give steam inhalation treatment to young children.
> - Older children should undergo steam inhalation treatment only if supervised.

ADMINISTERING EYE OINTMENT

To a child

- Wash your hands thoroughly before using the ointment.
- Draw the child's lower eyelid away from the affected eye.
- Squeeze a thin line of ointment along the inside of the lower eyelid.
- Ask the child to close the eye briefly.
- Explain to the child that his or her vision may be temporarily blurred.

To yourself

- Wash your hands thoroughly before using the ointment.
- Draw your lower eyelid away from the affected eye.
- Squeeze a thin line of ointment along the inside of the lower eyelid.
- Close your eye briefly.
- You may find that your vision is temporarily blurred.

ADMINISTERING EYEDROPS

To a child

- Wash your hands thoroughly before using the drops.
- Sit down and lay the child across your lap, holding his or her head steady. Ask another person to help you if necessary.
- Draw the lower eyelid away from the affected eye and drop the eyedrops on to the inside of the lower lid, taking care not to touch the eye or the skin around it with the dropper.
- Ask the child to try not to blink right away.

To yourself

- Wash your hands thoroughly before using the drops.
- Tilt your head backward and draw the lower eyelid away from the affected eye.
- Drop the eyedrops onto the inside of your lower lid, being careful not to touch the eye itself or the skin around it with the dropper.
- Try not to blink right away.

ADMINISTERING NOSEDROPS

To a child

- Lay the child on her back with her head tilted back. If she is a very young child, hold her arms.
- Hold her head still and drop the nosedrops into the nostril.
- Encourage her to sniff up the drops, so that they do not run out when she sits up.

To yourself

- Lie down on a bed with your head tilted backward.
- Drop the nosedrops into the nostril.
- Sniff up the drops, so that they do not run out when you sit up.
- Lie still for a few minutes to allow the drops to settle.

ADMINISTERING EARDROPS

To a child

- If the drops are being kept in the refrigerator, allow them to warm to room temperature before using them.
- Lay the child on his side. Hold his head firmly as you squeeze the drops into the ear canal.
- Keep his head still for a minute to allow the eardrops to settle.

To yourself

- If the drops are being kept in the refrigerator, allow them to warm to room temperature before using them.
- Lie down or tilt your head and squeeze the ear drops into the ear canal.
- Keep your head still for a minute to allow the eardrops to settle.

Hold child's head still

GIVING ASTHMA MEDICATION TO CHILDREN

1 Reassure

- Stay calm and reassure the child or baby because he may be frightened by the mask.
- An asthma attack can be frightening not only for the child or baby but also for the adult caregiver.

2 Prepare spacer

- Check that the inhaler is working by shaking it and depressing it once.
- Place the inhaler in the hole at one end of the spacer.
- Attach the mask (for a baby or young child) or mouthpiece (for an older child) to the other end of the spacer if it is not already in place.

3 Deliver dose

- Sit the child or baby on your lap, place the mouthpiece in the child's mouth or the mask over the baby's face and depress the inhaler.
- Hold the spacer in place until the child or baby has taken five deep breaths, which should be sufficient to inhale all of the medicine.

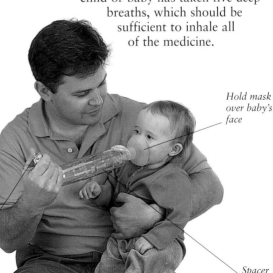

Hold mask over baby's face

Depress inhaler

Spacer

GIVING LIQUID MEDICINES TO CHILDREN

1 Measure dose

- Use a syringe or dropper to avoid spillage and to ensure that you give the correct dose.
- If you are unsure how to use the syringe or dropper, ask your doctor or a pharmacist to show you how to measure and give a dose of medicine to a baby or child.
- Always measure out the dose before you pick up the child or baby; otherwise, you may not be able to do the job.

3 Place in mouth

- For a child, place the tip of the syringe or dropper well inside the mouth and angle it toward a cheek.
- For a baby, touch his lips with the syringe or dropper to encourage him to open his mouth.

2 Reassure child or baby

- Hold the child or baby securely on your lap to give reassurance and prevent possible struggling.
- Have a drink ready in case the taste is unpleasant to the child or baby.
- If the child or baby is nervous about taking the medicine, explain that the drug will help him feel better and stress that it will all be over very quickly.

4 Deliver dose

- Slowly press the plunger or squeeze the dropper, allowing the child or baby time to swallow. Do not aim directly down the child or baby's throat; this could cause choking.
- If the child or baby spits out the medicine, wait until he has calmed down and then try again.
- Mix the medicine with a little jam, if this helps, but do not add it to a drink because it may stick to the sides of the cup.

DEALING WITH A PANIC ATTACK

1 Calm person

- Stay calm yourself and take the person to a quiet place.

2 Treat hyperventilation

- If the person feels tingling in the fingers, it may be caused by too much carbon dioxide in the blood.
- Encourage her to breathe more slowly and to imitate you.
- Try holding a paper bag against her mouth, so that she rebreathes her own expired air, until her symptoms stop.

RELAXATION EXERCISES

1 Get ready

- Performing breathing and muscle relaxing exercises can help rid you of feelings of anxiety.
- Wear comfortable, unrestrictive clothing.
- Choose a warm, quiet room for your relaxation exercises.
- Prepare a firm yet comfortable surface, such as an exercise mat or folded blanket, and have some cushions nearby for extra support.

2 Start with breathing exercises

- Put one hand on your chest and the other on your abdomen.
- Inhale slowly, hold your breath for a moment, then exhale slowly.
- Try to breathe using your abdomen muscles so that the lower hand moves more than the upper hand.
- Once you are breathing from your abdomen, feel your lower hand rise and fall with your abdomen.

Feel the gentle movement of your abdomen

Sit on a cushion for comfort

3 Relax muscles

- Lie down, put your arms by your side, and let your feet fall open.
- Shut your eyes.
- Take one or two slow, deep breaths. Focus on your breathing.
- Starting with your feet and working up to your head, tense the muscles in each part of your body, hold for a count of three, then release the tension.

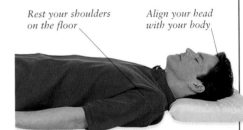

Rest your shoulders on the floor

Align your head with your body

4 Finish by resting

- When you have completed the exercises, lie still for a few moments, keeping your eyes shut, then roll over onto your side.
- Draw your knees up slightly and bend your arms to support your body in a comfortable position.
- After a few minutes, open your eyes and get up slowly.

Use your arms to support your upper body

Rest on a pillow for comfort

3
HOUSEHOLD EMERGENCIES

Fires, burst water pipes, sink blockage, and roof leakage are just a few of the many household incidents that can occur in any home at any time. By knowing how to cope with a wide range of household problems, and having the right equipment for the job, you can minimize any damage to your home and danger to your family. Follow the instructions to fix simple problems yourself by performing tasks such as releasing air from a radiator or replacing a pane of glass. For jobs that are less straightforward, learn how to create a temporary solution until you can arrange for a professional to make a permanent repair.

Home safety

Your home should be a place of safety and security, yet every year household accidents cause countless serious injuries and many deaths. By being aware of the potential dangers and taking action to make your home as safe as possible, you can do a great deal to reduce the risk of accident. The following room-by-room guide highlights potential trouble spots and provides practical advice on sensible safety precautions. Most household accidents derive from carelessness, so work cautiously and wear safety equipment when undertaking do-it-yourself projects.

MAKING YOUR HOME SAFE

1 Be prepared

- Assemble a basic emergency repair kit (see box, right) and keep it in an accessible place.
- Make sure that all family members know where the equipment is kept.
- Check that the adults know where to find and how to operate the main controls for gas (by the gas meter), electricity (by the fusebox), and water (often located under the kitchen sink).
- Draw up a family evacuation plan (p.173) and practice it regularly.
- Near the telephone, keep a list of phone numbers of an emergency plumber and electrician, your family doctor, and 24-hour helplines for reporting gas and water leaks.

2 Prepare for fire

- Install smoke and carbon monoxide alarms or detectors (p.173).
- Keep a fire blanket and a dry powder fire extinguisher that weighs at least 2 lb (1 kg) near the stove in the kitchen. Have the extinguisher serviced regularly.
- Buy a metal fire ladder to use when escaping.

ESSENTIALS

EMERGENCY REPAIR EQUIPMENT
- First-aid kit (p.60)
- Flashlight and spare batteries
- Lightbulbs
- Candles and matches
- Plugs and fuses (p.197)
- Screwdriver

3 Work safely

- If you are doing emergency repairs, take all necessary safety precautions, especially if the work involves electricity.
- Wear safety equipment: goggles to protect eyes from flying debris; dust mask to prevent dust from entering the lungs; and ear plugs to protect ears from the noise of power tools.

Wear goggles and a mask to protect against dust

Hold tools firmly for maximum control

MAKING A FAMILY EVACUATION PLAN

1 Plan escape routes

- Decide on the best route for escape – this should be the usual way in and out of your home.
- Plan an alternative route to use if the normal way is blocked.
- If doors or windows need to be unlocked to escape, make sure that everyone knows where to find the appropriate keys. Ensure that the doors and windows open easily.

2 Plan meeting point

- Decide on a safe assembly point outside the home where everyone can meet following an evacuation.
- Make sure that the whole family is aware of how to escape and where to meet after evacuation.

3 Practice your plan

- Walk through the escape routes with family members so that everyone knows what to do.
- Practice these escape routes on a regular basis, especially after making changes in your home.
- Wear blindfolds during one practice, to simulate dark and smoky conditions, but be careful with young children and the elderly.

! Important

- Keep all escape routes free of furniture and clutter.
- If you have overnight guests, tell them about your evacuation plan so that they will know what to do in the event of a fire.

INSTALLING SMOKE ALARMS

1 Choose alarms

- Buy battery-operated or electrical smoke alarms and take care to choose a reliable brand.
- For added safety, choose linked alarms, which set each other off when smoke is detected.

2 Install

- Attach alarms securely to the ceiling at least 12 in (30 cm) away from any wall or light fixture.
- If your home is on one level, put a smoke alarm in the hall; if it has more than one story, install one at the bottom of the stairs and another on each landing.

3 Test regularly

- Check once a month by pressing the test button. Change the battery in each alarm every 6 months.
- Vacuum the inside of each regularly to keep the sensor chamber free of dust.

INSTALLING CARBON MONOXIDE ALARMS

- Install one or two carbon monoxide alarms near sleeping areas and in any room with a boiler or a gas fire; these alarms emit a loud noise when they detect the gas.
- Place carbon monoxide detectors next to boilers and gas fires; these detectors change color if carbon monoxide is present.

MAKING YOUR KITCHEN SAFE

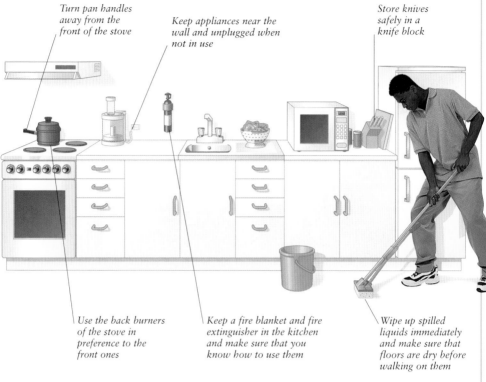

Turn pan handles away from the front of the stove

Keep appliances near the wall and unplugged when not in use

Store knives safely in a knife block

Use the back burners of the stove in preference to the front ones

Keep a fire blanket and fire extinguisher in the kitchen and make sure that you know how to use them

Wipe up spilled liquids immediately and make sure that floors are dry before walking on them

- If you have a water heater in the kitchen, make sure that the flue is kept clear. If you use gas, install a carbon monoxide alarm in the kitchen, as close to the water heater as possible (p.173).
- Unplug or switch off electrical appliances at the wall when they are not being used. Kettles, electric knives, and blenders are particularly hazardous.
- Use a ladder to reach high shelves instead of standing on a stool, which could tip over.
- Never leave a skillet or deep fryer unattended on the stove (p.183).
- Ensure that work surfaces and sinks are well lit so you can work safely.
- If you have young children, install simple security latches on cabinets and drawers that contain hazardous liquids or objects.

- Store matches, sharp items, and household chemicals well out of the reach of children.
- Try to keep young children out of the kitchen when you are cooking.
- Turn pan handles toward the wall so that children cannot grab them or accidentally knock them.
- Install guard rails around the stove to keep children away.
- Warn children that stovetops – especially electric burners, which may show no signs of being hot – can burn even when the power is off.
- Store sharp knives well out of the reach of children, ideally in a wooden knife block.
- Always switch off the electric iron and move it out the reach of children when it is unattended.
- Wipe up spills as soon as possible.

MAKING YOUR LIVING ROOM SAFE

Do not overload electrical outlets

Keep fire guards around the fire at all times

Do not let electric wires trail across the floor or under the carpet

Put children's toys away after use

Put nonslip mats under rugs to prevent slipping

Secure bookcases and other heavy furniture to the walls to prevent them from falling over

- Avoid running electric wires across the floor: these could be tripped on.
- Never run wires under a carpet where people walk; with wear, the carpet may expose bare wires.
- Check all electrical wiring regularly: frayed insulation can cause fires.
- Don't overload electric sockets with multi-point adaptors. Use an extension cable with four or six socket outlets instead.
- If you have an open fire, make sure that you use a fire guard, especially when children are present.

- Secure carpets and rugs firmly so that people cannot trip on them. If you have polished wooden floors, place nonslip mats underneath rugs so that they do not move.
- Always check an open fire before going to bed at night and make sure that a fire guard is in place.
- Install a carbon monoxide detector beside a gas fire (p.173).
- Unplug or switch off electric fires and televisions at the wall socket at night.
- Empty all ashtrays and dispose of their contents safely at night.

MAKING YOUR HALL AND STAIRS SAFE

- Ensure that halls and stairways are well lit – especially if children or elderly people are likely to use them.
- Leave a nightlight on at night.
- If you have young children, install safety gates at the stairway entrances, and keep them closed.
- Check for worn areas of carpet, which could cause trips or falls.

- Mats and rugs on parquet or polished wood flooring can be dangerous. Place nonslip mats underneath them to prevent them from sliding.
- Install extra grab rails on the stairs to assist elderly people.
- Keep the areas at the top and bottom of the stairs clear at all times.

MAKING YOUR BATHROOM SAFE

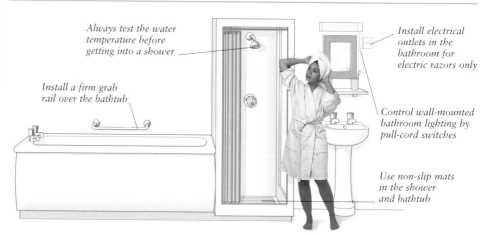

Always test the water temperature before getting into a shower

Install electrical outlets in the bathroom for electric razors only

Install a firm grab rail over the bathtub

Control wall-mounted bathroom lighting by pull-cord switches

Use non-slip mats in the shower and bathtub

- Secure a grab rail on the wall above the bathtub to provide extra support – especially for elderly people.
- Run the cold water first when preparing a bath for young children.
- Never leave young children on their own in a bath.
- Make sure that shower units are fitted with efficient thermostatic controls, so that there is no risk of anyone being scalded.
- Store medicines in a locked cabinet out of the reach of children.
- Never use an electrical appliance, such as a hairdryer or radio, in a bathroom.

- Never touch an electrical item with wet hands.
- Make sure that bathroom lights and wall-mounted heaters are controlled by pull-cord switches or switches outside the room.
- Check gas water heaters regularly to ensure that flues remain clear. Install a carbon monoxide detector or alarm (p.173).
- Never mix two types of household chemicals, such as bleach and bathroom cleaner. The combination can produce poisonous fumes.
- Keep all such chemicals out of the reach of children.

MAKING YOUR BEDROOM SAFE

- Service electric blankets regularly and check their wiring for wear and deterioration.
- Never leave electric blankets on overnight unless the instructions make it clear that it is safe to do so. They may overheat and catch fire.
- Keep a flashlight and your cellular phone (if you have one) by the bed at night, for use in an emergency.
- Never smoke in bed. You could fall asleep with a lit cigarette.

- Never drape a cloth over a bedside light to reduce glare. The heat from the bulb could cause a fire.
- Keep bedroom floors clear of clutter, especially if elderly people or young children may get up to use the bathroom at night.
- If bedroom windows have locks, keep the keys nearby – you may need to use windows as emergency exits. If possible, leave bedroom windows unlocked at night.

MAKING YOUR CHILD'S BEDROOM SAFE

- Never use pillows or comforters in cribs for babies under 1 year old.
- Do not allow very young children to sleep on the upper level of a bunk bed; they may fall out.
- Make sure that there is no gap between the mattress and bed rail through which a child could slip.

- When a young child moves out of a crib, secure guard rails to the bed so that she cannot fall out.
- Make sure that there are no lamps within reach of a child's crib or bed. Lightbulbs get hot, and pulling on the wire could be dangerous.
- Install plastic covers over electrical outlets that are not in use.
- Use plug-in nightlights so that children can find their way if they need to get up in the night.
- Install removable window guards that allow windows to normally open only slightly for ventilation, but fully during an emergency.

Put nonslip mats under rugs

Avoid feather pillows and comforters as they can provoke allergies

Keep bedroom floors clear of clutter

MAKING YOUR ATTIC SAFE

- Never use freestanding stepladders to ascend into the attic space: they tend to be unstable and are likely to tip over. Instead, install an attic ladder with a hand rail.
- Install a light in the attic, preferably controlled from the landing below. Choose a lightswitch that indicates whether the attic light is on or off.
- Line the attic floor with floorboards, or attach veneered chipboard to the rafters, so that you can store items and move around safely.
- Before storing heavy items, have a carpenter check that the rafters are strong enough to support the extra weight.

- Protect ceilings underneath by distributing the weight of stored items. Put heavier boxes at the sides.

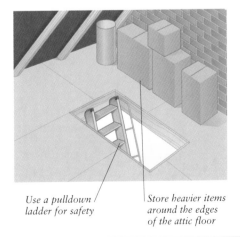

Use a pulldown ladder for safety

Store heavier items around the edges of the attic floor

Yard safety

Yards and outside buildings present many hazards, so safety is an essential part of yard maintenance. Check that garden yard boundaries are secure, especially if children or animals are likely to be outside; that paths and patios are free of debris; and that toolsheds and equipment are securely locked. Gardening itself can be a dangerous pastime, so make sure that you also take the necessary precautions when working with tools and machinery.

PREVENTING ACCIDENTS IN THE YARD

- Remove or fence off any poisonous plants or trees in your yard.
- Keep children and animals away from any area that has been sprayed with weedkiller.
- Cover outside drains with metal grills so that children's feet will not get caught inside them. Grills will also help prevent garbage from blocking drains.
- Fence off ponds, swimming pools, and any other water features in the yard if the space is used by children.
- Do not attempt to use a wheelbarrow to move heavy equipment; it will be very unstable. It is much safer to use a cart instead.

- Don't risk injuring your back by lifting a heavy load on your own – ask someone to help you.
- Never run a powerline along a fence or bury it underground when running electricity to a shed or workshop. Use special shielded cable underground, or run cable overhead, supported by a special wire. When in doubt, consult an electrician.
- For outside lighting and water-feature pumps, use a 12-volt system with a transformer and house it in a dry shed or other outdoor building.
- When you are operating electrical power tools, such as lawnmowers or hedge clippers, always secure a circuit breaker between the piece of equipment and the power source. Make sure that you wear the appropriate safety gear, such as safety goggles, protective gloves and if necessary ear protectors.

! Water danger

- Young children can drown in as little as a few inches of water. Even a bucket of water poses a danger.
- If you have a pond, take the precaution of stretching strong plastic netting over the pond and securing it firmly with wooden pegs.
- For complete peace of mind, consider filling in a pond and choosing a safer water feature, such as a small fountain.
- Make sure that any water barrels have secure lids.

Wear safety goggles to protect eyes

Wear ear protectors if tools are noisy

Choose protective gloves for yard work

MAKING PATHS AND PATIOS SAFE

- Uneven or broken pavement can cause people to trip and fall. Mend or replace cracked pavement as soon as possible.

- Icy steps are dangerous. Lay self-adhesive strips of abrasive material on step treads.

- Alternatively, coat the treads with a mix of sharp sand and exterior-grade PVA adhesive.

Use a wire brush to remove slippery algae

- During the winter, watch for a build-up of algae slime, which can make surfaces extremely slippery. Clean algae-coated walkways with a stiff brush and soapy water, or use a high-pressure washer.

- Prevent algae from building up again by treating the surface with a herbicide.

SECURING BOUNDARIES

- Make sure that boundary gates are kept locked and that bolts are well out of the reach of young children.

- If a gate leads onto a road, secure a latch that a young child cannot operate. Alternatively, fit a small bolt out of sight on the outside of the gate.

- If you have dogs or young children who use the yard, block off any gaps in hedges or fences through which they could escape.

- Remember that as dogs and children get bigger, fences may need to be raised or strengthened.

MAKING GARAGES AND SHEDS SAFE

- Always keep garages, workshops, and sheds securely locked.

- Store hoes, rakes, shovels, electrical equipment, and sharp tools, such as saws and knives, well out of the reach of children.

- Label all dangerous materials and ensure that container lids or caps are firmly closed.

- Store garden chemicals, such as pesticides and fungicides, out of the reach of children. Never pour expired chemicals down sinks or drains; dispose of them safely.

- Keep chemicals in their original containers. Never store them in other bottles.

- Never install fluorescent lighting near moving machinery, because it produces a faint strobe effect that can confuse the senses, making the use of such machinery dangerous.

DO'S AND DON'TS	
DO	**DON'T**
• Use a garage ramp when you are working beneath a car.	• Run a car engine in an enclosed space.
• Wear a dust mask and goggles to protect yourself from dust when sanding.	• Leave a hot tool on a work bench to cool down. Hang it up somewhere out of reach until it is cool.
• Store garden chemicals and tools safely out of the reach of children.	• Leave unattended power tools plugged in or switched on.

Fires in the home

Statistics show that once fire takes hold, you have less than 3 minutes to escape the flames and toxic smoke, and get to safety. With such a limited period of time, it is vital to have organized safe escape routes from your home and to have regular fire drills with the whole family. Install fire ladders to give you a better chance of escaping from upper floors. If a fire is small, try to put it out yourself using water, a fire extinguisher, or a fire blanket. However, if the flames are still burning after 30 seconds, you should leave the building immediately. To give yourself advance warning of a fire, install smoke alarms on every floor of the house and make sure that they are tested regularly.

ACTION PLAN

START

Are you in the same room as the fire?

Yes

No

Is the fire small?

Yes

No

Do you have a fire blanket or extinguisher that you know how to use?

Yes

No

Have you managed to put out the fire within 30 seconds?

Yes

No

Can you safely enter the room to assess the fire?

Yes

No

ACTION

EVACUATE BUILDING AND DIAL 911 OR CALL THE FIRE DEPT (see Escaping from a domestic fire, p.181).

ACTION

OPEN WINDOWS AND DOORS TO CLEAR REMAINING SMOKE.

ESCAPING FROM A HOUSE FIRE

1 Alert the family

- A smoke alarm may warn you of smoke or fire, or you may see a fire start. Check that everyone in the home is aware of the fire and is leaving quickly.
  - Follow the escape route chosen in your evacuation plan (p.173).

Close doors behind you

Guide children to safety

DO'S AND DON'TS

DO	DON'T
• Feel doors and door handles with the back of your hand before opening them.	• Use elevators.
• Close doors and windows behind you.	• Jump from upstairs windows unless forced or told (by the fire department) to do so.
• Keep keys by all locked windows.	• Underestimate the speed at which a fire can spread.

2 Evacuate building

- If possible, close internal doors and windows as you go, to confine the spread of smoke and fire.
- Do not open a door without first touching the door or its knob with the back of your hand to see if it is hot. Heat indicates fire within that room, so choose another route.
- If there is thick smoke, place a handkerchief over your mouth and nose, and crawl as low as possible.
- If fire or smoke blocks your escape route, find another way out.
- Once you are out of the building, meet at your agreed assembly point and check that no one is missing.

! If you are trapped upstairs

- Move into a room where rescuers will be able to see you.
- Close the door and wedge a blanket at its base to prevent smoke from entering.
- Open a window and shout for help.
- Use a fire ladder (see box below).

3 Dial 911 or call the fire department

- Tell the dispatcher your address, if anyone is still inside the building, and if anyone is injured.

USING FIRE LADDERS

- Following the instructions, extend and attach the ladder to the building's facade. If possible, attach the ladder so that it does not pass over lower windows; otherwise, there is a risk that you might climb down into flames.

- Help the elderly and children get onto the ladder and climb down safely. Reassure them and tell them not to look down.
- Use the children's harness that accompanies the fire ladder for a baby or young child.

TACKLING A FIRE

1 Sound the alarm

- Do not attempt to put out a fire yourself unless the fire is small, you discover it early, and you have a fire extinguisher or fire blanket.
- If you have doubts, dial 911 and, if necessary, evacuate.

2 Protect yourself

- Make sure that you can retreat quickly and safely from the area if the fire gets out of control.
- If the fire is still burning after 30 seconds, evacuate the house at once and dial 911.

USING FIRE EXTINGUISHERS AND BLANKETS

- Point the nozzle of a dry chemical fire extinguisher at the base of the flames and sweep it from side to side. **OR**
- Take the fire blanket out of its container and give it a shake to open it up.
- Hold the blanket up so that it shields your hands from the fire.
- Drop the blanket onto the flames and leave it there until the fire is out.

PUTTING OUT CLOTHES ON FIRE

1 Prevent flames from rising

- If someone else's clothes are on fire, force the person to the ground so that the flames do not rise up and burn his face and air passage.
- If your own clothes are on fire, lie down immediately to prevent the flames from rising up and burning your face and air passage. If you try to run for help, the movement will simply fan the flames.

Use a thick woolen rug or blanket to smother the flames

2 Smother flames

- Wrap yourself or the victim in a thick wool or cotton blanket, rug, or coat to smother the flames. Do not use materials that contain synthetic fibers to tackle the fire.
- Roll yourself or the victim around on the ground until you are sure that the flames are extinguished.

Roll the victim on the ground to ensure the flames are out

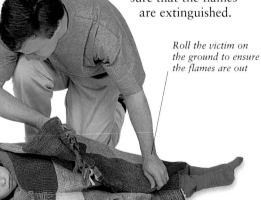

PUTTING OUT AN ELECTRICAL FIRE

1 Switch off power

- Unplug the burning appliance or, if you cannot safely reach the wall socket, turn the power off at the fusebox.
- If a computer monitor or television is on fire, the screen could explode: protect yourself by approaching it from the back or the side.

2 Smother flames

- Drape a fire blanket over the appliance to stifle the fire, or douse the flames with a dry chemical fire extinguisher (see box opposite).

Place the fire blanket over the burning monitor from behind

DEALING WITH A CHIMNEY FIRE

1 Evacuate

- Many chimney fires are explosive; bricks become projectiles that move like cannonballs.
- Do not try to extinguish the fire. Evacuate the house immediately.

2 Summon help

- Dial 911 or call the fire department immediately.
- Ensure that the chimney is checked and cleared by a chimneysweep before you light another fire in the grate.

PUTTING OUT A SKILLET FIRE

1 Approach fire

- Turn off the heat supply.
- Do not attempt to move the pan: the flames may blow toward you.
- Do not put water on a fire that is in a skillet or deep fryer: the water will disperse the burning fat and spread the fire.

2 Smother flames

- Cover the flames with a fire blanket (see box opposite). If you do not have a fire blanket, use a towel or dishcloth that has been wrung out in water.

Protect your hands as you approach a burning skillet

Gas leaks

Natural gas is not poisonous but when combined with air, it becomes highly explosive and can destroy a home. Do not attempt to do gas repairs yourself. This is one of the few areas of domestic maintenance in which any kind of repair or remedial work must be performed by a professional. Because natural gas has no smell, an artificial odor (methyl mercaptan) is added to both gas lines and tanks so that leaks can be detected quickly. If you smell escaping gas, you should take immediate action.

ACTION PLAN

START

Can you smell gas inside or outside the home?

Outside

Inside

ACTION
CALL GAS COMPANY IMMEDIATELY.

ACTION
WHEN THE ROOM IS WELL VENTILATED AND YOU CAN NO LONGER SMELL GAS, RELIGHT THE PILOT LIGHT.

Are any electrical appliances or lights turned on?

Yes

No

ACTION
LEAVE THEM ON, WITH THE EXCEPTION OF AN ELECTRIC FIRE, WHICH SHOULD BE TURNED OFF. EXTINGUISH ANY FLAMES AND VENTILATE THE ROOM.

ACTION
DO NOT TURN ON ANY APPLIANCES OR LIGHTS. EXTINGUISH ANY FLAMES.

Has a stove, boiler, or pilot light gone out?

Yes

No

Has a gas stove burner been left on?

Yes

No

ACTION
TURN THE BURNER OFF AND OPEN WINDOWS TO VENTILATE ROOM.

ACTION
TURN THE GAS OFF AT THE MAIN AND CALL YOUR GAS COMPANY IMMEDIATELY.

IF YOU SUSPECT A GAS LEAK

1 Avoid danger of explosion

- As soon as you smell gas, or if you suspect that a gas appliance is leaking but you cannot smell anything, immediately extinguish any flames, such as cigarettes or candles.
- Switch off any electric fires.
- Do not touch any other electrical appliances, including light switches. Operating anything electrical could create a spark that could ignite a concentration of gas.

DO'S AND DON'TS	
DO	**DON'T**
• Extinguish any flames and cigarettes.	• Turn on any lights or electrical appliances.
• Ventilate the room.	• Use your home or cellular telephone until you are outside.
• Check gas appliances and pilot lights.	
• Turn off the gas supply at the main or on the gas cylinder.	• Forget to relight pilot lights once the leak has been fixed.

2 Ventilate room

- If you find a gas jet left on, turn it off immediately. Open windows and any external doors.

3 Check for leak

- Check all gas appliances and turn off the gas supply at the main (next to the meter) or on the gas cylinder for bottled gas.
- Send family members outside until the smell of gas has disappeared.

4 Summon help

- If you cannot identify the source of the leak, or can identify it but realize you should not attempt to fix it, evacuate the home.
- Call your regional gas supplier's emergency number from outside your house.
- Keep the family out of the home until the gas company advises you that the danger has passed.
- Warn neighbors that you have detected a gas leak.
- Once repairs are complete, do not forget to relight all the pilot lights in the house.

! Carbon monoxide alert

- Carbon monoxide detectors either set off alarms or they change color when they sense the presence of the gas in the air. These detectors should be installed near boilers or other appliances using gas, such as gas stoves.
- When the siren sounds or the detector changes color, ventilate the room by opening external doors and windows.
- Switch off the leaking appliance (or turn off the gas at the main if you are unsure of the source). Call a professional to repair it.

Plumbing problems

Water in the wrong places can cause considerable damage, but the ability to make emergency repairs can prevent a minor problem from becoming a disaster. In a plumbing crisis, knowing the basics, such as where to find your main shutoff valve and how to drain the system, can make the difference.

ACTION PLAN

START

Is water leaking from the ceiling?

Yes

No

Is water leaking from a kitchen appliance?

Yes

No

ACTION

IF A DISHWASHER OR WASHING MACHINE IS LEAKING, CHECK DOOR SEALS, SUPPLY AND DRAIN PIPES

ACTION

IF THE RADIATOR IS LEAKING, REPAIR IT (see Radiator leaking, p.193). IF A PIPE HAS BURST, REPAIR IT (see Burst pipe, p.188)

Is water coming from the attic or roof?

Yes

No

ACTION

GO UP TO THE ATTIC AND CHECK FOR A BURST PIPE OR DAMAGE TO A WATER TANK. REPAIR IF NECESSARY (see Burst pipe, p.188, or Fixing a leaking water tank, p.187). CHECK THE ROOF AND REPAIR LEAK (see Leaking roof, p.206)

Is a radiator or pipe leaking?

Yes

No

ACTION

GO UPSTAIRS AND CHECK THAT ALL THE UPSTAIRS FAUCETS ARE TURNED OFF

Do you have access to the floor above?

Yes

No

ACTION

CALL THE BUILDING SUPERINTENDENT OR CONTACT YOUR LOCAL WATER DEPARTMENT

ACTION

IF YOU ARE STILL NOT SURE OF THE CAUSE OF THE LEAK, TURN OFF THE WATER AT THE MAIN SHUTOFF VALVE, DRAIN THE TANK, AND CALL A PLUMBER

LEAKING CEILING

➊ Turn off water main

- Go to the main shutoff valve and turn off the water.

➋ Drain system

- Turn off the boiler to keep the pipes from overheating.
- Run the faucets upstairs and flush toilets fed by the water tank to reduce the water level in the tank.

➌ Relieve pressure

- Use a bucket to catch water leaking from the ceiling.
- If there is a hairline crack, enlarge it with a screwdriver to increase the flow and reduce the weight of water on the ceiling.
- If the ceiling is bulging, put more buckets in place, then punch a hole.

Enlarge the crack in the ceiling with a screwdriver

➍ Find source of leak

- If the water is coming through the ceiling, check the room or the apartment above.
- If the water is coming from the attic area, check for a burst pipe or damage to the water tank and fix any leak (p.188 and below). If the pipes and tank are sound, look for holes in the roof itself and repair if necessary (p.206).

❗ Dangers of water and electricity

- If water is dripping from a light fixture or onto an electrical appliance, do not touch the switch, the light fixture, or the appliance. Turn off the power at the circuit breaker or fuse box and call an electrician immediately.

FIXING A LEAKING COLD WATER TANK

Some homes have a tank with a pump for constant house pressure. Others may have a repairable reservoir in the attic or basement.

- Shut the main valve. Arrange for disposal of cold water.
- Close the hot water valve at the hot water tank. Then

open the drain valve of the cold water tank.

- Flush toilets, then open all cold water faucets.
- Plug a small hole by drilling and inserting a bolt with rubber stops on either side. For corner hole, wipe dry; use an epoxy resin sealant.

Put rubber and metal washers on both sides of the hole

Insert a bolt into the hole

BURST PIPE

1 Locate frozen pipe

- Water expands as it freezes, which can cause old pipes to split open or a compression joint (where two lengths of copper piping are joined) to push apart.
- If you have copper pipes, check the compression joints to see if any have been pushed apart.
- If you have lead pipes, look for ice where the pipe wall has cracked.
- Water pipes will freeze only in an uninsulated roof space, outside, or in a house with no central heating.

2 Repair burst pipe

- If the pipe wall is damaged, wrap pipe repair tape around the crack.
- Thaw pipe (see box below) if necessary.
- Call a plumber to make a permanent repair.

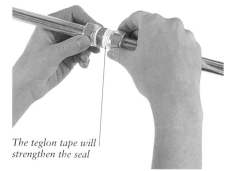

Wrap pipe repair tape around the damaged pipe to seal it

3 Shut off water supply

- If a compression joint is destroyed, it will need to be replaced.
- If the joint is damaged, shut off the water supply to the pipe by closing the gate valve. If the pipe does not have one, turn off the main and drain the entire water system by turning on all the faucets.

4 Repair joint

- Thaw the joint (see box below).
- Unscrew the joint, wrap teglon tape around the threaded parts, then refasten the joint.

The teglon tape will strengthen the seal

THAWING FROZEN PIPES

- If, during winter, you turn on a faucet and no water comes out, the pipe may be frozen.
- Find the pipe that feeds it, and tap it gently with a mallet; you will hear a dull thud at the frozen section, which may be bulging under the pressure of the ice.
- Check the pipe carefully for any cracks.

- If there are cracks, then proceed to step 2 above before thawing the pipe.
- Use a hot-water bottle, hot cloths, or a hairdryer to gently heat the pipe or joint. If the water inside boils, the pipe may burst.
- Do not use a blowtorch to thaw any type of pipework: the intense heat is likely cause damage.

Apply gentle heat to the frozen area

BLOCKED SINK

1 Use sink plunger

- Smear petroleum jelly around the rim of a sink plunger.
- Block the overflow outlet with a piece of cloth, then position the plunger over the drain. Run 2 in (5 cm) of water into the sink.
- Pump vigorously for a few minutes to clear a minor blockage.
- If this fails, use a commercial drain cleaner or pour carbonated soda dissolved in hot water down the drain.

Block the overflow outlet with a cloth

Pump the plunger over the drain

CLEAR BOTTLE TRAP

- If the sink is still blocked, place a bucket underneath the bottle trap below the sink and unscrew the base.
- Push a clotheshanger or "snake"(a flexible length of metal) down the drain to try to push the blockage out.
- If this is unsuccessful, try working up through the trap bottom and along the waste pipe. Try to pull any debris back toward you rather than pushing it further away.
- Replace the trap base and fasten securely.

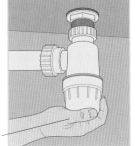

Remove the base of the bottle trap

2 Check U-bend

- For a U-bend with a drain plug (a small capped outlet at the bottom of the U section), put a bucket in place, then unscrew the plug using a wrench.
- Wedge a piece of wood in the U-bend to keep it steady as you work. Clear any debris, then replace the drain plug.
- For a removable U-bend, unscrew the joints and lift out the U section, draining the water into a bucket. Clear debris from the pipe, then replace the U section.

3 Check main drain

- If the pipe remains blocked, there could be a problem in the drain.
- Call a drain cleaner to come and clear the drain.

Unscrew both sides of the U-bend to remove blockage

Place a bucket underneath to catch water

LEAKING FAUCET

1 Turn off water

- A leaking faucet is both a nuisance and a waste of valuable water.
- In cold weather, dripping water can freeze in the pipes overnight, which may cause pipes to burst.
- In hard water areas, a faucet that keeps dripping may stain sinks and baths with mineral deposits.
- Before starting on any repair work, turn off the water supply.
- Close the "speedy" on the pipe, if it has one.

2 Call plumber

- Most leaking faucets are caused by faulty washers.
- You will need to remove the faucet cover to replace a washer, which may be tricky if you have modern faucets that are complex in design. If you feel unsure about tackling the job, call a plumber.

SILENCING DRIPS

- Until a faucet can be repaired, silence the noise by tying a piece of string around its spout. Put the other end of the string in the drain. The water should now trickle down the string and into the drain.

AIRLOCK IN PIPE

1 Release air

- If no water comes out and the pipe makes a banging noise when you turn on a faucet, there is probably an air lock in the pipe.
- You may be able to release the air by using a rubber mallet to tap along the pipe leading from the faucet.

Tap the pipe gently to dislodge the airlock

2 Turn on faucets

- If you cannot find the air lock in this way, turn all the faucets on full to try to drive out the air.

3 Use garden hose

- If this fails, connect one end of a garden hose to the faulty faucet and the other end to a main-fed faucet, such as the kitchen sink faucet.
- Turn on the faulty faucet, then the main-fed one. The pressure of the main water as it enters the faulty faucet should drive the air lock out of the pipe.
- When the pipe stops banging, turn off the faucets and remove the hose from the main faucet.
- Drain off the water in the hose, then disconnect the hose from the faulty faucet.
- If air locks occur repeatedly, call a plumber.

BLOCKED TOILET

1 Try to clear toilet

- If the contents of the toiletbowl do not flow away when the toilet is flushed, the toilet is blocked.
- Do not keep flushing in the hope that this will remove the blockage: water may build up in the bowl and overflow.
- Use a bent wire coat hanger or a snake to remove a blockage just beyond the bend.

2 Try water force

- If this fails, bail some water out of the bowl to reduce the level.
- Pour a bucket of water into the toilet. If the blockage is minor, the force of the water rushing down into the bowl can be enough to dislodge it.

3 Use plunger

- If the toilet is still blocked, get a toilet plunger or improvise by tying a plastic bag around the head of an old mop.
- Pump the plunger up and down in the bowl, but be careful not to use too much force: you risk cracking the bowl.
- If the toilet remains blocked, or you prefer not to try any of these techniques, call a plumber.

Plunge firmly but carefully so that you do not crack the bowl

DRIPPING OVERFLOW PIPE

1 Locate problem

- A dripping overflow pipe from a water tank or toilet cistern indicates that the correct water level is not being maintained.
- Do not ignore a dripping overflow: the drip could suddenly turn into a serious leak, which could cause a flood, or the water may freeze and result in a burst pipe.
- Look in the water tank or lift the cover of the cistern. Floating on the water is an object attached to the tank or cistern side. This float is joined to a float valve, which should close off the supply from the main when the tank or cistern is full.

2 Check float valve and float

- Check the float valve first. If the washer is worn, water will continue to trickle into the tank or cistern even when the float has reached its uppermost position.
- Examine the float to see if it is leaking. Give it a shake to see whether there is water inside.
- If necessary, buy a new washer or float to replace the faulty one.

3 Call plumber

- If the valve is broken, you will need to call a plumber to repair it.

Central-heating problems

A hot-water heating system – which is composed of a boiler and circulator, radiators or baseboard, and an expansion tank – can stop working if the circulator jams, or if a radiator develops a leak or has air trapped in it. Dealing with these problems is usually straightforward. Use the action plan to identify the problem, then follow the instructions on the opposite page. Alternatively, call a plumber or heating specialist.

ACTION PLAN

START

What is your heating problem?
- Single radiator not working
- No radiators working
- Radiator or joint leaking

Are the timer and thermostats set correctly?
- Yes
- No

ACTION
RESET THERMOSTATS OR TIMER

Is the circulator pumping water?
- Yes
- No

ACTION
TRY RELEASING AN AIR LOCK IN THE PUMP (see Circulator jammed, p.193)

Is any part of the radiator warm?
- Yes
- No

Is the joint or the radiator itself leaking?
- Joint
- Radiator

ACTION
CALL IN A PLUMBER TO FIX YOUR SYSTEM

ACTION
SEAL HOLES IN RADIATOR (see Radiator leaking, p.193)

ACTION
BLEED RADIATOR (see Radiator not working, p.193)

ACTION
REPAIR JOINT (see Radiator leaking, p.193)

ACTION
CHECK VALVE IS OPEN (see Radiator not working, p.193)

RADIATOR NOT WORKING

1 Check valve

- Check that the valve at the bottom of the radiator is fully open.

2 Check thermostats

- Look at the main central heating thermostat and the radiator's own thermostat (if present) to check that both are set correctly.

3 Bleed radiator

- Install an air bleed key on the air bleed valve at one end of the top of the radiator.
- Hold a cloth underneath the valve and turn the key counterclockwise until you hear air hissing out.
- Turn the key clockwise as soon as water, which may be hot, starts dripping out.

RADIATOR LEAKING

1 Find leak

- Pinpoint the source of the leak. Water can escape through a loose joint between the pipe and radiator; or through tiny holes in the radiator, caused by corrosion.

2 Repair joint

- Tighten the nut with a pipe wrench.
- If water still leaks, turn off the heating and call a plumber.

3 Seal small hole(s)

- Run a hose from the central heating drain valve (usually under the boiler or on the last radiator in the system) to a drain or sink, then drain the system. The sealant flows through and seals the leak.
- The sealant is only a temporary repair, so replace the radiator soon.

CIRCULATOR JAMMED

1 Find valve

- Turn off the circulator (this will be near the boiler) and find the bleed valve.
- Place a screwdriver in the bleed valve and have a cloth ready to catch the water that will be released when the air lock is released.

2 Release air lock

- Expel any air from the circulator as if you were bleeding a radiator (see above).
- If the circulator is still jammed, call a plumber or central heating specialist.

Turn bleed valve to release air lock

Air-conditioning problems

There are two main types of air conditioning: central systems and single-room units. Both circulate clean air that is cool in the summer and warm in the winter. Problems with central air conditioners are generally best dealt with by an air-conditioning specialist, but you can usually perform basic maintenance of room units yourself, such as checking thermostat settings, cleaning the filter, repositioning the sensor, and cleaning the condenser.

ACTION PLAN

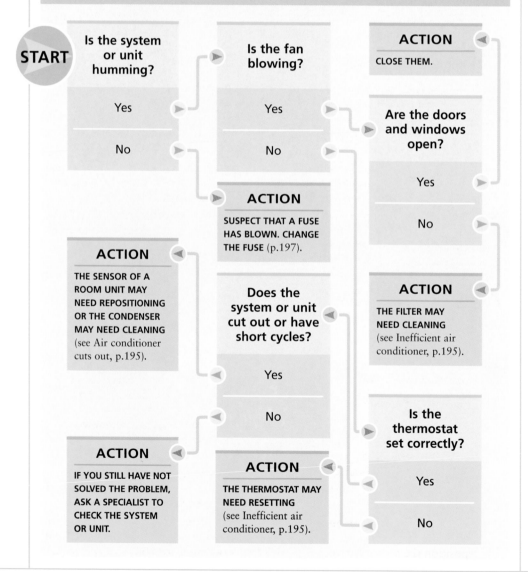

START

Is the system or unit humming?

Yes

No

Is the fan blowing?

Yes

No

ACTION
SUSPECT THAT A FUSE HAS BLOWN. CHANGE THE FUSE (p.197).

ACTION
CLOSE THEM.

Are the doors and windows open?

Yes

No

ACTION
THE SENSOR OF A ROOM UNIT MAY NEED REPOSITIONING OR THE CONDENSER MAY NEED CLEANING (see Air conditioner cuts out, p.195).

Does the system or unit cut out or have short cycles?

Yes

No

ACTION
THE FILTER MAY NEED CLEANING (see Inefficient air conditioner, p.195).

Is the thermostat set correctly?

Yes

No

ACTION
IF YOU STILL HAVE NOT SOLVED THE PROBLEM, ASK A SPECIALIST TO CHECK THE SYSTEM OR UNIT.

ACTION
THE THERMOSTAT MAY NEED RESETTING (see Inefficient air conditioner, p.195).

INEFFICIENT AIR CONDITIONER

1 Reset thermostat

- If the air conditioner is switched on but the fan is not blowing, check the temperature setting on the thermostat. If the thermostat is set too high for the current conditions, the air conditioner will not be stimulated to operate.
- Reset the thermostat to a lower temperature. The fan should start to work right away.

2 Remove filter

- If the fan is working efficiently but the room or house is still too warm, the filter may need either cleaning or replacing (depending on the type of air con ditioner).
- For a central system, a:k an air-conditioning specialist to clean or replace the filter, as appropriate.
- For a room unit, unplug the unit at the wall. Remove or lift up the front panel, depending on the design, and remove the filter.

3 Clean filter

- Clean the filter with some warm water containing a mild detergent, then rinse it in clean water and dry it thoroughly.
- Replace the filter and turn the unit back on.

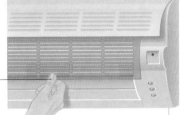

Clip filter back into place after cleaning

4 Install new filter

- If your unit has a disposable filter, check its condition. If it has turned black, is warped, or has holes in it, then it needs replacing.
- Remove the old filter and replace it, following the manufacturer's instructions. Then replace the front panel, and turn the unit back on.

AIR CONDITIONER CUTS OUT

1 Reposition sensor

- For a room unit, unplug the unit at the wall. Remove the front panel and filter.
- Check the thermostatic sensor; it should be near, but not touching, the evaporator coils. Move it away from the coils if necessary.
- Replace the filter and front panel and plug in the unit.
- For a central system, get an air-conditioning specialist to reposition the sensor for you.

2 Clean condenser

- For a wall-mounted room unit, remove the condenser (the part of the unit outside the room) first. The condenser in a window-mounted room unit can be cleaned in place.
- Use a vacuum cleaner to remove the dust and lint that has collected on the condenser.
- For a central system, get an air-conditioning specialist to clean the condenser for you.

Electrical problems

We all take electricity for granted – flick a switch and a light comes on, plug in the television and it works – but fuses can blow, electrical equipment can malfunction, and wiring can become damaged or overheated, posing a potential fire hazard. By equipping yourself with some basic electrical knowledge, you will be able to rectify common problems quickly when they occur.

ACTION PLAN

START

Has one electrical appliance or several failed?

Several

One

Have you checked both the plug and fuse (p.197)?

Yes

No

ACTION

PLUG A WORKING APPLIANCE INTO THE OUTLET. IF APPLIANCE FAILS, REPLACE THE OUTLET (p.199)

ACTION

REPLACE FUSE OR REWIRE PLUG IF NECESSARY (p.197)

ACTION

CHECK THE CIRCUIT BREAKER BOX FOR A BLOWN FUSE OR "OFF" CIRCUIT (p.198)

Are lights or appliances in only one area affected?

Yes

No

Have you lost electricity throughout the house?

Yes

No

ACTION

CALL AN ELECTRICIAN

ACTION

TURN ON MAIN SWITCHES AND CIRCUIT BREAKERS

Are the main switches and circuit breakers switched on?

No

Yes

Do your neighbors have power?

Yes

No

ACTION

THERE IS PROBABLY A LOCAL POWER FAILURE. REPORT PROBLEMS TO YOUR ELECTRICITY SUPPLIER

FAULTY APPLIANCE

1 Check plug

- Loosen the large screw between the pins and remove the plug cover.
- Check the wiring inside the plug for loose connections.
- Check that each wire is securely attached to the correct terminal – black to Hot, white to Neutral, and brown (if present) to Ground (see Rewiring a plug, below).
- If the plug is a sealed unit, you will have to call an electrician to check why the appliance is not working.

DO'S AND DON'TS

DO	DON'T
• Turn off appliances at the wall outlet when not in use.	• Touch plugs, outlets, or switches if your hands are wet.
• Switch off the wall outlet and remove the plug before you attempt to repair an appliance	• Replace a blown fuse with one of higher amperage: this can result in overheated wiring and fire.
• Have your wiring checked by a professional at least once every 5 years.	• Attempt electrical work unless you are confident that you know what to do.

2 Check fuse

- Turn off appliances on the circuit, if known.
- Locate the fuse box and examine the filament strips visible through the mica window of each fuse.
- A blown fuse has a melted strip, seen through a halo of smoky metallic residue.
- Unscrew the threaded ceramic fuse from its receptacle, and replace it with one of the same amperage.
- Turn fixtures and appliances on again, one by one.

REWIRING A PLUG

- Remove the plug cover, loosen the terminal screws, and ease out the cord.
- Position the cord on the plug with the wires placed in their correct positions to gauge whether you need to remove any of the cord's outer insulation.
- If necessary, use wire strippers to cut away 2 in (50 mm) of the outer insulation, then reposition the cord.

- Cut each wire to length (each one should be long enough to reach its terminal) and use wire strippers to remove ¼ in (6 mm) of insulation from the end of each wire.
- Replace the cord in the plug, fit the cord grip loosely, and push each wire carefully into its terminal.
- Tighten each terminal screw down on to its wire and refit the plug cover.

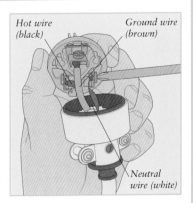

Hot wire (black)   Ground wire (brown)

Neutral wire (white)

ELECTRICAL CIRCUIT FAILURE

1 Look for faulty cartridge fuses

- When power fails in one part of the house, turn off the affected appliances and lights right away and then go to the service/fuse box.
- If the service has cartridge fuses, turn off the fuse box toggle switch and open its cover.
- You will need to determine which fuse has blown using a continuity tester. Remove each fuse, touch one end with the alligator clip of the tester, and the other with the probe. If the bulb of the tester does not light, the fuse is blown.
- Replace the blown fuse(s) with one of the same amperage.

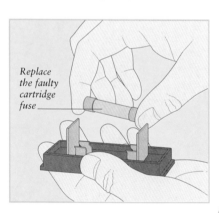

Replace the faulty cartridge fuse

2 Check circuit breakers

- Most modern homes are now equipped with circuit breaker switches instead of less consumer-friendly ceramic, cartridge, or rewirable fuses. Many local codes require them because they are not as prone to consumer error in replacement.
- Most circuit breakers have a key identifying the rooms affected by each switch.
- If your unit has miniature circuit breakers (MCBs), look for one in the "off" position and simply flick it back on, or push the reset button.

Push the switch back to the "on" position

! Replacing fuse wire

- Rarely, some homes will have fuses with replaceable wires. These must be replaced with wires rated with the same gauge as the melted one! Call an electrician to check the service and to replace fuse wires.
- Never use any conductor (wire, strip, coin, or foil) as a substitute for a fuse or fuse wire.

3 Identify recurrent fault

- If the MCB switch will not stay in the "on" position, or the fuse blows again when you turn the power back on, try to identify the fault.
- Check to see whether any light bulbs have blown, then switch off all appliances on that circuit and switch them back on one at a time.
- If you cannot find the cause of the problem, call an electrician.

FAULTY WALL OUTLET

1 Look for signs of damage

- Check for scorch marks on an outlet or around the base of plug pins; these indicate poor connections.
- If you have already checked or fixed the plug (p.197), and the appliance works in another socket, the outlet is probably faulty and will need to be replaced.
- If any part of the outlet is wet, do not attempt to replace it – ask an electrician to do it for you.

2 Replace outlet

- If possible, buy a new outlet that is identical to the old one so the wires will be in the same place.
- Switch off the power at the circuit breaker/fuse box and take out the relevant fuse (or flip the switch to the "off" position if your unit has MCBs).
- Remove the fixing screws from the outlet and pull it out of its bracket. Note which wires lead to which outlet terminals.
  - Loosen the terminals to free the conductor wires, then connect the wires to the correct terminals of the new outlet.
  - Put the new outlet into the old mounting bracket and screw it into place.

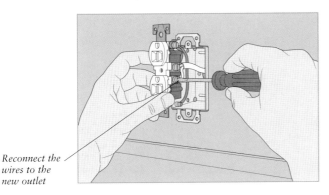

Reconnect the wires to the new outlet

WORN ELECTRICAL WIRE

1 Look for signs of damage

- If the sheathing on an electrical cord is damaged or worn, you could be electrocuted if you touch the exposed inner wires.

2 Check inner wires

- Unplug the cord at the wall.
- If the inner wires are damaged, do not use the appliance until an electrician has replaced the cord.

3 Make repair

- If the inner wires are undamaged, wrap insulating tape around the cord as a temporary measure until an electrician can replace it.

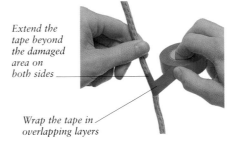

Extend the tape beyond the damaged area on both sides

Wrap the tape in overlapping layers

Structural problems

Most structural problems can be prevented by performing regular internal and external maintenance checks. Look at the condition of your windows, doors, roof, walls, fences, and drains, and deal with minor defects immediately before they become major problems. Even in a well-maintained home, however, there is plenty that can go wrong – windows get broken, doors stick, roof tiles fall off, and holes appear in gutters – but the advice here will help you at least make a temporary repair before seeking expert advice.

SECURING BROKEN PANE OF GLASS

1 Make cracks safe

- If the glass is cracked, cover the crack(s) with clear, self-adhesive waterproof repair tape on both sides of the glass to hold it together temporarily.
- Either replace the pane yourself (see opposite) or get a glazier to do the job for you.

Tape over the cracks carefully to avoid breaking the glass

2 Cover shattered pane

- If the glass is shattered, cover the outside of the hole with a sheet of polyethylene and secure it to the frame with battens and pins or strong tape.
- For greater security, screw a sheet of ½-in (12-mm) thick plywood over the inside of the broken door or window pane.
- If you feel that you can do the job, replace the glass yourself (see opposite), or ask a glazier to do it for you.

CHOOSING AND MEASURING FOR REPLACEMENT GLASS

- Safety glass is reinforced in manufacture and must be used when glazing a very large area, such as a patio door or picture window, where it could be mistaken for an opening, or where glass will be fitted within 31 in (80 cm) of the floor.

- There are three types of safety glass: toughened glass, laminated glass, and wired glass. If you need to use safety glass, discuss with your glass merchant which type is most suitable for the window or door in question.

- If the glass is patterned, take a piece to match with the new glass.

- Measure the height and width of the opening, going right into the groove cut for the glass in the frame. Cut away any old putty or remove old bead to make sure. Since the cavity may not be square, take two measurements on each dimension and use the mid-point as your figure.

- Measure the two diagonals of the opening. If they are not the same, make a cardboard template to give to your glass supplier.

- Buy a pane of glass that is ⅛ in (3 mm) smaller than the cavity on each dimension; also buy some putty and some glazing points.

REPLACING DAMAGED PANE OF GLASS

1 Remove old glass

- Put on strong protective gloves and safety glasses.
- If the glass is only cracked, run a glass cutter around the edge about 1 in (25 mm) from the frame. Place self-adhesive tape across the cracks, then tap the glass with a hammer. It should come away in one piece.
- If the glass is shattered, sweep up the debris, then pry out any loose pieces still in the frame. Use an old chisel and hammer to remove pieces from around the edges, with the old putty. Work from the top of the frame downward.
- Use pliers to extract the glazing sprigs (the tiny nails used to hold the glass in place), then brush the frame to remove small fragments.
- Dispose of the broken glass safely.

2 Insert new glass

- Wet your hands and then knead some putty to make it pliable. Working on the outside of the window, press a continuous putty line all around the edge where the glass will rest using your thumb.
- Place the glass, lower edge first, on to the putty and press it firmly into place, leaving a ⅛-in (3-mm) gap all around.

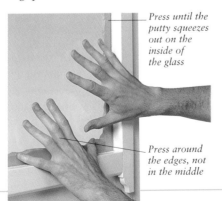

Press until the putty squeezes out on the inside of the glass

Press around the edges, not in the middle

3 Secure new glass

- Fix the glass into position with glazing points spaced about 20 cm (8 in) apart. Tap them gently into the frame with a small hammer, ideally a pin hammer.

Keep the hammer head parallel to the pane of glass

- Remove any surplus putty on the inside edge of the glass with a wet putty knife (a small, pointed, wide-bladed knife).
- Roll some more glazing putty into a thin sausage and press it into the join between glass and frame all around the outside of the window.
- Smooth it by holding the putty knife at a 45° angle to the frame, with the flat of its blade on the putty, and pulling it along. Miter the corners.
- Allow the putty to dry for at least 2 weeks before painting.
- If the glass is held by beading, apply a strip of self-adhesive plastic foam around the outside edge of the glass before pinning on the beading.
- Repaint the frame, brushing a ⅛-in (3-mm) margin of paint onto the glass to ensure that rainwater will not get behind the putty and into the wood frame.

DOORS AND WINDOWS THAT STICK

1 Remove paint layers

- A build-up of paint layers can cause doors and windows to stick.
- Strip off all the paint back to bare wood, then repaint.

2 Plane door

- If a door or window catches as you close it, take it off its hinges, plane a little off the top, bottom, or side, depending on where it catches, then rehang it.

Plane to bare wood on the edge that is sticking

3 Prevent dampness

- A door that is sticking in damp weather but fits perfectly well in dry weather is absorbing moisture, probably through an unpainted top or bottom edge. Ideally, wait for dry weather before painting it.
- If the bottom edge of a door is unpainted, take the door off its hinges, then paint all the surfaces and rehang it.
  - If this does not solve the problem, plane the sticking edge, smooth it with sandpaper, if necessary, then paint and rehang as before.

DAMAGED WINDOW JOINTS

1 Make temporary repair

- Joints that shrink as the wood dries out can cause a window to sag.
- A sash window will need to be removed for repairs (see step 2).
- A prominent casement window can be temporarily repaired in place until you have time to make a permanent repair (see step 2). If the window is not in a prominent position, most repairs can be done in place.
- Unscrew the frame a little and then pry the loose joint open slightly. Squeeze some PVA woodworking adhesive into the gap.
- Screw an L-shaped metal bracket across the joint to hold it together.

2 Make permanent repair

- For a permanent, and more sightly, repair, remove the window and unscrew the frame.
- Pry the loose joint open and squeeze some PVA woodworking adhesive into the gap.
  - Hold the joint in an adjustable sash clamp until it has set, then replace the window.

Place the joint in a pipe clamp and leave until the adhesive has dried

DAMAGED SASH WINDOWS

1 Ease sticking parts

- If a sash window sticks a little, rub a candle on to the sliding parts and put oil on the pulleys.
- If the window is sticking badly, it is likely that a joint has dried out and needs repairing (p.202).

Rub candle wax against the recess

2 Damaged or broken sash cords

- If the sash cords have broken, so that the top window crashes down, you will need to get them removed and replaced.
- In the meantime, you can make the window safe by using lengths of wood to wedge it shut.
- Replacing sash cords is not easy or a job for the amateur because replacement cords must be fitted with the correct weights. Get a window repairer to do the job for you.

BADLY FITTING HINGES

1 Replace protruding screws

- Check the hinge screws. If the heads are protruding, a door or window will not close properly against the frame. Try screwing them in more tightly.
- If this is unsuccessful, replace any protruding screws with smaller-diameter, longer screws.

2 Shim a hinge

- If a hinge is recessed too far into the frame, the door or window will not close properly.
- Take the door or window off its hinges and remove the hinge.
- Shim the recess with a piece of card the same size as the hinge.
- Replace the hinge and rehang the door or window.

3 Tighten screws

- If a hinge is too loose, the door or window will not hang properly. Tighten loose screws or replace them with longer screws.

4 Gain a hinge

- If a hinge is insufficiently recessed into the frame, the door or window will not close properly.
- Take the door or window off its hinges and remove the hinge.
- Use a wood chisel to carefully cut a deeper recess for each affected hinge, then replace the hinge.

Enlarge the hinge recess

DEALING WITH WOOD ROT

1 Assess damage

- Rotten wood at the foot of doors or around window frames is usually caused by wet rot.
- Wet rot occurs when wood gets damp, often when water has seeped through damaged paint. A first sign is often peeling paint.

A sign of wet rot is wood that is dark brown and crumbly when dry

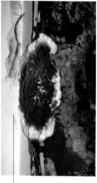

A cotton-wool like material and rust-colored spores indicate dry rot

- If you can detect a strong, musty, mushroomy smell indoors, or see a white, cottonlike material below kickboards or through floor-boards, you may have dry rot.
- Dry rot affects wood in badly ventilated confined spaces, and it spreads rapidly. Call in rot treatment specialists immediately.

2 Treat cause of wet rot

- Before repairing damaged wood, try to find out why the wood has become damp. Check for a leaky pipe or blocked drain.
- Fix the cause of the dampness and let the wood dry.

3 Cut away damaged wood

- Chisel out all the decaying material until you reach sound, solid wood.
- Coat the sound wood and surrounding woodwork with a chemical wet rot treatment.

4 Apply wood hardener

- Brush a coat of wood hardener on to the exposed wood. This varnishlike liquid binds the loose fibers of wood together and seals the surface, making it ready for replacement wood or filler.

5 Fill hole

- For extensive damage, use new wood, treated with preservative, to fill the main gap.
- For smaller gaps, use a special two-part wood filler, following the manufacturer's instructions. Use wood filler also to fill any gaps around new wood.
- Once the filler is dry, rub it down with sandpaper until smooth, then paint, stain, or varnish.

BROKEN OR UNSTABLE FENCING

1 Replace panel

- If a fence panel has been damaged by an impact, blown over by high winds, or is in a state of disrepair, you will need to replace it.
- For a panel supported by wooden posts or recessed concrete posts, remove the nails or angle brackets holding the panel in place at each end and remove the panel. Hold a new panel in place and reattach it.
- For a panel supported by grooved concrete posts, slide the old panel out and slide a new one in.

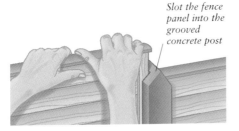

Slot the fence panel into the grooved concrete post

2 Replace post

- If a fence post wobbles, it is rotten at the base and needs replacing.
- Detach the fencing on either side. If the fence is closeboarded, wedge strong wood props under the top edge to hold the fence in place while you work on the post.
- For a post set in concrete, cut it off at ground level, drive a metal repair socket into the centre of the stump, then insert a new post cut to the right length. Reattach the fencing panels on either side.
- For a post not set in concrete, dig it out and replace it with a new one.
- Before inserting the new post, soak it in chemical preserver overnight to protect it against rot.
- Anchor the new post firmly into the ground then reattach the fencing panels on either side.

BROKEN OR UNSTABLE GATE

1 Replace post

- A rotten gate post should be replaced by a new wooden post (see Replace post, above).

2 Make gate stable

- If a gate is generally unstable, check the diagonal brace on its back. If the brace is not sound, replace it with a new one.
- Alternatively, if a joint is loose, open the joint slightly and squeeze some waterproof adhesive into it. Use a metal bracket to keep the joint together, fixed with 1-in (25-mm) galvanized or alloy screws.

3 Secure hinges

- If a gate is sagging, the hinges may need to be secured using longer or thicker screws.

Reattach the hinges with stronger screws

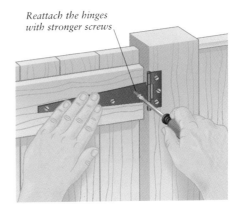

LEAKING ROOF

1 Inspect the roof

- Look at your roof from the ground, using binoculars if necessary, to see if you can spot any slipped or missing tiles or slates.
- Go to the loft with a flashlight and inspect the roof from the inside.
- If the roof is lined, check the lining for damp stains.
- If the roof is unlined, look for rays of daylight between tiles.
- Check roof timbers for dampness.
- If the source of the leak is at a junction between the roof and other parts of the building, such as a wall or chimney, inspect the metal strips (flashing) that seal the join from the outside.
- Once you have identified the source of the leak, make a temporary repair from inside (see box) if you can. Then call a roofing contractor to make a permanent repair.

TEMPORARY ROOF REPAIR

Push the plastic under the damaged area

Patch the hole
Cut a sheet of strong plastic, at least 12 in (30 cm) larger than the hole. Slide it between the roof battens and the tiles surrounding the missing or damaged tile.

Use the lower edge of the plastic sheet to drain water away from the roof

Secure sheeting
Push the lower edge of the plastic out over the lower edge of the hole, so that it directs water down the roof. Secure it with strong waterproof tape.

2 Remove tiles/slates

- Wedge up the tiles or slates that overlap the damaged one, then rock it loose and slide it out carefully.
- Buy a matching tile or slate from your local construction store.

3 Install new tile or slate

- Slide the new tile or slate into place on a builder's trowel until the two nibs on the back of the tile or slate hook on to the roof battens.
- Remove the wedges that were propping up the surrounding tiles or slates.

4 Repair flashing

- If flashing has deteriorated, it needs to be replaced by a roofing contractor. Cracks or shrinkage, however, can be repaired relatively easily.
- If the edge of the flashing has come away from the wall, push it back into the mortar course and apply new mortar to secure it.
- If the flashing is cracked, cover it with aluminum self-adhesive flashing tape, following the manufacturer's instructions.

LEAKING GUTTERS AND LEADERS

1 Check gutters and pipes

- If rainwater is overflowing from the gutter, check both the gutter and the leader leading from it for blockages. Obstructions are commonly caused by a build-up of leaves, birds' nests or balls falling into leaders.
- If water is leaking through the gutter, check the dripping area of the gutter for cracks, holes, or bad joints.
- If the gutter is not damaged, check to see if it is sagging, which prevents it from draining properly.

2 Clear blockages

- Put on protective gloves, and clear the gutter of leaves and debris so that water can flow freely.
- Clear both ends of the leader.
- If the blockage is caused by a bird's nest, make a hook out of a length of stiff galvanized wire. Slide the wire down one side of the nest to hook it up and out of the pipe.
- For a blockage that is out of reach, use a long, flexible rod to clear it.

! Good maintenance

- If leaves are a nuisance, secure protective mesh over the gutter and in the mouth of the leader. You will need to ensure that there is no build-up of leaves over the mesh, as this could cause rainwater to pour over the edge of the gutter.
- Repaint metal drains and gutters frequently to prevent them from rusting and developing holes or cracks.

3 Repair faulty gutter

- If the gutter is plastic, seal a leaking joint by wrapping gutter repair tape around it. If the gutter is cracked, place tape over the crack inside the gutter.
- Repair a sagging gutter temporarily by hammering a wooden wedge in between the gutter and each bracket to hold each section in place.

- If the gutter is metal, scrape off any rust, then paint the leaking area with a sealing compound. Protect the repair until the sealant has dried, then repaint.

- To treat holes in metal gutters, first put on safety goggles, then wire-brush away any loose rust.
- Apply a rust-proof primer, then seal small holes with a sealing compound and large holes with a special glass-fiber filler. To finish, apply tar or gloss paint.

Insects and pests

As well as being a nuisance, insects can sting or bite; cockroaches, mice, and rats create unhygienic conditions; and woodworm can ruin woodwork. Take steps to eliminate insects or pests or call an exterminator.

FLEAS

1 Identify source

- Fleas are usually brought into the house by the family pet. Make sure that all pets are regularly treated with flea killer.
- Flea eggs can lie dormant in carpets until they are activated by movement or warmth.

2 Apply flea killer

- Buy a flea repellent/insecticide, preferably from a veterinary office.
- Vacuum carpets, then spray carpets and furnishings with flea killer, especially under sofas and beds.
- Treat your pets and wash their bedding regularly.

ANTS

1 Use insecticide

- Sprinkle ant insecticide powder into the nest entrance or where ants are entering the house.

Sprinkle ant powder into any cracks where ants appear

2 Use gelatin bait

- If the insecticide is ineffective, put down poisoned gelatin bait; this will be taken back to the nest, killing the other ants.

COCKROACHES

1 Use insecticide

- If you can find where cockroaches are hiding, spray the area well with an insecticide.
- If the cockroaches persist, contact an exterminator.

2 Repeat treatment

- New cockroaches are likely to appear at 4-monthly intervals; be prepared to repeat the treatment.
- Keep work surfaces clean and clear of any food.

BEES, WASPS, AND HORNETS

1 Stay safe

- If you see a swarm of bees close to your house, get everybody inside and shut all doors and windows.
- Contact an exterminator.

2 Have nest sprayed

- If wasps or hornets bother you often, there is probably a nest.
- Contact an exterminator to deal with the nest.

3 Treat stings

- Try not to antagonize bees, wasps, or hornets by spraying them with insecticide; they are more likely to sting you if they are angry.
- If you are stung, refer to p.59 for treatment. Bee stingers can be removed, but wasps do not leave a stinger. If you develop a minor allergic reaction, seek medical help.
- If you develop symptoms of anaphylactic shock (p.28), seek medical help immediately.

WOODWORM

1 Identify signs

- If you spot $\frac{1}{16}$-in (2-mm) holes in furniture or structural timbers, you have woodworm. Sawdust is a sign that woodworm are active.
- Minor woodworm attacks are easy to treat (see step 2), but if an infestation is severe, you should seek professional help.

2 Treat infestation

- Brush surfaces with woodworm fluid. On furniture, use an aerosol with a nozzle to inject the fluid.
- To treat structural timbers effectively, use a large sprayer.
- To treat flooring, lift every third or fourth floorboard and spray thoroughly underneath.

MICE AND RATS

1 Block entry holes

- Small pellet-shaped droppings in your home indicate mice.
- Look for any obvious entry holes into your home and block them.

2 Put down bait

- Put down poisoned mouse bait wherever you find droppings. Be prepared to repeat if necessary.

3 Set traps

- Set three or four baited mouse traps where droppings are found in the house.
- Use peanut butter, chocolate, or cooked bacon as bait for traps.

4 Call rodent control

- Larger droppings indicate rats; call your local health department.

Furniture and furnishings

When accidents happen, it pays to clean up spills and stains quickly in order to avoid lasting damage to upholstered furniture and furnishings, especially carpets. Equip your home with a basic stain removal kit (see below) and you will be well-prepared to effectively tackle even the most stubborn stains.

GREASE ON CARPETS

1 Absorb grease

- Place a piece of brown paper over the mark. Put the tip of a warm iron onto the paper and press it until the grease is absorbed into the brown paper.

2 Use carpet cleaner

- To remove the remainder of the mark, rub carpet cleaner gently into the carpet with a sponge.

- If you have not used the cleaner on a particular carpet before, check for color fastness first by testing the cleaner on an unobtrusive area of the carpet.

- Wipe off the foam with a clean sponge or cloth and inspect the mark. If you can still see a stain, or the stain reappears later, repeat the stain removal treatment.

GREASE ON UPHOLSTERY

1 Apply talcum powder

- Sprinkle a thick layer of talcum powder over the mark, covering it completely, and leave until the grease begins to be absorbed.

Cover grease with talcum powder

2 Brush off talcum powder

- After 10 minutes, brush off the talcum powder.
- Repeat if necessary.

GREASE ON WALLPAPER

1 Blot grease

- Use white kitchen towels to blot the splash, working quickly so that the grease is not absorbed.
- Hold a piece of brown paper or wallpaper against the stain.

2 Use iron

- Warm an iron, switch it off, then press it onto the covering paper to draw out the grease.
- Use an aerosol grease remover on any remaining traces.

RED WINE ON CARPETS

1 Flush spill

- Blot the spill immediately with white kitchen towels then sponge it with warm water to flush out the stain. Pat the area dry.
- Alternatively, pour white wine on to the spill, blot up both liquids, then sponge with clear, warm water and pat dry.

Flood the red wine stain with white wine

2 Clean stain

- Apply carpet cleaner. Work some of the foam into the stain with a sponge, always rubbing from the edge of the stain inwards to prevent it spreading.
- Sponge the stain with clear water to rinse it. Repeat the treatment until the stain has disappeared.

Rub the foam gently into the stained area

PET STAINS ON CARPETS AND UPHOLSTERY

1 Remove droppings

- Wear rubber gloves.
- Remove the dropping with a spoon, always scraping into the stain to avoid spreading it.
- Pour a few drops of ammonia into warm water and use the mixture to sponge the stain clean. Repeat the treatment if necessary.

2 Remove urine

- Clean the stain from a carpet or upholstery using a cleaner that contains a deodorant.
- Alternatively, sponge the stain with cold water and pat dry. Follow this by sponging the stain again with cold water containing a little antiseptic.

Home security

By identifying vulnerable areas of your home and taking adequate precautions, you can dramatically reduce the risk of being burglarized. Installing additional locks and bolts is an effective way of deterring thieves. Security devices such as peepholes, door chains, and alarms are also easy to install; and they not only safeguard your property but also provide peace of mind, particularly when you are away from home.

ASSESSING YOUR HOME SECURITY

1 Identify vulnerable areas

- Check all your doors and windows for strength and security. Imagine that you have locked yourself out: which window or door would you choose to force open or break?
- Look at your house again and reassess your security.
- Contact your local police department for advice.

2 Install main door security devices

- Install locks on the front, back, and any side doors. For added security, you should install heavy bolts at the top and bottom of the inside of each door.
- Back and side doors must have sturdy locks because they are often hidden from view and badly lit, which means that a burglar can attempt entry unobserved.
- For security when answering the door, install a strong door chain and peephole (p.213).
- If a door opens outward, install hinge bolts to the back edge (p.214) so that the door cannot be levered open on the hinge side.

3 Install patio door locks

- Install locks and deadbolts (p.214) at the top and bottom of patio doors and French windows to prevent them from being forced open.

4 Install window security devices

- Windows are popular points of entry for burglars.
- Secure windows with locks or deadbolts to prevent the catches being released through a smashed window. There are several types for metal and wood windows.

5 Assess lighting

- If you install security lighting to help you unlock your door on dark nights, remember that this could be equally useful to a burglar.

6 Consider an alarm

- For the best security, either install a burglar alarm yourself or have one installed professionally.

SELECTING LOCKS

1 Check for quality

- Always invest in high-quality locks. Cheap locks are more likely to rust and stick, which means that they are not cost-effective in the long term.

2 Use strong fasteners

- If you install locks on your doors and windows, use long, strong screws for maximum strength.
- If you are unsure, get a locksmith to do the job for you.

INSTALLING A DOOR CHAIN

1 Choose chain

- Choose a strong door chain and the longest and heaviest-gauge screws possible. The chain's strength depends upon how well it is anchored to the door and frame.

Screw the fixing plates to the door and frame

2 Attach plates

- Hold the chain against the door, ideally just below the lock.
- Make pilot holes with a bradawl or drill so that both sections of the chain are aligned, then secure both fixing plates.

INSTALLING A PEEPHOLE

1 Select viewer

- Choose a telescopic viewer with as wide an angle of vision as possible. You should be able to see someone standing to the side of the door or even crouching down.
- Before you buy the peephole, make sure that the viewer is adjustable to fit any door.
- Mark the best position for the peephole, ideally in the center of the door at eye level.

Drill the hole for the peephole at eye level

2 Fit peephole

- Using the correct-sized drill bit, usually ½ in (12 mm), drill a hole right through the door.
- Insert the barrel of the viewer into the hole from the outside and screw on the eyepiece from the inside.
- Check that the lighting outside your front door is bright enough for you to be able to see out clearly at night.

INSTALLING HINGE BOLTS

1 Position bolts

- Wedge the door fully open and mark the center of the hinge edge of the door about 3 in (75 mm) in from both hinges.
- Drill holes at the marked points to the width and depth specified by the manufacturer.
- Fit the bolts into the holes and partially close the door so that the bolts mark the door frame.

Insert the bolts into the drilled holes

2 Install cover plates

- At the marked points, drill holes into the door frame to the width and depth of the protruding bolts, allowing a little more for clearance.
- Close the door to check that it shuts easily. Enlarge the width or depth of the holes as necessary.
- Open the door and hold cover plates over the holes. Mark the edge of each plate with a pencil.
- Chisel out the recesses so that the plates lie flush with the cover frame.
- Screw the plates in place.

INSTALLING A DEADBOLT

1 Drill holes for the barrel and key

- Mark a central point on the front edge of the door where you want to install the bolt.
- Drill a hole at the marked point to the width and depth given on the manufacturer's instructions.

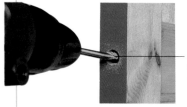

Drill into the opening edge of the door

- Use a square to mark a line transferring the center of the hole to the inside face of the door.
- Mark the keyhole, then drill a hole (see manufacturer's instructions for width and depth) through the inside face of the door only.

2 Install bolt and plate

- Screw the keyhole plate to the door.
- Insert the bolt into the hole. Then draw around the faceplate to mark its recess. Gain the wood with a chisel. Screw the bolt to the door.
- Insert the key and turn the bolt to mark the door frame. Then drill a hole to a depth that matches the length of the bolt.
- Fit the escutcheon over the hole.

Mark the shape of the faceplate recess

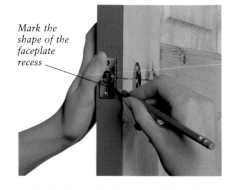

JAMMED LOCK

1 Add lubricant

- If a lock is jammed, do not try to force the key to turn: you could break the key in the lock.
- Apply a few drops of penetrating oil to the key, or dry lubricant, such as graphite powder, to the lock, to ease the problem.

2 Work key

- Work the key gently in and out of the lock, adding a little more lubricant if necessary.
- If this fails, either replace the cylinder if it is a cylinder lock (see below) or replace the lock body of a mortise lock (see below).

JAMMED CYLINDER LOCK

1 Remove cylinder

- If a cylinder lock is jammed (see above) or if you are worried about the security of your existing lock, replace the cylinder.
- Unscrew the lock body on the internal side of the door, then unscrew the cylinder.
- Remove the cylinder from its cavity by pulling it from the external side of the door.

2 Install new cylinder

- Insert a new cylinder by sliding it into the cylinder hole and screwing it into place.
- Put the lock body back in position and refix the holding screws.

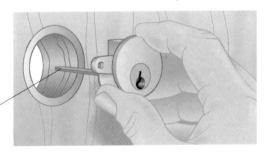

Slide the new cylinder into the existing cylinder hole

DAMAGED MORTISE LOCK

1 Replace striker plate

- If a striker plate is damaged, causing a door to stick as it closes, buy a replacement.
- Unscrew the damaged striker plate from its position in the door jamb.
- Insert a replacement striker plate in exactly the same position and screw it into place.

2 Replace lock body

- If a mortise lock is jammed (see above) or if you are worried about the security of your existing lock, replace the lock body.
- Unscrew the lock body and remove it from its mortise in the door.
- Insert a replacement lock body into the mortise and screw it into place. If the fit is too tight, use a wood chisel to enlarge the recess slightly.

DEALING WITH INTRUDERS

1 Be vigilant

- If you arrive home and see anyone loitering outside, pass by your house and ask a neighbor to accompany you to the door.
- If you return home to find that the front door is open, do not enter your home. Move a safe distance away and, if you have a cellular phone, call the police. Alternatively, go to a neighbor's and phone the police from there.
- If you come home and your key won't open the door, it could mean that an intruder has secured the door from inside so as not to be disturbed. Move away quickly and call the police.
- If you return home to find that your home has been ransacked, call the police immediately. Do not touch anything until the police arrive so as not to destroy any fingerprints left by burglars.

2 Make a noise

- If you do enter your home and meet an intruder, run out and shout or scream as loudly as you can.
- Don't try to apprehend him or her.

3 Stay calm

- If you must face the intruder, keep calm and try not to provoke a reaction by making threats.
- Try to memorize as much as you can of the intruder's appearance, mannerisms, and speech so that you can provide the police with an accurate description.

4 Call the police

- Dial 911 or call your local police station.
- Try to give the police as much information as possible.

DEALING WITH A NIGHT INTRUDER

- If you are woken in the night by unusual noises or the sound of breaking glass, call the police.
- Keep your cellular phone turned on by the bed so that you can still call for help if the telephone line has been cut.
- If you are alone in the house, talk loudly as if you have a companion in the room. You could also switch on the lights and make a lot of noise. Most intruders will leave as soon as they hear noise.
- Do not go downstairs to investigate.

- Do not keep an offensive weapon or try to defend your property. No items, however valuable, are worth serious injury or death.
- If you meet the intruder, stay calm and try to memorize his or her appearance.

Responding to a disturbance
When you dial 911, you will be advised on whether to make a noise or to pretend that you are asleep. Stay in bed until the police arrive.

COPING AFTER A BREAK-IN

1 Don't move anything

- If you discover that your home has been broken into, try to keep calm.
- Do not touch anything. The police will want to check the crime scene and look for fingerprints.

2 Call police

- Dial 911 or call your local police station.
- When the police arrive, they will talk to you about the burglary, ask what has been taken, then take a statement. They will then provide you with a complaint number for your insurance company.

3 List missing items

- Start to make a list of what you think has been taken. This process can go on for days, because many items will be missed only when you try to find or use them. The police should supply you with a form for your list.
- Give as clear a description as you can of all items, and provide photographs of valuables, if you have any.
- Indicate on the list which, if any, items have been owner-labeled.

SEEKING ADVICE

- If you are the victim of a burglary or assault, you will be contacted by Victim Support, an organization that provides counselling and help for victims of crime.
- Talk to friends and family about your experience. They may be able to offer you reassurance and comfort.

4 Secure premises

- If burglars have forced entry by smashing glass, make a temporary repair for security (p.200).
- Determine how the burglar(s) gained access to your home and take steps to make it more secure by installing additional locks or bolts (p.214).

5 Contact insurers

- Contact your insurance company and explain what has happened.
- The insurance company and/or claims adjuster will require the complaint number and a detailed list of what has been stolen.

Give your insurance company details of what has been stolen

6 Keep in contact with police

- If you move while the investigation is still ongoing, notify the police of your new address.
- If you discover more damage or missing items, contact the officer handling your case as well as your insurance company.

4

NATURAL DISASTERS

Surviving any kind of natural disaster depends largely on being prepared. If you know how to protect your home and family, how to understand the early warnings, and how to evacuate if advised to do so, you will be ready for most disaster situations. Once a disaster is over, life may not return to normal for some time, so you also need to know how to cope with the consequences, including power cuts, damage to your home, and water shortages. If evacuated, you may even have to survive outside for a while before help arrives.

Planning for disaster

If you live in an area that is prone to certain types of natural disaster, planning and preparing for an emergency will help protect you and your family. Take steps to safeguard your home and property. Choose a safe place indoors to take shelter. If hurricanes are a threat, find out where your local shelter is, and assemble essential equipment that may help you survive the aftermath.

ACTION PLAN

START

Do you know if any disasters are likely (p.221)?

Yes

No

ACTION

CONTACT YOUR CITY/TOWN COUNCIL.

ACTION

PROTECT YOUR PROPERTY.

ACTION

CHECK AND REPLENISH SUPPLIES REGULARLY.

ACTION

PREPARE A KIT FOR THE TYPE OF DISASTER YOUR AREA FACES.

Have you sought information on the disaster(s)?

No

Yes

Have you protected your property (p.222)?

Yes

No

Do you have a disaster emergency kit (pp.224–5)?

Yes

No

ACTION

PROTECT YOUR FAMILY.

Have you protected your family (p.223)?

No

Yes

Do you have an evacuation plan (p.224)?

Yes

No

ACTION

MAKE SURE YOU AND YOUR FAMILY KNOW WHAT TO DO.

ASSESSING YOUR RISK

- Volcanic eruptions and earthquakes occur around geological fault lines; both can produce tsunamis.

- Hurricanes mostly affect areas around the Atlantic basin and the Pacific basin, where they are known as tropical cyclones. They are often accompanied by tornadoes.

- Flooding can occur almost anywhere, although the most serious floods are usually caused by very high tides.

- Wildfires occur in many countries – 80 percent are started by humans.

- Extreme cold occurs in much of the Northern Hemisphere but many countries experience freezes in winter.

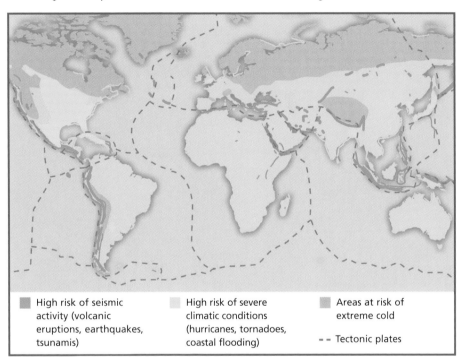

■ High risk of seismic activity (volcanic eruptions, earthquakes, tsunamis)	■ High risk of severe climatic conditions (hurricanes, tornadoes, coastal flooding)	■ Areas at risk of extreme cold – – Tectonic plates

1 Be informed

- Contact your town/city council to find out whether your area is prone to any specific types of disaster. Ask for information about each type.

- If your area is prone to flooding, contact your city/town council to find the height to which a flood could rise.

- Before moving or traveling abroad, find out about potential disaster risks in that area.

- Learn about the effects of disasters that may strike your area.

2 Reduce risk

- Take steps now to protect your property against natural disasters. Your home will be less vulnerable if you take sensible precautions and carry out routine building maintenance (p.222).

- Protect your family by coming up with a family disaster plan (p.223) and making sure that you are all prepared for evacuation (p.224).

- Always keep abreast of the weather situation and local plans regarding shelters and evacuation.

PROTECTING YOUR HOME

- Have unsafe or old chimney stacks removed or repointed.
- Replace cracked or broken slates or tiles on the roof (p.206). Check that roof flashings are watertight. If any are loose or damaged, have them repaired or replaced (p.206).
- Keep gutters and leaders clear and in good repair (p.207).
- If you live in an area prone to tornadoes or hurricanes, install special hurricane shutters.
- Alternatively, install wooden frames on the windows so that you can board them up quickly (p.234).
- Check and, if necessary, repair any obvious weaknesses, such as cracks that are wider than ⅛ in (3 mm), in the structure of your house.
- If your area is at risk of flooding, make sure that you have sufficient sandbags to block all potential water entry points, such as external doors and vents (p.228).
- Ensure that all adults in the home know how to turn off gas, electricity, and water at the main, in case you need to do so quickly.
- Check that you have adequate insurance coverage for damage caused by local disasters.

PROTECTING YOUR POSSESSIONS

- Make sure that shelves are securely fastened to the wall.
- Keep heavier items on lower shelves so that if a disaster occurs and they fall, they are less likely to injure anyone.
- If flooding is a risk in your area, keep precious items on higher shelves to protect them from water damage. Alternatively, move your most valuable possessions upstairs.
- Bolt tall pieces of furniture, boilers, and other heavy items to the wall or floor (p.238) to ensure that they are stable and secure.
- Install additional devices to secure heavy light fixtures to ceilings.
- Keep a supply of bricks that you can use to raise heavy furniture out of reach of flood water.
- Keep a fire extinguisher and blanket to put out minor house fires.

PROTECTING YOUR YARD

- Remove any diseased or broken tree branches that could be blown about by high winds. Thin out crowded branches to reduce wind resistance.
- If you live in an area that is prone to wildfire, create a safety zone around your home (p.232).
- During hurricane/tornado seasons, bring indoors or move into the garage any garden furniture or children's play equipment that is not anchored to the ground.

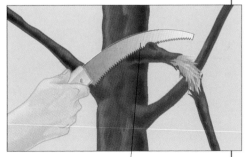

Cut off any broken branches before high winds rip them off

PROTECTING YOUR FAMILY

1 Be informed

- Contact your city/town council to find out if warning signals will be issued and what action you should take (see box below) in a disaster.
- If you live in an area that is prone to certain disasters, you may be given a telephone number to call for up-to-date information and warnings. You may also find advice on the Internet (see pp.250–251 for recommended websites).
- Prior to a disaster, public address systems such as bulhorns may be used to inform people quickly and provide instructions.
- If you are likely to be evacuated to an emergency shelter, find out beforehand where the nearest shelters are and how to get to them.

2 Think ahead

- Keep emergency contact numbers near the telephone and ensure that everyone knows where they are.
- Consider how to help the elderly and physically disabled.
- Plan how you are going to look after pets. Keep pet carriers for small family pets if necessary.
- Assemble essential items that you will need if disaster strikes (p.225).

3 Make a family disaster plan

- Discuss how to prepare for disaster.
- Make sure that any children understand the dangers of severe weather and other disasters that threaten your area.
- Some natural disasters, including lightning strikes, earthquakes, and volcanic eruptions, can cause house fires. Have a meeting place just outside the home where you can check that everyone is safely out of the building in the event of a fire.
- Arrange a second meeting place some distance away, such as at a friend's or relative's home, should you have to leave the immediate area. Make sure that everyone has the address and telephone number.
- Choose at least two escape routes from your home and each room.
- Identify safe places in your home where you could take shelter if you are advised to stay indoors or if you do not have time to leave before a disaster strikes.
- Make a family evacuation plan (p.224).
- Discuss how to make contact and reunite family members should a disaster occur when you are not all at home together.

UNDERSTANDING EARLY WARNINGS

- If you live in a hurricane or tornado zone, be prepared for a "watch" (indicates possible disaster) and then a "warning" (indicates probable or imminent disaster) as the hurricane or tornado approaches your area.
- If you live in a tsunami area, an "advisory" is the first alert, followed by a "watch" (possible) and "warning" (imminent).

- If you live in an area prone to flooding, a "watch" (possible) may be followed by a "warning" (imminent) and then a "severe warning" (imminent and severe).
- In areas of particular risk, there may be a system for sending warning messages by telephone, fax, or pager directly to people whose homes are threatened.

EVACUATING SAFELY

1 Follow instructions

- Prepare to evacuate if you are told to do so by your city/town council or emergency services, or if you feel in danger in your own home.
- Follow evacuation instructions carefully: there may be limits on what you can take with you.

2 Gather family members

- Assemble family members quickly, collect your disaster emergency kit (p.225), and decide whether you should leave by car or go on foot.
- Help the elderly and children evacuate. Leaving home in a disaster situation is distressing, so remain calm and be reassuring. Older people might require particular help, such as the aid of a wheelchair.
- Put small pets into pet carriers; take dogs with you in the car or put them on leashes if you are on foot.

3 Take precautions

- If high winds are forecasted, bring children's play equipment and garden furniture indoors (p.222).
- Call the friend/relative whose home serves as your second point of contact in your evacuation plan. Explain where you are going.
- Use telephones and cellular phones only if it is essential to get in touch with family or friends; otherwise, keep lines free for emergency calls.
- Always turn off the gas, electricity, and water before leaving.
- Close and lock all your external doors and windows as you leave, including doors to outbuildings.

4 Be a good neighbor

- Make sure that your neighbors are aware of the need to evacuate.
- Help elderly or disabled neighbors who may be unable to evacuate without your assistance.

PREPARING A DISASTER EMERGENCY KIT

1 Organize basic items

- List the items you would need to take with you in an evacuation (see p.225 for suggestions).
- The amount of equipment you will need depends on the type and extent of disaster likely to affect your area.
- Assemble these items.
- Encourage your children to help with the planning and packing of your family emergency kit.

2 Consider extras

- If your area is at risk of a major disaster, you may well have to survive outside for several days. Plan to take water-purifying tablets. Have garbage bags and a plastic bucket with a lid (to be used as a toilet) and rolls of toilet paper.
- If you live near a volcano, add a disposable dust mask and goggles for each family member.
- If you have a small pet, keep a pet carrier.

3 Keep kit ready

- Keep your disaster emergency kit in a safe, accessible place, such as in the garage, and ensure that all family members know where it is.
- Practice evacuating your home; loading the kit into the car, and leaving as quickly as possible.
- Replace your water supplies every 6 months and regularly check the sell-by dates of all foods.
- Test batteries regularly.
- Note the expiration dates of first-aid and prescription medicines. Replace those that have expired.

4 Assess situation

- If evacuating by car, load your kit into the trunk.
- If evacuating on foot, decide how much of the kit your family can carry.
- In the case of a mass evacuation, emergency shelter will be provided in local community buildings. In such situations you do not need to take food, water, or bedding.
- In situations where it may be some time before you can return home, take plenty of clothing and toys or games to keep children busy.

DISASTER EMERGENCY KIT

MEDICAL EQUIPMENT
Pack a first-aid kit and any over-the-counter or prescription medicines needed

FLASHLIGHTS AND BATTERIES
Have one flashlight per family member, plus plenty of spare batteries

CANDLES AND MATCHES
These are for backup lighting during a prolonged poweroutage

BATTERY-POWERED RADIO
Use this for news of the disaster and emergency radio broadcasts

WATER
Store 8 pints (4.5 liters) of water per person per day

FOOD AND CAN OPENER
Store enough canned or dried food for 3 days

FAMILY DOCUMENTS
Keep passports and family documents in a waterproof wallet with emergency money

BEDDING
Keep one sleeping bag or blanket per person for sleeping outside

BABY FOOD AND MILK
Take jars, cans, formula mixes, bottles and spoons

DIAPERS AND CREAMS
Keep supplies of disposable diapers and diaper cream

SHOES AND CLOTHES
Keep a change of footwear and clothing for each person

RAINWEAR
Have a lightweight, waterproof jacket for each family member

Severe storm

➤ For FLOOD see p.228

High winds during a severe storm can cause damage to roofing, chimneys, and windows, while heavy rain can cause leakage and flooding. Lightning can also be dangerous if you are out in the open. But there are steps you can take to cope with and protect against storms and lasting damage.

COPING WITH A SEVERE STORM

1 Take precautions

- Stay inside during the storm.
- Fasten doors and windows tightly and check that doors to garden sheds and garages are also secure.
- Keep flashlights, candles, and matches in case of power outages.
- If a thunderstorm is on the way, disconnect television antennae and unplug computers and televisions. Power surges from lightning can start fires and cause considerable damage.
- Keep some buckets that you can place under ceiling leaks if the roof is damaged.
- Store garden furniture.

Take inside anything that could be damaged by the storm

2 Deal with leaks

- Water dripping through the ceiling indicates that the roof is damaged or that flashing has worked loose, allowing water to seep through.
- Place buckets under the drips and go into the attic to look for a leak.
- If a roof tile or slate is damaged or missing, make a temporary repair with plastic sheeting (p.206).
- If water is coming in around the chimney stack, repair or replace flashing after the storm (p.206).
- If water is pooling outside your house, use a stiff broom to sweep it away, preferably downhill.
- If the water continues to rise, block all gaps under and around doors with sandbags (p.228).

3 Minimize damage

- If a window is blown in, move valuables out of that room. Block the window with boarding, nailing it from the inside. Alternatively, move a large piece of furniture, such as a wardrobe, in front of it.
- If a chimney stack is blown off, water may find its way down the chimney. Use boards to block all fireplaces, preventing rubble from coming down into the room.

BEING OUTSIDE IN LIGHTNING

1 Get to safety

- If you are out in a lightning storm, seek shelter in a low area, such as a ditch or hillside, away from tall trees and poles, and water.
- Remember that any thunderstorm may produce lightning.
- Stay far away from metal objects, such as fences or pylons, which pose a particular danger: lightning sparks can arc off metal, and strike anyone standing nearby.
- If you are riding a bicycle, get off, leave the bicycle, and take shelter.
- If you are riding a horse, get off, tether the horse safely to whatever is available, then seek shelter.
- If you are in a car with a metal roof, stay where you are: the car's metal shell and rubber wheels will protect you.
- If you are out in a boat, head for land immediately.

DO'S AND DON'TS

DO	DON'T
• Get to open land.	• Stand on high ground, such as on top of a hill.
• Stay away from tall trees or rocks.	• Think that you are protected by wearing rubber-soled shoes or boots.
• Get as small and low you can.	
• Protect your head from a possible strike.	• Kneel or sit down on wet material.
• Stay in your car if you can.	• Carry metal objects.

2 Protect yourself

- Do not carry anything with a metal rod, such as an umbrella or golf club, that might conduct lightning.
- If you feel your hair stand on end, lightning is about to strike.
- If you are near trees or rocks, run for open ground, if you have time. Kneel down, bend forward to protect your head, and put your hands on your knees.
  - It is important to protect your head, the most vulnerable part of the body, and to minimize contact with the ground.

Keep your head lower than the rest of your body

! If someone is struck by lightning

- A bolt of lightning can be fatal if it strikes someone on the head and then travels down to the ground. It can also cause severe burns, broken bones, cuts, and unconsciousness; and it can set clothing on fire.
- Do not touch someone who has been struck by lightning if he or she is very wet or in water: you could be electrocuted because the electrical discharge is still within his or her body.
- Dial 911 or call EMS immediately, even if the person appears to be unharmed.
- If the person's clothing is on fire, follow the instructions on p.182.
- Treat the burns (pp.48–9).
- If the person is not breathing, start rescue breathing (pp.16–17).
- If the person has no signs of circulation, start CPR (pp.18–20).

Flood

◀ For SEVERE STORM see p.226   ▶ For TSUNAMI see p.242
Heavy rainfall, melting snows, rivers changing course, dams collapsing, and high tides in coastal areas can all cause floods. If you live in an area prone to flooding, know the difference between a "flood watch" (flooding is possible), a "flood warning" (flooding is expected), and a "severe flood warning" (severe flooding is expected). Take the necessary measures to protect your family and home.

PREPARING FOR A FLOOD

1 Plan ahead

- Contact your city/town council to find out the height to which a flood could rise.
- Be alert to flood warnings issued by weather forecasters and the Environmental Protection Agency.
- Keep enough bricks with which to raise wooden or upholstered furniture off the floor and out of the flood water.
- Buy sandbags and sand if water is likely to rise above door level.
- Keep your important documents in plastic wallets in a safe place.

2 Prepare home

- Block all gaps under and around external doors with sandbags (see box below).
- If flood water is expected to rise up to window height, place sandbags along windowsills too.
- Take up your carpets and store them upstairs along with all the valuables you can move.
- Fill clean baths, sinks, and plastic bottles with cold water.
- Turn off electricity and gas supplies; flooded wiring can cause fires.
- Use bricks to raise furniture.

PROTECTING YOUR HOME WITH SANDBAGS

- Use sandbags to seal entry points around doors and vents. Also seal windows if the water is likely to rise that high.
- Half-fill the sandbag casings with sand. If you run out of casings, make your own from plastic shopping bags, pillow cases, or even stockings.
- Place the first row of bags in position, butting them up against each other, end to end, and then stomp down on them to mould the ends together.
- Lay the second row on top, staggering the bags, and stomping down on them to mould them into the row below. This will prevent seepage through gaps.
- If your wall of sandbags needs to be three or four layers, lay two rows side by side, followed by a second double row, then one or more single rows on top.

Using sandbags
Lay the second row of bags in place, staggering the bags over the first row in a brickworklike formation.

SURVIVING A FLOOD

1 Stay inside

- If you can, move upstairs, taking with you food, water, emergency supplies, pets, valuables, and important papers.

Take plenty of water with you

Take small pets upstairs in pet carriers

If your child is upset by the flood, carry her to safety

- If flood water rises quickly, leaving you no time to move your valuables upstairs, put them on high shelves to keep them out of the water.
- Be aware that flood water can weaken structural foundations, causing buildings to sink, floors to crack and, in severe cases, walls to collapse. Regularly check for cracks in what you can see of your walls, floors, doors, staircases, and windows.
- Listen to your radio for updated local information and follow all official instructions.
- Observe outside water levels to see how fast the flood is rising.
- Use your drinking water supply until you are told that the main water is safe to drink.

2 Evacuation

- If you are told to evacuate, follow the instructions carefully.
- In addition to taking your disaster emergency kit (p.225), take all the clothing you can. It may be days or, in some situations, weeks before you are able to return home.

3 Signal for help

- If the water has risen to the point that you are unable to leave safely on foot, or you feel that your life is in danger if you stay where you are, signal for help.
- Lean out of an upstairs window or climb onto the roof and call for help by shouting and/or waving something bright.

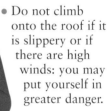

- Do not climb onto the roof if it is slippery or if there are high winds: you may put yourself in greater danger.

Attract attention by shouting and waving

! If you are outside

- Be very careful when walking through flood water: just 6 in (15 cm) of fast-flowing water can unbalance you and cause you to fall.
- If possible, use a stick to feel the ground before you step on it: hazards hidden under the water could be highly dangerous.
- Avoid riverbanks and sand dunes, which could collapse. Also beware of large waves.
- Minimize contact with flood water: it could be contaminated with sewage.

Extreme cold

Heavy snowfall and very low temperatures can produce difficult conditions both in the home and outside, especially if cold weather is prolonged. Prepare for wintry conditions well in advance by checking in summer or early autumn that your house is well-insulated. During a freeze, keep warm, stay safe, indoors if you can, and be a good neighbor to the elderly or frail.

PREPARING FOR EXTREME COLD

1 Check insulation

- Attach self-adhesive foam strips around loose-fitting doors and windows to prevent drafts.
- Fit draft protectors across the bottoms of external doors.
- Hang a heavy curtain at the front door to keep the hall draft-free.
- To improve insulation, secure sheets of glass in frames across single glazed windows. Alternatively, use a special heat-sensitive plastic film as a temporary measure (see box right); the film is cheaper, but less efficient.
- Check that outdoor pipes and faucets are properly insulated.
- Check that the attic, and pipes and water tanks within it, are well insulated.

2 Check heating

- Before winter arrives, turn on your central heating to check that it works. If you discover problems see p.192 for advice.
- Stick aluminum foil sheets behind radiators to reflect heat back into the room. This is particularly important for radiators against external walls.

3 Take precautions

- Buy low-wattage electric heaters that you can leave on overnight to keep rooms above freezing.
- If you depend on electricity, buy a portable gas heater to use should power lines come down.
- If you have a wood or coal fireplace, stock up on fuel and matches.
- Maintain medicine supplies.
- If your stove is electric, stock up on foods that do not need cooking.

TEMPORARY INSULATION

Attach lengths of tape

Apply adhesive tape
Attach lengths of double-sided adhesive tape down the sides and across the top and bottom of the window. Allow adhesive to harden for 1 hour.

Keep the hairdryer moving to smooth film

Stretch plastic
Press heat-sensitive plastic film across the window and onto the adhesive strips. Hold a hairdryer a few inches away and warm the plastic until the film is quite taut.

SURVIVING EXTREME COLD

1 Stay warm

- Keep the heating on day and night at a low setting so that your home does not become cold and water pipes do not freeze. Alternatively, use low-wattage electric heaters.
- If you are worried about costly fuel bills, heat only the rooms that you need to use, and close the doors to unheated rooms.
- Close the curtains to keep the heat in, but air rooms daily so that they do not become stuffy.

2 Stay inside

- When outside conditions are icy, do not venture outside unless need be. If you must go out, see the box on the right for sensible advice.
- Do not drive unless absolutely necessary. If you will be driving on rural or hilly terrain, go prepared to be caught in a snowdrift or blizzard (see below).
- Check that you have a cold-weather kit (see box right) in your car in case of emergency.
- Always take a cellular phone, whether you are on foot or in a car.
- If you live in an avalanche area and an avalanche warning is issued, stay inside unless told to evacuate.

IF YOU HAVE TO GO OUT

- Dress warmly in layers of light clothing, a jacket or coat, hat, scarf, and gloves.
- Wear sturdy boots with deep treads. Be careful to take small, firm steps; point your toes inward on downhill slopes and bend your knees slightly if the going is steep.
- Be careful on icy surfaces; try to find something, such as a railing, to hold onto.
- Be particularly careful if you are elderly: brittle bones fracture easily.

Cover your hands and head

Preventing heat loss
A hat is the most important item of clothing, because most body heat is lost through the head

ESSENTIALS

COLD-WEATHER CAR KIT
- Shovel
- Blankets and coats
- Gravel or canvas
- Flashlight, batteries
- High-energy food
- Water

! If your car gets stuck in snow

- Drive very slowly backward and forward, moving only slightly each time, allowing your car to gradually make a track for itself.
- If this does not work, use a shovel to clear away snow from around the wheels, then put down gravel or canvas to give the tires something to grip. Drive forward very slowly. Once the car is clear of the snow, drive until you have reached safety.

- If you are unable to move the car, do not try to walk to safety: stay inside the vehicle.
- Wrap yourself in blankets or newspaper.
- Turn on the engine and run the heater for 10 minutes every hour to conserve gasoline.
- Open a window occasionally to let in air.
- Try to stay awake; the risk of hypothermia (p.54) is greater if you fall asleep.

Wildfire

Most wildfires, which include bushfires and fires in woods, forests, and prairies, occur in hot, dry weather. These fires can spread rapidly, covering vast areas, and once they have taken hold, are very difficult to control. Protect your home against wildfire by creating a safety zone, take sensible precautions to safeguard your family, and know what to do in the event of wildfire.

PROTECTING AGAINST WILDFIRE

1 Create a safe zone

- Remove all flammable vegetation, dead branches, leaves, and twigs, and mow grass within 30 ft (9 m) of your home (100 ft/30 m if you live in a pine forest).
- Keep this zone clear to ensure that wildfires will have little to burn and pass by your house instead.
- Consider felling trees other than fire-resistant hardwoods, such as oak, beech, or ash, inside the zone.
- Store flammable items, such as old newspapers, firewood, and wooden garden furniture, well outside the safety zone.

2 Be prepared

- Make sure that gutters and drains are clear of debris (p.207).
- Install a garden hose that is long enough to reach the full extent of your house and garden.
- Store in a handy, safe place tools, such as brushes and spades, that could be used to beat out fire.
- Plan several escape routes from your home by car and by foot.
- Arrange to stay elsewhere in case you have to evacuate the area.
- Keep plenty of fuel in your car so that you can escape quickly in the event of an emergency.

SURVIVING WILDFIRE

1 Be ready to evacuate

- If a wildfire appears to be heading in your direction, check that your car has ample fuel, then park it facing your main route of escape.
- Place your disaster emergency kit (p.225) in the trunk, then close all the doors and windows and leave your key in the ignition.
- Assemble your pets and fire tools (see Be prepared, above).

2 Protect your home

- Bring wooden garden furniture inside the house, if necessary.
- Use your garden hose to soak both the safety zone and the house.
- Close all the windows, doors, and air vents. Draw heavy curtains, pull down blinds, and take down any lightweight curtains.
- Move flammable furniture into the center of the house, away from any windows and glass doors.

3 Get to safety

- Keep the radio on and listen for updated local information and official instructions.
- If you are told to evacuate, follow the instructions carefully.

- Put on a hat and gloves, strong shoes, and cotton or woolen clothing that covers your arms and legs.

Take a brush to beat out small fires

Wear gloves to protect your hands

Wear your sturdiest shoes

- Take your pets, disaster emergency kit, and fire tools with you.
- Choose a planned route that will take you away from the fire, but be alert to changes in the fire's speed and direction.

4 Use your car as protection

- If you are overtaken by flames when in the car, stay inside your vehicle. You are safer inside your car than outside in the thick smoke and fierce heat, even with the risk that the fuel tank may explode.
- Explain to any passengers the risks of leaving the car.

5 Follow official instructions

- Do not return home until you have been given the all-clear.
- When you are allowed to return home, proceed with caution – small fires may still be blazing.
- As a precaution against more fires, resoak your house and the entire safety zone with water.
- If your house has been damaged by fire, check with the fire department that it is safe to enter the building.
- If necessary, arrange temporary accommodation elsewhere.
- If the fire has passed by your house, check for any smoke damage that may call for an insurance claim. Take photographs, if you can, to support future claims.

! If you are outside

- Try to run diagonally away from the fire to get out of its path. Aim for an open area; a road, or a river, if possible. If the fire comes close, lay down, curl into a ball, and cover your head, hands, and as much of your body as possible with a jacket.
- If your clothing catches fire, quickly smother the flames with a coat and then roll around on the ground to extinguish them (p.182).

Emergency action
If fire is blocking all your escape routes, head for a dip or hollow and roll into a ball.

Hurricane

◀ For FLOOD see p.228   ▶ For TORNADO see p.236

Hurricanes are extremely violent storms that produce torrential rain and strong winds of up to 190 mph (305 km/h). Tornadoes may occur simultaneously or in the hurricane's wake. Flooding may also follow. Many hurricanes can be predicted, enabling people to protect their homes and evacuate their families in good time. If you live in an area that is prone to hurricanes, make sure that you know the difference between a "hurricane watch" (a hurricane is possible within 36 hours) and a "hurricane warning" (a hurricane is likely within 24 hours).

PREPARING FOR A HURRICANE

1 Plan ahead

- Install hurricane shutters or buy sheets of plywood and strips of wood for boarding windows (see box below). Nail the frames in position and prepare the plywood sheets for installation when necessary.
- Know the location of the nearest hurricane shelter.

2 Take precautions

- Keep alert for a "hurricane watch" and listen to local radio stations for updates on the situation.
- If a "hurricane watch" turns into a "hurricane warning," make final adjustments to your home.
- Choose a safe part of the house where family members can gather, ideally in a room in the center of the house (such as a hallway) that does not have windows.
- Close the hurricane shutters or fix boards in place (see box right).
- Secure external and garage doors.
- Fill clean baths, sinks, containers, and plastic bottles with water to ensure an uncontaminated supply.

3 Get to safety

- If you live in a mobile home, leave immediately and head toward a hurricane shelter or open ground.
- If you live in a house and you are advised to evacuate, follow all the instructions carefully.
- Avoid coastal and riverside roads on your way to a hurricane shelter: these routes may be flooded.

BOARDING WINDOWS

Predrill screw holes

Secure frame in place

Make outer frame
Cut strips of wood to fit around the outside of the window frame. Predrill with holes 6 in (15 cm) apart. Nail the strips in place to form a frame.

Screw board in place

Align screw holes

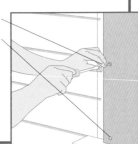

Attach cover
Cut sheets of ½-in (1-cm) plywood to fit window frame. Predrill holes to align with the frame. Screw cover in place.

DURING A HURRICANE

1 Stay informed

- Keep your radio on and listen for updated local information and official instructions. You may be asked to turn off utilities or to evacuate at any point.
- If you are advised to evacuate, follow all the instructions carefully.

2 Stay indoors

- Do not evacuate unless advised to do so, or you feel that it would endanger life to remain at home.
- Close all interior doors and place doorstops under them.
- Close all curtains and blinds.
- Turn off major appliances if advised to do so, or if power fails.
- Make sure that all household pets are inside and keep them in pet carriers with adequate water.
- Go to your chosen safe place and stay under a table, if there is one.
- If you feel that the house is starting to collapse around you, try to move quickly under a sturdy bed or a pile of mattresses; if there is no time to move, stay under the table.

3 Stay safe

- Be aware that when the eye of the storm passes overhead, it may appear that a hurricane is over. However, winds will start blowing again from the opposite direction within the hour; this can often be the worst part of the storm.
- Listen for warnings of tornadoes (p.236) or severe flooding (p.228), both of which often occur in the wake of a hurricane.
- Stay where you are until you are sure that the hurricane has passed.

! If you are outside

- Lie flat on the ground and crawl on your stomach to shelter, such as an outcrop of rock, a ditch, or a low wall.
- Cover your head with your hands or a coat.
- Do not take shelter close to trees because branches may break off or trees may even be uprooted, and fall on top of you.
- During the eye of the storm, move to the other side of your shelter, since the wind will now come from the opposite direction.
- After the winds die down, wait for at least 1½ hours before leaving your shelter.

HELPING CHILDREN COPE

Children may find a hurricane terrifying, especially if their home and belongings are damaged or an evacuation is necessary. To help them feel more secure, try the following.

- Explain that a hurricane is a very bad storm and that the family might need to go to a safer building.
- Ask children to help you with simple tasks.

- Take playthings, such as cards, into the safe room or hurricane shelter to keep children busy.
- Write each child's name, address, and contact number on a piece of paper and place it in the child's pocket.

Comforting children
Reassure young children and calm their fears by holding them and giving them plenty of attention.

Tornado

◀ For **SEVERE STORM** see p.226 ▶ For **HURRICANE** see p.234

Tornadoes, tall columns of spinning air moving at high speeds, can cause immense damage. Tornadoes usually occur in warm, humid, unsettled weather, but they can develop anywhere at any time, particularly after a thunderstorm or hurricane. If you live in a tornado area, make sure that you are familiar with the early warning system: a "tornado watch" indicates that a tornado is possible; and a "tornado warning" that a tornado has been seen and could be heading in your direction. Depending on the severity and path of the tornado, either stay under shelter or evacuate your home.

PREPARING FOR A TORNADO

1 Take precautions

- Keep alert for a "tornado watch" and listen to local radio stations for updates.
- Close hurricane shutters or board your windows (p.234) to protect yourself from flying glass (but see point 2 below).
- Choose a safe part of your house where family members can gather if a tornado is on the way (p.234, Take precautions).
- Fill clean baths, sinks, containers, and plastic bottles with water to ensure an uncontaminated supply.
- Fill your vehicle's tank with fuel.

2 Listen for warning

- If a "tornado watch" turns into a "tornado warning," be prepared to evacuate your home. If you are in a car, van, or mobile home, get out (see Stay safe, p.237).
- If warnings predict that your home will be in the tornado's direct path, open doors, shutters, and windows on the side away from the storm to prevent a buildup of air pressure.

3 Get to safety

- If you are told to evacuate, follow the instructions carefully.
- Act promptly, but calmly. You may have only a short time to get to the nearest hurricane shelter.

SIGNS AND WARNINGS

- Certain changes in weather conditions, such as blowing debris or a sudden wind drop and unusually still air, may herald a tornado.
- In some circumstances, a low rumbling noise, the sound of an approaching tornado, may be audible.
- Tornadoes can be seen approaching, often from a great distance, moving at speeds of up to 30–40 mph (50–60 km/h).
- A tall funnel shape of whirling air and dust will descend from underneath a storm cloud.

Violent tornado
The characteristic twisting funnel of air and dust indicates an approaching tornado.

DURING A TORNADO

1 Stay safe

- If a "tornado watch" turns into a "tornado warning" but you are advised not to evacuate, go to your chosen safe place in your house.
- Protect yourself and your family by crawling under a heavy piece of furniture, such as a table or desk.
- If you are unable to hide under furniture, sit down in the center of the room and protect your head with your arms.
- If you are in a car, van, or mobile home, get out at once and head for open ground. Lie down flat and cover your head. Vehicles can be picked up by a forceful tornado and then dropped again, so they are not safe places for shelter.

2 Stay informed

- Listen to your radio for updated local information and official instructions. You may be asked to turn off utilities or evacuate if the tornado alters course.
- If you are advised to evacuate, follow all instructions carefully.

3 Return home

- Once the tornado has passed, wait at least 5 minutes before leaving your place of shelter.

Choose a sturdy piece of furniture as your shelter

Take your radio with you to stay informed

! If you are outside

- Find the nearest sturdy building and head for the basement or lay down on the ground floor.
- If you are close to a bridge, get underneath it.
- If there is no obvious shelter, lie flat on the ground, away from trees or structures that could collapse, and ideally in a ditch. Cover your head with your hands.
- Be aware of the dangers of flying objects, falling trees, buildings that may collapse, and damaged power lines.

- If you are in a car, do not try to outdrive a tornado: if it changes course you will be in danger of being picked up in your vehicle.
- Get out of the car immediately and either find shelter or lie in a ditch or other low-lying land with your hands over your head.

Protecting yourself
If you are unable to locate a shelter, find a low-lying area and lie down, taking care to protect your head.

Protect your head from flying debris

Earthquake

◄ For **WILDFIRE** see p.232 ► For **TSUNAMI** see p.242

Earthquakes may strike along fault lines without warning, causing deaths and major damage. Often quakes last for only seconds, but in that time, they can destroy buildings and roads, and crush people. Fires resulting from broken gas pipes can rage for days afterward, and aftershocks are a further danger. If you live in an earthquake area, prepare your home as best you can.

PREPARING FOR AN EARTHQUAKE

1 Identify potential hazards

- Check structural elements in your home (see p.222) to ensure that they are sound and see that heavy furniture is secure (see box below).
- Place large, heavy objects on lower shelves and rehang heavy mirrors or pictures that are currently positioned over seating or beds.
- Store fragile items in low cabinets that are fitted with latches or locks.

2 Identify safe places

- In every room, identify safe spots where you could take shelter. Ideal places are under sturdy desks, tables or strong internal doorway wells away from windows, or places where glass could shatter.
- Identify at least one safe outdoor location that you could escape to if necessary. Try to find a spot that is out in the open, well away from buildings, trees, power lines, and elevated roads and bridges, all of which are dangerous because they could fall or collapse.
- Make sure that every member of your family knows what to do in the event of an earthquake (p.239).

3 Be ready

- Be alert for small tremors, known as foreshocks. These indicate that a larger earthquake is on its way. If you do feel a foreshock, warn family members and head for a safe location at once.
- Be prepared to experience a ripple of aftershocks following the main earthquake. These aftershocks can also be severe and may cause additional damage.

SECURING FURNITURE

Screw the bracket into the wall and the bookcase

Attach furniture
Attach exterior angle brackets at the top or sides of tall furniture like bookcases and wardrobes

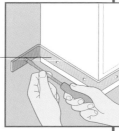

Attach steel straps at top and bottom of the boiler to secure it to the wall

Secure boiler
Use galvanized steel straps, with holes punched through them, to attach a boiler to the wall

DURING AN EARTHQUAKE

1 Take cover

- If you feel the ground shake, drop under a heavy desk or table, press your face against your arm to protect your eyes, and hold on.
- If you cannot reach a table, take shelter in an internal doorway.

Brace yourself against a support

Cover your eyes with your arm

- If you cannot move quickly to a safe place, stay where you are but keep well away from windows.
- If you are in bed, stay there and protect your head with a pillow.
- Stay exactly where you are until the shaking stops.

2 Expect aftershocks

- Put out candles or naked flames in case of gas leaks. If you smell gas, turn off the supply at the main.
- Each time you feel an aftershock, take cover and hold on, as before.
- Be aware that aftershocks can topple structures already weakened by earthquakes. Inspect your home for damage after each aftershock, and move everyone out of the building quickly if you suspect that it is unsafe.

DO'S AND DON'TS

DO	DON'T
• Keep away from windows: they could be shattered.	• Use stairs or elevators.
	• Run into the street: falling bricks or glass could injure you.
• Take cover wherever you are.	
• Stay away from items that might fall on you, such as tall furniture.	• Think that you are safe once the ground stops shaking: always expect aftershocks.
• Put out cigarettes in case of gas leaks.	• Use telephones unless the call is essential.

3 Stay safe

- If you are outside, do not go back into your home until it has been checked for structural safety.
- If you are inside and your home seems to be structurally sound, wait there until you are given the official all-clear. Then, prepare to leave. Stay elsewhere until your home has been checked by a professional.
- Check everyone for injuries and give first-aid treatment as necessary.
- If water pipes are damaged, turn off your supply at the main.
- If you can smell gas or suspect that electrical wiring is damaged, turn off supplies at the main.
- Keep listening to your radio for official instructions.

! If you are outside

- Lie down as far away as possible from buildings, trees, and power lines, or seek shelter in a doorway. Stay where you are until the shaking stops.
- Do not go into any form of underground shelter, such as a cellar or tunnel, because it could collapse.
- If you are driving, stop your car carefully and stay in your car until the shaking stops.

Volcanic eruption

◄ For **EARTHQUAKE** see p.238 ► For **TSUNAMI** see p.242

Often with little or no warning, volcanoes erupt, sending molten lava and mud flowing down the sides, clouds of ash billowing into the sky, and rock fragments hurtling down to earth. You increase your chances of escaping unharmed if you leave the area as soon as you are advised to do so.

ESCAPING A VOLCANIC ERUPTION

1 Be prepared

- If you live anywhere near a volcano, whether it is dormant or active, keep a pair of goggles and a disposable dust mask for each family member.

VOLCANO

- Make sure that you have planned at least two routes out of the area, and arranged a place to meet family members.

! Warning signs

Professional vulcanologists study grumbling volcanos for indications of activity. The following are all warning signs that a volcano is active and about to erupt:

- An increase in seismic activity, ranging from minor tremors to earthquakes.
- Rumbling noises coming from the volcano.
- A cloud of steam hanging over the top of the volcano.
- A smell of sulfur from local rivers.
- Falls of acidic rain.
- Fine dust suspended in the sky.
- Occasional bursts of hot gases or ash from the volcano top.

2 Evacuate

- If a volcano erupts without advance warning, you may be advised to evacuate the area, in which case you should leave immediately. Make sure that you follow all evacuation instructions carefully.
- Put on goggles and a disposable dust mask. If you do not have a mask, then improvise by wrapping either a wet scarf or handkerchief around your face.
- To avoid skin irritation caused by ashfall, put on clothing that covers your entire body.

Goggles protect the eyes; make sure they fit snugly

Wear a mask to protect against poisonous gases and dust

- Avoid areas that are downwind of the volcano because burning hot ash and clouds of gases may be blown in your direction.
- Avoid river valleys and low-lying areas, where mudflows may occur.

DURING A VOLCANIC ERUPTION

1 Follow instructions

- If a volcano erupts while you are at home, make sure that all family members and household pets are accounted for, and close all your doors, windows, and vents.
- If you are not advised to evacuate, stay inside.
- Listen to your radio for official instructions. A period of calm may follow an eruption. Be prepared because you may be told to leave then to escape further eruptions.

! If you are outside

- Try to get inside a building.
- If you are caught in a rock fall, roll into a ball to protect your head.
- If you suspect that you are in the path of a nuée ardente (see box below), you can survive only by finding shelter underground or submerging yourself in water. The danger usually passes in just 30 seconds.
- If you are caught near a stream, beware of mudflows (see box below). Do not cross a bridge if a mudflow is moving beneath it because the bridge could be swept away.

2 Beware of ashfall

- If you have breathing problems, such as asthma, stay inside.
- Press damp towels firmly around doors and windows, and any other draft sources.
- Avoid driving: heavy ashfall clogs engines, often causing cars to stall.
- Clear volcanic ash from the roof of your house: its weight can cause buildings to collapse. Be careful when working on the roof, and put on protective clothing, goggles, and a dust mask before going out.

3 Stay safe

- If you were evacuated, stay out of any restricted areas until you are given the official all-clear.
- Be aware that mudflows, ashfall, flash floods, and wildfires can reach you even if you are far from the volcano and are unable to see it.
- When you return home, or if you never left, dampen and clean up ash that has settled around the house, being careful not to wash it into drains. Put on your protective clothing, goggles, and a dust mask.

UNDERSTANDING THE DANGERS

- Ash and other debris rain down from the sky, covering buildings, land, and people.
- Debris flows are a mixture of water and volcanic debris that flows down the volcano sides. They can travel long distances and destroy whole villages.
- Mudflows are fast-moving rivers of mud that flow from volcanoes down river valleys and over low-lying areas.

- Lava flows are fairly unlikely to kill you because they move slowly, but anything that stands in their path will be burned, crushed, or buried.
- Pyroclastic surges are mixtures of rock fragments and hot gases that move rapidly across land like hurricanes. Anyone caught in their paths is likely to be burned, asphyxiated, or crushed.

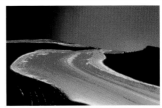

RED-HOT LAVA FLOW

- Nuées ardentes are rapidly moving, red-hot clouds of ash, gas, and rock fragments that flow down the side of a volcano at speeds of over 100 mph (160 km/h).

Tsunami

◄ For **FLOOD** see p.228   ◄ For **EARTHQUAKE** see p.238

An earthquake, volcanic eruption, or underwater landslide can cause a tsunami: a series of underwater waves that sweep towards shore, sometimes rising to heights of over 100 ft (30 m), and causing immense damage. A "tsunami advisory" indicates that a tsunami is possible; a "tsunami watch" that a tsunami may be 2 hours away; and a "tsunami warning" that giant waves may be imminent. If you live within 2 miles (3.2 km) of the shore and your house stands less than 100 ft (30 m) above sea level, evacuate as soon as you receive a "tsunami warning" and move to high ground as far inland as you can go.

PREPARING FOR A TSUNAMI

1 Be aware

- Keep alert for a "tsunami advisory" or "tsunami watch," and listen to local radio stations for updates.
- Check that your planned escape route is clear.
- Familiarize yourself with warning signs, such as a sudden change in the level of coastal waters.
- Tsunamis often cause severe floods; make sure that you are prepared to cope (p.228).

2 Take precautions

- Keep your car filled with fuel so that you can drive to safety at a moment's notice.
- If a "tsunami watch" turns into a "tsunami warning," prepare to evacuate your home.
- Coastal areas within 1 mile (1.6 km) of the sea and less than 25 ft (7.5 m) above sea level are most at risk; make an early assessment of the best route to higher ground.

UNDERSTANDING TSUNAMIS

- Earthquakes, underwater landslides, or volcanic eruptions can cause tsunamis.
- Each tsunami consists of a series of waves travelling at speeds of up to 600 mph (970 km/h).
- These waves are hundreds of miles (kilometers) long but only a few feet (about a meter) "tall" as they travel the ocean floor. Hence, they cannot be detected from the air or at sea until they near the shore.
- Seismic activity may be the only advance warning of an approaching tsunami.
- As the tsunami nears the coast, the waves slow down and increase in height.
- Before the first wave reaches the shore, the sea may be dramatically "sucked" away from the shoreline.
- Successive waves appear at intervals of 5 to 90 minutes.
- The first wave is usually not the largest; the following ones cause the most damage.

Sea-borne disaster
Vast sea waves crash onto the shore, causing damage and claiming lives.

DURING A TSUNAMI

1 Get to safety

- If you are advised to evacuate, follow all instructions carefully and leave as quickly as possible.
- Go to your planned evacuation place or follow instructions for a recommended evacuation route, if issued. Your place of safety should be at least 100 ft (30 m) above sea level or 2 miles (3.2 km) inland.

2 Stay informed

- Keep listening to your radio for updated local information and official instructions.
- Stay inland and on high ground until the official all-clear is given.

- Be aware that a tsunami is not just one wave, but a series of waves, so the risk of danger may continue for hours. People who return to their homes after the first wave (often not the biggest) risk drowning.

3 Check damage

- When you are allowed to return to your home, inspect the structure of the building carefully for cracks or weaknesses. Tsunami waters often damage foundations and walls.
- Enter cautiously because there may be hazards hidden under the water.
- Check for potential fire hazards, such as broken gas pipes or flooded electrical circuits.

! If you feel an earthquake on the coast

- Drop to the ground, crawl to a sturdy shelter, if possible, and put your hands over your head to protect it.
- When the shaking stops, gather your family and evacuate. Move inland and to higher ground as quickly as possible: a tsunami may be only minutes away.
- Stay away from any structures that may have been weakened by the earthquake.
- Do not leave your place of safety until an official all-clear has been issued.

4 Stay safe

- Do not use tap water unless you have been officially advised that it is safe to do so.
- Open doors and windows to help the building dry out.
- Inspect all your food and drink supplies and throw away wet items.
- If you smell gas, turn off the supply at the main, open your doors and windows, and leave at once.
- If electrical wiring has become wet or damaged, turn off the electricity supply at the main.

DO'S AND DON'TS

DO	DON'T
• Go as far inland and as high as you can to escape the water.	• Try to watch the giant waves come ashore.
• Be careful returning home: the tsunami may have caused structural damage.	• Leave your place of safety after the first wave: wait for the official all-clear before returning home.
• Use bottled water until you are told that tap water is safe.	• Enter your home with a naked flame: there may be a gas leak.

Post-disaster survival

Once a severe natural disaster is over, life may not return to normal for some time; in the case of an earthquake or volcanic eruption, it may be weeks before normal life resumes. In the meantime, keep out of danger, find temporary shelter, if necessary, and conserve food and water supplies. Check your home for damage, and find temporary accommodation if you suspect that it may be unsound.

ACTION PLAN

START

Are you in your home?

Yes

No

ACTION

IF YOU EVACUATED, WAIT UNTIL THE ALL-CLEAR BEFORE RETURNING HOME.

Is it safe to turn on main supplies (p.248)?

Yes

No

ACTION

TURN ON WATER AND ELECTRICITY AND GET YOUR GAS PROVIDER TO TURN ON THE GAS.

Are any family members injured?

Yes

No

Might your home have been damaged?

No

Yes

ACTION

CHECK FOR DAMAGE (p.248).

ACTION

GIVE APPROPRIATE FIRST AID (pp.8–63) AND SEEK MEDICAL HELP IF NEEDED.

Is the family together?

Yes

No

ACTION

TRY TO CONTACT MISSING MEMBERS OF THE FAMILY. MAKE ARRANGEMENTS FOR FAMILY MEMBERS UNABLE TO RETURN HOME (p.245).

ACTION

WAIT UNTIL THE SITUATION HAS IMPROVED OR SEEK ADVICE FROM YOUR SERVICE PROVIDERS.

IMMEDIATE AFTERMATH

1 Assess situation

- If the disaster was severe but you remained in your home, you will usually be advised to stay there unless you think that the building is structurally unsound.
- You are generally safer in your home, away from external dangers. By staying inside, you will not obstruct the emergency services.
- Check your home for minor damage, some of which you may be able to repair, and for the safety of main supplies (p.248).
- Listen to your radio or watch television (if you have electricity) to assess the scale of the disaster and its aftermath.
- If the incident had minor or no effects on your home and family, resume your normal daily activities, but be aware that nearby areas may have been more seriously affected and could be dangerous.

2 Treat injuries

- If any members of the family have been injured during the disaster, give them appropriate first-aid treatment (pp.8–63). Always seek medical help if injuries are severe.

3 Make contact

- If you have been separated from family members who were unable to find shelter in the house with you, you will want to make contact as soon as possible.
- Try to get in touch by cellular phone or call the friend or relative at the second emergency meeting place in your disaster plan (p.223).
- Keep calls to a minimum to avoid blocking lines badly needed by the emergency services.
- If you can move around safely in the local area, visit neighbors, especially the elderly or disabled, to see if they need help or supplies.
- If you were not at home when the disaster struck, contact family members as soon as possible to reassure them that you are safe.

4 Try to reach help

- If you or your family were not at home and now cannot get home, to your second meeting place, or to an evacuation shelter, you may have to survive outside until help arrives. (See pp.246–7 for advice on surviving outside.)

DEALING WITH STRANDED FAMILY MEMBERS

- If the disaster has caused local damage, such as roads blocked by fallen trees or flooding, school children may not be able to return home that evening. Ask a friend to collect them and keep them for the night.
- If the situation is severe, you may need to make arrangements for your children for a few days until travel is possible.

- If you cannot make contact with your stranded children for any reason, ask the emergency services for help.
- Family members working outside the immediate area may also be stranded and unable to return home. They will need to make alternative accommodation arrangements until the situation improves.

SURVIVING OUTSIDE

1 Avoid danger

- Any post-disaster area will be full of potential hazards, so stay alert and move around carefully.
- Keep well away from damaged power lines: high-voltage electricity is very dangerous and can cause electrocution and fire.
- Leaking gas pipes are also a danger. If you smell gas, you should leave the area immediately.
- If sewage pipes are damaged, there is the risk that raw sewage could spill out in the open, leading to the rapid spread of disease.
- Buildings that are unstable due to a natural disaster could topple at any time. Keep away from tall buildings and structures.

! Heat exposure

- Prolonged exposure to strong sunlight can lead to sunburn (p.50), heat exhaustion (p.51), heatstroke (p.52), and resulting illness.
- Move the victim of any of these conditions to a cool place.
- Cool sunburned skin with cold water and give the person cold drinks to sip.
- Symptoms of heat exhaustion are headache, dizziness, nausea, and rapid pulse. Give the person an isotonic drink or a weak salt and sugar solution (p.51).
- Symptoms of heatstroke are headache, dizziness, flushed skin, and, in serious cases, unconsciousness. Remove the victim's outer clothing, lay him or her down, then cool the skin by repeatedly sponging cold water over it.

! Cold exposure

- If the weather is very cold and you cannot find shelter, you are at risk of developing frostbite (p.55) and/or hypothermia (p.54).
- Symptoms of frostbite include "pins-and-needles," followed by numbness. Skin may be white, mottled and blue, or black.
- Symptoms of hypothermia include very cold skin, shivering, apathy, poor vision, and irritable behavior.
- For either condition, put the victim in a sleeping bag or wrap her in a survival blanket (covering the head too). Frostbitten fingers may be tucked under the armpits for extra warmth. Give warm, sweet drinks.

Keeping warm
Wrap the victim in a survival blanket, and cover her head if she is not wearing a hat.

2 Find shelter

- If you had to evacuate your home but did not manage to reach either your chosen place of evacuation or a local emergency shelter, you will need to find some form of shelter for your family.
- If you are in a town, try to find an empty building to take shelter in. Avoid buildings that look as though they may be structurally unsound, especially following an earthquake.
- If you are in the countryside, look for a manmade structure, such as a bridge, barn or shed. As a last resort, trees will at least protect you from extremes of temperature, wind, rain, or snow.
- Use the bedding supplies in your disaster emergency kit (p.225) to keep warm at night.

3 Create shelter

- If you cannot find shelter, try to build something with materials you have or find.
- You need to build a structure that will provide adequate protection from the wind, rain, and sun.
- If you are in the countryside, you could use vegetation and branches to construct a lean-to shelter.
- If you are in a town, hunt around for sheets of metal, plastic sheeting, pieces of wood, or anything else that could be used to create a shelter.
- Involve all family members in constructing the shelter. Not only will the work be done more quickly, but it will keep you all occupied.

Make a roof out of vegetation strapped to a wooden frame

Find something water-resistant to use as a floor

4 Keep positive

- Unpack your disaster emergency kit and find places for everyone to spread out their sleeping bags. Make your shelter as comfortable as possible.
- Comfort young children by telling them how exciting your "camping" experience will be.
- Try to keep up morale with the thought that you are all safe and that this is only a temporary situation until help arrives.

5 Build fire

- If it is cold, build a fire. If you are in the countryside, use twigs and small branches, but be aware of the dangers of starting a wildfire. If you are in a town, use whatever materials are available.
- If you have suitable containers with you, you may be able to heat up some of your emergency food.

6 Conserve food and water

- If you are unable to reach safety or help fails to arrive within 2 days, think about conserving your supplies of food and water.
- Restrict adult rations but give children, the elderly, and pregnant women normal supplies, if possible.
- Be aware that water is more vital than food: a healthy adult can survive without food for a week with no serious health effects, but more than 1–2 days without water can be highly dangerous.
- If water supplies run low, collect rainfall to drink.
- Alternatively, find the cleanest-looking source you can and purify water to make it drinkable (p.249).
- Do not drink water from streams or damaged pipes: it could be contaminated and could seriously damage your health.

CHECKING YOUR HOME

1 Check for damage

- Do not enter your home if there is water around it. Flood water can undermine foundations, causing buildings to sink, floors to crack, or walls to collapse.
- Check the outside of your home for signs of structural damage, such as cracks in walls, a leaning chimney, and walls at angles.
- If you are certain that it is safe to enter your home, go inside and inspect the walls, floors, windows, doors, and staircases for damage.
- Do not enter your home carrying any naked flame, such as a lighted cigarette, in case of gas leaks.
- If you are unsure, ask a structural engineer to inspect your home.

2 Check safety of main supplies

- If you remained in your house and did not turn off main supplies, be aware of the possible dangers.
- If wiring has been damaged, turn off electricity at the main and ask an electrician to inspect it.
- If you can smell gas, turn off the supply at the main, open doors and windows, and leave at once.
- If sewage pipes are damaged, turn off your water supply at the main shutoff valve (outside your house) to prevent contaminated water from entering your water system.
- Do not drink tap water unless you have been officially told it is safe.
- If you turned off main supplies before the disaster, and are certain that they are safe, turn on the water and electricity, and ask your gas supplier to turn on the gas.

3 Make repairs

- Check for minor damage, such as cracked or missing roof tiles and leaks, in your home. Remedy any problems as quickly as possible. If necessary, use short-term solutions until proper repair work can be undertaken.
- If your home has been shaken by the disaster, causing breaks and spills, clean up dangerous debris as quickly as possible. Shattered glass and spilled flammable liquids and bleaches are potentially dangerous.

Clear up any breaks and spills

4 Contact your insurance company

- Call your insurance company's emergency helpline as soon as possible. You will be given advice on what to do.
- If immediate repairs are necessary, arrange for them to be carried out straight away. Keep the receipts to give to your insurers later.
- Your insurance company will send a loss adjuster to assess extensive damage and the cost of reparation.
- Take photographs or videos of the damage to corroborate insurance claims. Keep copies of all your correspondence with insurers.

LOOKING AFTER YOUR FAMILY

1 Cope with power loss

- You may have to cope without supplies of gas and electricity for a period of time, particularly if the disaster has been serious enough to affect the local infrastructure.
- Use flashlights or candles at night, but conserve supplies by using them only if absolutely necessary.
- If you have a working hearth and chimney, forage for wood to burn, but be aware of the danger of chimney fires in a dirty chimney.

2 Use food sensibly

- Without electricity to power refrigerators and freezers, chilled or frozen foods will become inedible.
- In order to conserve the cold air inside, avoid opening fridge and freezer doors.
- A fully stocked, well-insulated freezer should keep foods frozen for at least 3 days, so use supplies from the fridge first. Only foods that do not require cooking will be usable, unless you have a camping stove.
- Once you have finished these supplies, eat canned and dried foods.

3 Keep up morale

- The aftermath of a major natural disaster will be a difficult period. Family members or friends may be unaccounted for, you may have to cope with injuries, and there will almost certainly be damage and suffering all around.
- Help your family remain positive and keep them focused on the issue of survival. Keep busy and try to work together as a team, making sure that you discuss all plans.
- Reassure young children that you have survived and that the worst is over. Keep them entertained to distract them.
- Bear in mind the comfort factor of food. In a time of great stress and upheaval, a familiar food or drink can be very reassuring.

PURIFYING WATER

If water supplies run low and main water is contaminated, you will have to purify water.

- If you can see particles floating in water, strain it through some paper towels then boil it, add purifying tablets, or disinfect it.
- Boil some water for 10 minutes to purify it, then allow it to cool before drinking.
- Use chlorine-based tablets to purify water.

- To disinfect water, use regular household bleach containing 5.25 percent sodium hypochlorite only. A stronger percentage is dangerous.
- Add two drops of bleach to 1 pt (500 ml) of water, stir and leave it to stand for 30 minutes. The water should smell slightly of bleach. If it does not, repeat the process and leave the water to stand for 15 minutes more.

Useful online sites and addresses

FIRST-AID ORGANIZATIONS

American First Aid
4306 State Route 51 South
Belle Vernon, PA 15012
Tel: (800) 831-9623
Online: www.amfirstaid.com

American Red Cross
P.O. Box 37243
Washington, DC 20013.
Tel: (800) 435-7669
Online: www.redcross.org

**National Safety
Organization**
1121 Spring Lake Drive
Itasca, IL 60143-3201
Tel: (630) 285-1121
Online: www.nsc.org

DIY HELP

**AmeriSpec:
Home Inspection Service**
The ServiceMaster Company
One ServiceMaster Way
Downers Grove, IL 60515
Tel: (800) WE-SERVE
Online: www.amerispec.com

**Arctic Council - Emergency
Prevention, Preparedness,
and Response**
Suite 301, 5204-50 Avenue
Yellowknife, NT XIA IE2
Canada
Tel: (867) 669 4725
Online: http://eppr.arctic-
council.org

**Emergency Services
WWW Site List**
Online: www.district.north-
van.bc.ca/eswsl/www-911.htm

**Southern Union Gas
Company**
Emergency Tel:
(800) 959-LEAK/959-5325

GENERAL HEALTHCARE

**Agency for Healthcare
Research and Quality**
2101 E. Jefferson St.,
Suite 501
Rockville, MD 20852
Tel: (301) 594-1364
Online: www.ahcpr.gov

**American Alliance
for Health, Physical
Education, Recreation,
and Dance**
1900 Association Dr.
Reston, VA 20191-1598
Tel: 1-800-213-7193
Online: www.aahperd.org

**American Health
Care Association**
1201 L St., N.W.
Washington, DC 20005
Tel: (202) 842-4444
Online: www.ahca.org

**American Institute
of Homeopathy**
801 N. Fairfax Street,
Suite 306
Alexandria, VA 22314
Tel: (888) 445-9988
Online: http://www.
homeopathyusa.org

**American Medical
Association**
515 N. State Street
Chicago, IL 60610
Tel: (312) 464-5000
Online: www.ama-assn.org

**American Medical
Women's Association**
801 N. Fairfax Street,
Suite 400
Alexandria, VA 22314
Tel: (703) 838-0500
Online: www.amwa-doc.org

Canadian Health Network
Online: www.canadian-health-
network.ca

Family Health International
P.O. Box 13950
Research Triangle Park
NC 27709
Tel: (919) 544-7040
Online: www.fhi.org

HealthNet Canada
4271 - 99 Fourth Avenue
Ottawa, Ontario K1S 5B3
Canada
Tel: (613) 220-0623
Online: www.healthnet.ca

National Institute on Aging
Building 31, Room 5C27
31 Center Drive, MSC 2292
Bethesda, MD 20892
Tel: (301) 496-1752
Online: www.nia.nih.gov

**The Emergency Medicine and
Primary Care Home Page**
Online: www.embbs.com

MASTER TRADESMEN

Lockmasters, Inc.
5085 Danville Rd.
Nicholasville, KY 40356-9531
Tel: (800) 654-0637
Online: www.lockmasters.com

Master Builders Association
2155 112th Ave NE
Bellevue, WA 98004
Tel: (800) 522-2209
Online:
http://www.mbaks.com

NATURAL DISASTERS

Alzheimer's Association
919 North Michigan Avenue,
Suite 1100
Chicago, Illinois 60611-1676
Tel: (800) 272-3900
Online: www.alz.org

American Red Cross
P.O. Box 37243
Washington, DC 20013.
Tel: (800) 435-7669
Online: www.redcross.org

**Disaster Survival
Planning Network**
669 Pacific Cove Drive
Port Huenene, CA 93041
Tel: (800) 601- 4899
Online:
www.disaster-survival.com

**Environmental Protection
Agency**
Ariel Rios Building
1200 Pennsylvania Avenue,
N.W. Washington, DC 20460
Tel: (202) 260-2090
Online: www.epa.gov/

**Federal Emergency
Management Agency**
Tel: (800) 480-2520
Online: www.fema.gov

**Geological Association
of Canada**
Department of Earth Sciences
Room ER4063, Alexander
Murray Building
Memorial University of
Newfoundland
St. John's, NF A1B 3X5
CANADA
Tel: (709) 737-7660
Online: www.gac.ca

Geological Society of America
P.O. Box 9140
Boulder, CO 80301-9140
Tel: (303) 447-2020
Online: www.geosoceity.org

**National Oceanic and
Atmospheric Administration**
National Weather Service
1325 East West Highway
Silver Spring, MD 20910
Online: www.nws.noaa.gov

**National Severe
Storms Laboratory**
1313 Halley Circle
Norman, Oklahoma 73069
Tel: (405) 360-3620
Online: www.nssl.noaa.gov

**The Global Earthquake
Response Center**
Online: www.earthquake.com

The Weather Channel Online
Online: www.weather.com

**The Weather Network
(USA and Canada)**
Online:
www.theweathernetwork.com

**United States
Geological Survey**
National Earthquake
Information Center
Box 25046, DFC, MS 967
Denver, Colorado 80225
Tel: (303) 273-8500
Online: http://neic.usgs.gov

**Vortech Storm
Research Organization**
P.O. Box 1233
Danbury, CT 06813-1233
Online:
http://vortechstorm.tripod.com

home SECURITY
American Society
for Industrial Security
1625 Prince Street
Alexandria, Virginia
22314-2818
Tel: (703) 519-6200
Online: www.asisonline.org

**Canadian Resource Centre
for Victims of Crime**
100 - 141,
rue Catherine Street
Ottawa, Ontario
K2P IC3
Tel: (613) 233-7614
Online: www.crcvc.ca

**National Organization
for Victim Assistance**
1730 Park Road NW
Washington DC 20010
Tel: (202) 232-6682
Online: www.try-nova.org

**The National Center
for Victims of Crime**
2000 M Street NW,
Suite 480
Washington, DC 20036
Tel: (202) 467-8700
Online: www.ncvc.org

SPECIFIC HEALTH PROBLEMS

American Academy of Allergy,
Asthma, and Immunology
611 East Wells Street
Milwaukee, WI 53202
Tel: (414) 272-6071
Online: www.aaaai.org

**American Academy
of Dermatology**
P.O. Box 4014
Schaumburg,
IL 60168-4014
Tel: (847) 330-0230
Online: www.aad.org

**American Academy
of Ophthalmology**
P.O. Box 7424
San Francisco,
CA 94120-7424
Tel: (415) 561-8500
Online: www.aao.org

**American Academy of
Orthopaedic Surgeons**
6300 North River Road
Rosemont,
Illinois 60018-4262
Tel: (847) 823-7186
Online:
http://orthoinfo.aaos.org

American Diabetes Association
1701 North Beauregard Street
Alexandria, VA 22311
Tel: (800) DIABETES
Online: www.diabetes.org

American Epilepsy Society
342 North Main Street
West Hartford,
CT 06117-2507
Tel: (860) 586-7505
Online: www.aesnet.org

**American Gastroenterological
Association**
7910 Woodmont Ave.,
Seventh Floor,
Bethesda, MD 20814
Tel: (301) 654-2055
Online: www.gastro.org

American Heart Association
National Center
7272 Greenville Avenue
Dallas, TX 75231
Tel: (800) AHA-USA-1
Online:
www.americanheart.org

American Lung Association
61 Broadway, 6th Floor
NY, NY 10006
Tel: (212) 315-8700
Online: www.lungusa.org

American Stroke Association
National Center
7272 Greenville Avenue
Dallas TX 75231
Tel: (888) 4-STROKE
Online:
www.strokeassociation.org

Crohns and Colitis Foundation of America
386 Park Avenue South,
17th Floor
New York, NY 10016
Tel: (800) 932-2423
Online: www.ccfa.org

Head Injury Resource Center
212 Pioneer Bldg
Seattle, WA 98104-2221
Tel: (206) 621-8558
Online: www.headinjury.com

Incontinence.org
Online: www.incontinence.org

International Society for Sexual and Impotence Research
Online: www.issir.org

P.O. Box 94074
Toronto, Ontario M4N 3R1
Canada
Online: www.ibsgroup.org

MAGNUM, Inc.
The National
Migraine Association
113 South Saint Asaph,
Suite 300
Alexandria, VA 22314
Tel: (703) 739-9384
Online: www.migraines.org

Meningitis Foundation of America Inc.
6610 North Shadeland
Avenue, Suite 200
Indianapolis, Indiana
46220-4393
Tel: (800) 668-1129
Online: www.musa.org

National Alliance of Breast Cancer Organizations
9 East 37th Street, 10th Floor
New York, NY 10016
Tel: (888) 80-NABCO
Online: www.nabco.org

National Eczema Association for Science and Education
6600 SW 92nd Ave., Ste. 230
Portland, OR 97223-0704
Tel: (800) 818-7546
Online:
www.nationaleczema.org

National Prostate Cancer Coalition
1158 15th St., NW
Washington, DC 20005
Tel: 202-463-9455
Online: www.4npcc.org

TRADE ASSOCIATIONS

American Society of Heating, Refrigerating, and Air-Conditioning Engineers, Inc.
1791 Tullie Circle, N.E.
Atlanta, GA 30329
Tel: (800) 527-4723
Online: www.ashrae.org

American Wood-Preservers' Association
P.O. Box 5690
Granbury Texas 76049-0690
Tel: 817-326-6300
Online: www.awpa.com

Canadian Security Industry
Online: www.csio.net

National Electrical Contractors Association
3 Bethesda Metro Center,
Suite 1100
Bethesda, MD 20814
Tel: (301) 657-3110
Online: www.neca-neis.org

National Glass Association
8200 Greensboro Drive,
Suite 302
McLean, VA 22102-3881
Tel: (866) DIAL-NGA
Online: www.glass.org

National Pest Management Association
8100 Oak Street
Dunn Loring, VA 22027
Tel: (703) 573-8330
Online: www.pestworld.org

National Roofing Contractors Association
10255 W. Higgins Road,
Suite 600
Rosemont, IL 60018
Tel: (847) 299-9070
Online: www.nrca.net

Plumbing-Heating-Cooling Contractors – National Association
180 S. Washington Street
P.O. Box 6808
Falls Church, VA 22040
Tel: (703) 237-8100
Online: www.phccweb.org

Plumbing Related Associations & Organizations on the Web
Online: www.plumbingweb.
com/assn.html

Security Industry Association
635 Slaters Lane, Suite 110
Alexandria, VA 22314-1177
Tel: (703) 683-2075
Online: www.siaonline.org

TRAVEL ADVICE

Travel Advice
5545 South 1025 East
South Ogden, UT 84405
Tel: (800) 854-3391
Online: www.traveladvice.com

Index

Acknowledgments

Cooling Brown would like to thank Derek
Coombes, Elaine Hewson, and Elly King
for design assistance, Kate Sheppard for
editorial assistance, Dennis Fell for advice
on air conditioning, and G. R. Coleman.

Dorling Kindersley would like to thank
Andrea Bagg and Martyn Page for their
editorial help, and Franziska Marking for
picture research.

MODELS
Philip Argent, Flora Bendall, Imogen
Bendall, Jennifer Bendall, Ross Bendall,
Alison Bolus, Eleanor Bolus, Dale Buckton,
Angela Cameron, Madeleine Cameron,
Shenton Dickson, Olivia King, Michel
Labat, Janey Madlani, Tish Mills

INDEX
Patricia Coward

ILLUSTRATORS
David Ashby, Kuo Kang Chen, Peter
Cooling, Chris King, Patrick Mulrey,
John Woodcock

PHOTOGRAPHERS
Matthew Ward, Trish Grant

PICTURE CREDITS
Colin Walton 210b, Corbis 236, Photodisc
240, 241, 242

JACKET PICTURE CREDITS
Pictor International front bl, front br;
Popperfoto front bc; Science Photo Library
BSIP, Laurent front tr; Stone/Getty Images
back tc, back tl, front tc, front tl, spine.

All other images © Dorling Kindersley.
For further information see:
www.dkimages.com